Through prayer and by God's grace...

Timothy

"*Prayer Coach* teaches excellent theology, but it is the most useful practical help I know to those wanting to develop the discipline of prayer."

—D. A. CARSON, Research Professor of New Testament,
Trinity Evangelical Divinity School

"This book had a singular effect on me. . . . It made me want to pray more."

—BILL HYBELS, Senior Pastor, Willow Creek Community Church
and Author of *Too Busy Not to Pray*

"The word *coach* always brings to mind the men who led me throughout my career. They possessed a combination of encouragement, challenge, humility, praise, instruction, and expectation toward me. May this book uplift and challenge you to take your prayer life to new heights, just as those men did for me and the game of football."

—MIKE SINGLETARY, Hall of Fame Chicago Bears Linebacker and Assistant Head
Coach of the San Francisco 49ers

"Our prayer life should be coached at the highest level to have the ultimate relationship with our Lord and Savior. Look no farther than *Prayer Coach*."

—JENNIE FINCH-DAIGLE, USA 2004 Olympic Gold Medalist, Softball Pitcher

"Get ready to be encouraged. Prepare to learn how to be intimate with the King of creation. There is nothing in my life that compares with drawing near to God. It is the deepest joy of my heart. So you can imagine my excitement to come upon a resource that equips me more effectively. There are scores of ideas and insights that *Prayer Coach* uncovers that promise to sustain an unquenchable desire for more of Jesus in my life."

—BILL MCCARTNEY, Founder, Promise Keepers and
Former Head Football Coach of the University of Colorado Buffaloes

"When I think of my friend Jim, the word *prayer* always comes to mind. I'm thankful he has distilled his lifetime of insights and practices into this wonderfully accessible and practical book."

—LEE STROBEL, Author of *The Case for the Real Jesus*

"Jim has done a masterful job of making prayer accessible while retaining its mysterious majesty."

—SANDY RIOS, Talk Show Host, WYLL Radio and FOX News Contributor

"One of the most inspiring books I have ever read! *Prayer Coach* gives practical steps to changing your prayer life. But don't let the easy application fool you. This book takes your prayer life from T-ball to the big leagues."

—MATT DALLY, Bassist/Vocalist, Superchick

"Are you wondering how to grow in your prayer life? Nicodem offers practical suggestions for you to consider, helpful tips that come straight from his own personal experience as a follower of Christ and a pastor. His insights will assist you in developing a deeper relationship with our heavenly Father. Nothing is more important."

—FRANKLIN GRAHAM, President and CEO,
Billy Graham Evangelistic Association and Samaritan's Purse

"At last a practical guide to prayer that avoids the ethereal heights to which most of us can never ascend. For all of us who say with the disciples, 'Lord, teach us to pray,' Jim gives us a clear and attainable path toward learning to enjoy the blessings and benefits of personal conversations with God."

—JOE STOWELL, President, Cornerstone University
and Former President, Moody Bible Institute

"Jim will motivate, encourage, and give you multiple, practical ways to improve your prayer life—with great joy. *Prayer Coach* is extremely practical, a joy to read, and loaded with easy-to-use tools for effective prayer habits."

—DANN SPADER, Founder, Sonlife Ministries
and President, Global Youth Initiative

"This is a magnificent book, and as a coach Nicodem would be hard to beat. He used to be my pastor, and he teaches lessons that few can forget."

—CLIVE CALVER, Former President,
World Relief and Senior Pastor, Walnut Hill Community Church

"With an honest, personal approach, Nicodem rallies people to prayer. You will find the book filled with 'game plan' suggestions, both offensive and defensive. We have seen even the enemies of Christ brought into the kingdom through prayer."

—TOM WHITE, Executive Director, the Voice of the Martyrs

"What most of us long for is instruction over inspiration. We know we need to pray; what we lack is knowing how to do it. Nicodem's work is inspiring because it's practical. Having worked with students ages 12 to 22 for over 20 years, I assure you that the principles in this book are applicable for youth as well as adults. Youth pastors, here's the book you've been waiting for to teach your students how to consistently pray!"

—TIMOTHY DOWNEY, Assistant Professor of Youth Ministry,
Moody Bible Institute

"Everybody prays—even unbelievers. And everybody struggles with prayer—even saints. *Prayer Coach* is aimed at helping real people learn to pray Jesus' way."

—JOHN ORTBERG, Pastor, Menlo Park Presbyterian Church and Author of *When the Game Is Over, It All Goes Back in the Box*

"Jim helps to eliminate the barriers some may have in speaking clearly to God. *Prayer Coach* has already made me a much more effective prayer warrior. Now I enjoy my prayer time with our awesome and powerful God."

—KEVIN R. CARR, Vice President of Automotive Sales Operations, Sears

"How surprising and refreshing—a pastor of a large church who loves prayer! Every chapter inspires readers toward prayer without 'guilting' them."

—LON ALLISON, Director, Billy Graham Center, Wheaton College

"Pastor Jim is easy to relate to. Prayer Coach made prayer enjoyable again. In any areas of prayer that I was lacking before, I now feel prepared to change."

—STEPHEN DREW, Senior, Larkin High School

FOREWORD BY
BOBBY BOWDEN

PRAYER COACH

For all who want to get off the Bench
and onto the praying Field

James L. Nicodem

CROSSWAY BOOKS
WHEATON, ILLINOIS

Published by Crossway Books
        a publishing ministry of Good News Publishers
        1300 Crescent Street
        Wheaton, Illinois 60187

Holy Spirit Take Control by Rory Noland. © 1984 Rory Noland, administered by Willow Creek Association. Used with Permission.

Design and typesetting by Lakeside Design Plus
Cover design by Jessica Dennis
Cover photo: iStock

First printing 2008

Printed in the United States of America

Scripture references are from *The Holy Bible: New International Version*®. Copyright © 1973, 1978, 1984 by International Bible Society. Used by permission of Zondervan Publishing House. All rights reserved.

The "NIV" and "New International Version" trademarks are registered in the United States Patent and Trademark Office by International Bible Society. Use of either trademark requires the permission of International Bible Society.

All emphases in Scripture quotations have been added by the author.

ISBN 978-1-58134-884-2

Library of Congress Cataloging-in-Publication Data
    Nicodem, James L., 1956–
      Prayer coach : for all who want to get off the bench and onto the praying field / James L. Nicodem.
        p. cm.
      Includes bibliographical references and index.
      ISBN 978-1-58134-884-2 (hc)
      1. Prayer—Christianity. I. Title.

    BV210.3.N54 2008
    248.3'2—dc22   2008000792

LB   16   15   14   13   12   11   10   09   08
           9   8   7   6   5   4   3   2   1

To some of the prayingest people I know:

Mom and Dad,
and
My Prayer Partners at Christ Community Church.

God's blessing on my life and ministry can be traced back to your
commitment to praying for me.

Contents

Foreword

I have had a lot of shortcomings during my seventy-eight years but lack of prayer has never been one. I have been praying for as far back as I can remember, thanks to my mother, father, and Ruhama Baptist Church. God has always answered my prayers, sometimes yes and sometimes no. It's amazing but some of the no's have been some of the wisest things that "never happened" to me.

Prayer must be the most neglected of powers available to humans. We have a God who gives us this opportunity to talk to him, tell him we love him, and ask that he take care of our needs. God wants to talk. God talks to us when we read the Bible. We talk to him when we pray.

Every person needs to set a time to pray. I arise each morning at 4:00 a.m. I set the coffee on and then my wife joins me. We start by reading Scripture. We began in Genesis and are now in the New Testament. When we finish Revelation we will go back and read the whole Bible again. We then have our prayer time together. This is my formal prayer time but I continue to pray throughout the day. God has answered yes to so many of my prayers I could write a book. Skeptics would say no, but that is their problem. How do I

9

pray? Same as I would talk to my daddy except I begin with "Dear God" and end with "in Jesus' name, Amen!"

That's enough about me; now on to this book. Read *Prayer Coach*. I believe you will be more empowered in prayer and worship with our almighty God. Dr. Nicodem has many intriguing thoughts on prayer. Read his book and I believe your desire to pray will increase. I know his people's prayers have been instrumental in the growth and quality of Christ Community Church. God is wonderful!

—Coach Bobby Bowden,
Head Football Coach, Florida State University Seminoles,
Winningest Coach in Major College Football History

Meet Your Coach

I magine this. You decide to take up golf as a hobby. (This may *really* stretch your imagination if you hate golf.) But every time you go out to play you end up discouraged by your performance. You slice your drives. You top your fairway iron shots. And you four-putt most greens. (If you aren't familiar with golf lingo, trust me—this is all bad!)

When you describe your frustrations to a friend, he hands you a book on golf he thinks might help. The book covers the history of the game, explains the rules and some basic strategies, gives the bios of a few popular PGA stars (like Tiger Woods), and includes photos of some of the world's most picturesque courses.

Will any of this help your golf game? No. And until your game is helped, you probably won't enjoy playing. You may even give it up. (Think of how often you've seen bags of barely used golf clubs at garage sales.)

Imagine, instead, that a friend who's a good golfer takes you out to the course and begins to work with you on your game. One aspect of it at a time. He shows you how to grip your driver, draw it back, and follow through—and your slice disappears! Your tee shots now travel down the middle of the fairway (which beats watching them disappear into the woods). Beginning to have some fun?

Just wait until your friend helps you with your fairway irons and your putting. Yeah!

What does any of this have to do with prayer? Ask any gathering of Christ followers, "How many of you wish that you were better prayers?" and almost every hand will go up. After all the sermons we've heard on prayer, all the books we've read on the topic, and all the Holy Spirit's promptings to pray—we just don't do a very good job of it. Neither do we enjoy it. (Can we even imagine using the words "prayer" and "enjoy" in the same sentence?)

Prayer Coach is a "nuts and bolts" approach to praying. My goal is to provide you with the sorts of practical tips (whether you're a beginner or veteran) that will improve your prayer life. There are all sorts of coaches these days. Financial coaches for those who want to manage their money well. Vocal coaches for those learning how to sing. Career coaches for those making job transitions. Why not a prayer coach?

Now, I'll have to admit, right up front, that the only thing I've ever coached—officially—is girls' soccer. That's pretty ironic, since I've never played soccer—it wasn't a known sport at the schools where I grew up. But when my young daughters signed up for park district soccer, and there weren't enough coaches to go around, and dads were being guilt-tripped into helping out—well, I ended up with the job. I've even got the T-shirt to prove it.

But prayer is an entirely different matter for me. I love to pray. And I'm passionate about teaching others (especially guys) how to do so with confidence and greater consistency. *Prayer Coach* begins with a frank discussion of the obstacles that keep many of us from praying like we wish we would—and how to overcome them.

Then we'll move on to a handful of basic strategies (part 2) that will breathe immediate life into your praying. *Patterns*—simple routines that will launch you into prayer when you're out on a morning jog or driving in the car with your kids. *Promptings*—you'll learn how to become more sensitive to the Holy Spirit's spontaneous leadings to pray. *Passion*—a good case can be made from Scripture that God won't respond to your prayers until they're offered with fervency.

Once these basics are under your belt, you'll be able to consider the building blocks of prayer (part 3). You may already be familiar with the acronym CHAT as an outline for talking to God: Confess, Honor, Ask, Thank. This is more than a clichéd summary of balanced praying. It's a call to a spiritual discipline, one that will bring depth to your prayer life. You'll learn how to *confess* sin in a way that gets the roots out; *honor* God with prayer that's more profound than the generic, "I praise you for who you are"; *ask* for your needs to be met—while discovering that every request is an opportunity to be drawn closer to God; *thank* God in every situation, especially trials (I'll stir up your creative juices when we get to this one).

Finally, you're going to expand your list of those who benefit from your prayers. The beneficiaries (part 4) are going to include spiritually lost friends, your kids (if you're a parent), the Christian leaders who most influence you—and, believe it or not, Satan (although I'll have to stretch the use of the word "beneficiary" to include him in this section).

This may be the most practical book on prayer that you will ever read. It's not meant to be the kind of book that you read through once and then put aside. That would be about as helpful as taking just one golf lesson and then expecting your game to improve. No, you'll want to turn to the tips in *Prayer Coach* again and again. I hope you'll even consider studying it with a small group.

Ready? Let's tee it up!

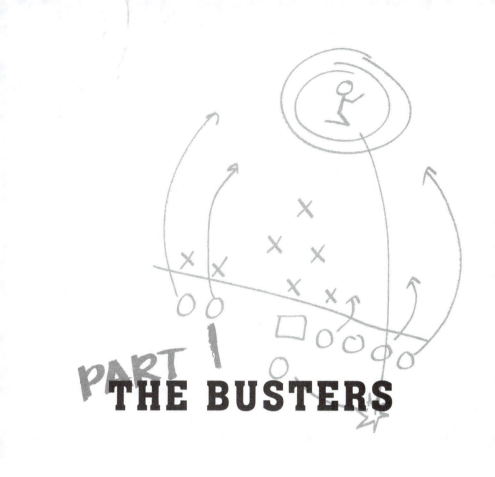

PART 1
THE BUSTERS

1

Obstacles

Fail to Plan, Plan to Fail

I stopped by the home of a friend recently. He's a relatively new believer who's been coming to our church for only a short time. At the end of our visit, I volunteered to pray about some of the things we'd been talking about—the uncertainty of his job, his growing relationship with God, his concern for his teenage daughter. When I finished, he looked at me somewhat wistfully and said, "Some day I'd like to be able to do that."

Not quite sure what he was referring to, I asked, "You'd like to be able to do *what*?"

"Pray!" was his emphatic response. He didn't mean it as flattery. And I didn't take it as such, because, after all, there is little skill involved in praying well. Praying is not a talent to be applauded, like piano playing or public speaking or golfing. It's more like . . . well . . . like mowing the lawn. It's something we just do. I wouldn't be flattered if my friend had said to me, "Someday I'd like to be able to mow the lawn just like you."

One of my major objectives in writing this book is to convince you that praying is not just for the pros. You don't have to be an apostle Paul or a John Wesley or a Billy Graham to pray well. There is no special skill involved. It is something, rather, that we become good at by just doing it.

And that's the problem. Most Christ followers don't do it. Often when I am speaking on the topic of prayer, I will ask my audience, "How many of you are satisfied with the amount of praying you do?" I have yet to see a single hand raised. We all wish we prayed more. We don't need another pep talk on the importance of prayer. We believe it's important. We just don't do it!

Why not? Let me begin with some prayer busters, or obstacles, that keep us from praying. These roadblocks are common to all of us and must be removed in order for prayer to take off in our lives.

The solutions I propose are simple and practical. If you find anything super deep in these pages it probably got there by accident. I have read many profound books over the years on the topic of prayer. Unfortunately, most of what I learned didn't translate into more praying on my part. The goal of this book, again, is to get you to actually do it.

That's what Jesus' example prompted the disciples to want for themselves. In the opening verse of Luke 11 we read: "One day Jesus was praying in a certain place. When he finished, one of his disciples said to him, 'Lord, teach us to pray, just as John taught his disciples.'" There is a sense of urgency to this request. Bible scholars tell us that the verb is an aorist imperative. An aorist imperative is often used to convey a demand for immediate action.

Having observed Jesus at prayer, the disciples were now imploring him, "Teach us to pray . . . right now! Don't put us off. This is something we need immediately. We're tired of being prayer deficient."

Interestingly, this is the only place in the four Gospels where Jesus' followers ask him, directly, to teach them something. Not that such a request would have been unusual. It was common, in the culture of that day, for students to ask for instruction on specific topics from their rabbis. And yet this is the only time we find Jesus' disciples making such a request of him. This is important. There is an urgency about it. *Teach us to pray!*

Please note, as well, that this is not, strictly speaking, a how-to request. The disciples are not asking for a lesson on prayer techniques (i.e., "Lord, teach us *how* to pray"). They are simply seeking help to get going. It's the same as when I ask the Lord, "Teach me to love So-and-so." Am I asking for ideas about how to do it? No, I just need a kick in the pants to start loving. Similarly, the disciples wanted a push to start praying. *Teach us to pray!*

If this is the cry of your heart, if you wish you prayed more than you do, if you're ready to remove the obstacles that keep you from just doing it, consider the common prayer busters which can be overcome with God's help.

No Plan

Stop and think for a moment about something you meant to do—but haven't gotten around to. Maybe it's the oil in your car that should have been changed three thousand miles ago. Or the important phone call that should have been returned last week. Or shouldn't you have taken the dog to the vet for his annual shots by now?

Why haven't you done these things yet? Chances are pretty good that your problem is as simple as not having a plan for getting the job done. You haven't officially put it on your "to do" list or written it on your calendar. You've heard it before: when we fail to plan, we plan to fail.

This is why my heating bill was so high this past winter. We have trouble with the airflow in our home, which makes it necessary for me to close all the first-floor vents in the summer (to force the cool air upstairs) and close the second-floor vents in the winter (since the heated air will rise anyway). When temperatures started to drop in late fall, I kept telling myself, *I've got to readjust all those vents.* But I never got around to it.

All winter long I pumped hot air up to the bedrooms, which meant that the first floor thermostat never warmed up enough to turn off the furnace. It ran and ran and ran. On bitter cold January nights I found myself perspiring and kicking off blankets. Each morning I'd think, *I've got to readjust all those vents.* But the job never got done. Why? Because it didn't make it to my chores list. I didn't write it in my Day-Timer to be done on my day off.

The things we get done are typically the things that we schedule to do. No plan, no action. This is just as true when it comes to the practice of prayer. Do we have a set time and place for this spiritual discipline? (This is not to suggest that we shouldn't be praying spontaneously throughout the day. But this sort of impromptu praying is more likely to happen if we have developed the habit of daily planned prayer.)

Jesus made plans to pray. He intentionally set aside time and had specific places he liked to go to talk with his heavenly Father. It is not surprising that his disciples observed him at prayer in Luke 11, because Jesus is frequently found praying in this Gospel. In fact, some have referred to Luke as "The Gospel of Prayer." Here's a quick survey:

3:21: When all the people were being baptized, Jesus was baptized too. And as he was *praying*, heaven was opened. . . .

5:15–16: Yet the news about him spread all the more, so that crowds of people came to hear him and to be healed of their sicknesses. But Jesus often withdrew to lonely places and *prayed*.

6:12–13: One of those days Jesus went out to a mountainside to *pray*, and spent the night *praying* to God. When morning came, he called his disciples to him and chose twelve of them. . . .

9:18: Once when Jesus was *praying* in private and his disciples were with him, he asked them, "Who do the crowds say I am?"

9:28–29: About eight days after Jesus said this, he took Peter, John and James with him and went up onto a mountain to *pray*. As he was *praying*, the appearance of his face changed, and his clothes became as bright as a flash of lightning.

22:39, 41, 44: Jesus went out as usual to the Mount of Olives, and his disciples followed him. . . . He withdrew about a stone's throw beyond them, knelt down and *prayed*, . . . And being in anguish, he *prayed* more earnestly, and his sweat was like drops of blood falling to the ground.

Prayer was routinely on Jesus' agenda. It was something he made plans to do. And if prayer is going to happen in our lives we will have to put it on our schedules. When and where will you pray each day? That's what a plan comes down to: time and location.

Start with the "when." If you were to inject fifteen minutes of prayer into your day, when would be the best time to schedule it? How about setting your alarm clock a quarter of an hour earlier and using that time to pray (after you've shaved or had a cup of coffee or done whatever it takes to wake you up)? Or maybe you have drive time on the way to work that could be spent in prayer. If you want to include the rest of the family in the venture, perhaps you'll want the fifteen minutes to be scheduled right after dinner. Some people like to wrap up their day by kneeling for prayer at the side of their bed.

What time works best for you? As basic as this decision sounds, I believe it's so critical that I would encourage you to stop reading for a moment and lock in a daily prayer time. Actually put it on your calendar or Day-Timer or PDA or wherever you schedule important activities.

Now that that's settled, where will you pray? It needs to be a distraction-free environment. And it helps to develop the habit if the location is the same each day. At the desk in your study? In the park near your home? By the side of your bed? In the parking lot where you work?

I always make my way, first thing in the morning, to my reading chair in the living room. Just sitting down in that familiar spot, cup of chai tea in hand, reminds me what I'm there for. God and I have a regularly scheduled appointment. Prayer happens because I've planned for it to take place.

No Praise

I like to think of praise as the spice of my prayers. Without praise my praying becomes bland. There is a sameness about it, which causes me to lose interest in it.

I recently made an appointment with an ENT specialist due to a problem with my throat. I was periodically losing my voice—not a good thing to happen to a preacher. The doctor numbed my sinuses and ran a scope through them in order to get a look at my larynx. (It gave new meaning to the old taunt, "up your nose with a rubber hose.") The good news was that there were no nodules on my voice box. But the bad news was that my throat was scarred by acid reflux.

The doctor gave me four steps for correcting the situation. First, he asked me to start on a certain medication. "I can do that," I told him. Next, he told me to put the head of my bed on wooden blocks so that I am slightly inclined at night. "I can do that," I responded. (My wife just loves sleeping downhill!)

Third, he instructed me to eat my dinner earlier so that my food is digested before I go to bed. "I can do that," I assured him. Finally, he asked me to stay away from spicy foods. "I *can't* do that!" I objected. No way am I going to give up Mexican, Indian, Szechwan, and Thai food. Spice is what makes eating enjoyable.

And the spice of praise is what gives flavor to our praying. No wonder the psalmist encourages us to begin our prayers in this way. "Enter his [the Lord's] gates with thanksgiving and his courts with praise," we are instructed in Psalm 100:4. This is how we're to come before the King of Kings and Lord of Lords. With praise on our lips.

Interestingly, I regularly hear from believers that praise is the most stilted aspect of their prayer lives. Confession may be difficult for us to do, but at least we don't have any trouble knowing what to say in this regard. Thanksgiving is often lacking from our prayers, but when we finally get around to it we can usually come up with a long list of things to express gratitude for. Petition (sometimes referred to as "gimme" prayers) flows quite easily from our lips.

But praise is a different matter. All it takes is a sentence or two before we run out of words. Why is that? Why do we find it so difficult to go on and on in praise of our awesome God? I believe that our biggest problem in this regard is our limited vocabulary. There are a handful of God's attributes that immediately come to our minds (he is holy, gracious, faithful, powerful), but after we have exhausted this short list we are stuck.

Sometimes we try to get out of this bind by praying a generic, "Lord, I praise you for who you are!" That's pretty lame, isn't it? Try that with your spouse if you're married: "Honey, I praise you for who you are." You'll probably get a strange look in response, or a "What's *that* supposed to mean?"

If we want to praise God for who he is we must expand our knowledge of the attributes and titles by which he goes in Scripture. Over the years I have gradually compiled a list of almost 250 of these descriptions. This A to Z list includes attributes such as patient, wise, angry, just, radiant, generous, exalted, sovereign, unchanging, zealous, and righteous. The titles range from King to Rock, Shepherd, Shield, Way, Trap and Snare, Living Water, Refining Fire, Brother, Refuge, Warrior, Song, and Morning Star. There is a lot to meditate on here and much to stimulate our praise.

This topic deserves additional treatment, so I will return to it later and provide some practical suggestions for turning this list of God's attributes and titles (see Appendix) into praise. But before we leave this prayer buster let me offer one final word of explanation as to why our neglect of praise tends to diminish our praying in general.

Imagine this. You have a neighbor to whom you are always appealing for help. Whenever you speak with him it's always to ask for a favor—to lend you a tool, or to watch your kids, or to give you a hand with a household project.

One day it dawns on you that this is the nature of every conversation you have with him. You wonder if he notices this as well. You reason (and rightly so), "He must get tired of seeing me coming." How do you remedy this situation? There are two ways to go about it. You could either correct the imbalance in your conversations (by talking to him about more than just your personal needs) or you could speak less frequently with your neighbor so that you don't wear him out with your requests.

Many of us take the latter approach in our relationship with God. Aware of the fact that all our prayers seem to be appeals for help, our tendency is to scale back these conversations so as not to be a bother to God. (Even we get tired of our self-centeredness.)

How much better it would be, instead, if we introduced some balance to our praying. Beginning our prayers with praise acknowledges that, "This is not all about me—God, too, will be blessed by these prayers." Such a realization encourages us to converse with him with greater regularity.

No Pattern

I like ruts. That's a strange thing to admit, but it's true. I have found that familiar ruts (maybe a more positive expression would be "routines") help me get started on tasks that I might otherwise put off because of simple inertia.

And when something breaks up one of my routines? I can be paralyzed with indecision. Happened not too long ago. My teenage son had a day off of school. I decided to bag my agenda for the day and do something with him. "What would you like to do?" I asked. "I dunno," he shrugged. "Go to a movie?" I suggested. "I dunno." "Bowling?" "I dunno." Take the train into the city?" "I dunno."

We were both stuck. The absence of routine had stopped us cold. In fact, we probably would have sat there indefinitely in indecision if my wife had not shown up and threatened to put us both to housework if we couldn't find something to do. That got us going.

I'm a big fan of ruts, routines, and patterns. When I exercise each day, for example, I know exactly what I am going to do. I know how many sets of push-ups I'll attempt and how far I'll run (3.1 miles exactly—not 3.2 or 3.0). I don't make up my workout as I go. I do it the same way, every time. And that's one of the reasons I don't hesitate to get started. I jump right in.

I've discovered that routines are equally helpful when it comes to prayer. There are certain patterns that I go to that launch me into intercession. Rather than getting hung up on the question of "what should I pray for?" I have a familiar way with which to begin.

I'll devote more attention to several helpful prayer patterns in a later chapter, but let me mention a few of these formulas now to give you a better idea of what I'm talking about. I'll start with the believer's armor. There are six pieces to this protective suit that Paul describes in Ephesians 6:13–17.

How does one put on "the belt of truth" or "the breastplate of righteousness" or "the helmet of salvation"? The writer of the old hymn, "Stand up, Stand up for Jesus" knew the answer to that question.[1] "Put on the gospel armor," his lyrics instruct us, "each piece put on with prayer." Good advice. Pray on the Ephesians 6 armor.

My kids and I made a practice of doing this on the short drive to school each morning. (My two oldest are now out of the home—and I miss sharing this routine with them.) Until just recently when he graduated, my youngest and I began many of our days with this prayer as we traveled to his high school. I'd ask him to choose one of the six pieces of armor and get us started. He might select the gospel shoes and begin with: "Lord, I'm putting on the gospel shoes. Help me to be a bold witness today. Let me run toward conversations about Jesus and the good news of his salvation."

Then it was my turn. Perhaps I'd choose the belt of truth. I'd pray something like: "We want to be honest men today, Lord. Characterized by your truth. Help us to walk in integrity—to be the same in private as we are in public. Keep us from using deceitful words. . . ."

Back and forth we'd go until we had prayed through all six pieces of armor (or as many as we could get to before we rolled into the parking lot). Anybody who has high schoolers knows the semi-comatose condition in which they head out the door most early mornings. Trying to engage them in coherent prayer could be a hopeless challenge. But I've found that the use of certain patterns, like the believer's armor, launches us into meaningful intercession in a brief period of time.

Let me give you two more examples. The A to Z list of God's attributes and titles has already been mentioned. Each day I move through this list by taking the next three entries and praising God for such. If I am in the *m*'s, I may be exalting God for being master, mediator, and merciful. Within half a minute of dropping into my prayer chair, I have already begun to extol God with heartfelt adoration. My pattern got me started.

The fruits of the Spirit (described as a singular, collective fruit in Gal. 5:22–23) provide another pattern. Knowing these nine traits by heart (love, joy, peace, patience, kindness, goodness, faithfulness, gentleness, and self-control) allows me to meditatively scroll through the list and choose one to focus on in prayer. "What do I need most today, Lord? Gentleness? Okay, take away my inclination to be harsh with others. Don't let my speech be filled with sarcasm. Remind me of how gentle you have been with me—like a shepherd with his little lamb."

Patterns help us overcome the obstacle of inertia and begin to pray. I'll cover several more of these in chapter 3. You'll learn the routines of "body parts," "a few friends," "persecuted believers," and others.

This is not a technique that I made up. I learned it from Jesus. We've already looked at the disciples' request in the opening verse of Luke 11: "Lord, teach us to pray." His response in the verses that follow has come to be known as "The Lord's Prayer." Most believers are familiar with this model prayer. If they hear the words, "Our Father, Who art in heaven," they know to continue, "Hallowed be Thy name."

Unfortunately, what was intended to be a model prayer has become a mantra to many who use it. High school football teams recite it for good luck in the locker room before big games. Others rattle it off in desperate circumstances as a means of protection.

But Jesus' intention was not to give us an incantation to repeat word for word. He was providing us with a pattern to follow when we pray. A road map that would get us started on our journey. The prayer begins with praise, continues with petition, and wraps up with confession. What a great example.

If we want prayer to play a more significant role in our lives we must overcome some common obstacles: no plan, no praise, and no pattern. Our next chapter will cover five additional roadblocks. But with God's help we can bust the busters.

Onto the Praying Field

1. On a scale of 1 to 10, how would you rate your prayer life? Explain your answer. What are some of the obstacles that you face to praying more consistently and effectively?

2. Luke 11:1 records that Jesus' disciples asked him to teach them to pray. What do you think they observed about Jesus' praying that motivated this request?

3. What are the advantages of having a plan for daily prayer? Are there any disadvantages to this approach?

   Do you have a time and place for daily prayer? If not, what time of the day would work best for you? Where could you go to pray each day that would be free from distractions and interruptions?

4. If God is so awesome, why do we have such a difficult time praising him in prayer?

   From the appendix, choose three entries that begin with the letter "A" and write a brief paragraph for each, describing what they tell you about God. Then make those paragraphs into prayers of praise to God.

5. Describe the prayer launchers in this chapter. Have you ever used one of them as an outline for your praying?

   Look up the *fruits of the Spirit* in Galatians 5:22–23. Choose a fruit that you greatly need and explain why you selected it. How do you see this same characteristic modeled by Jesus? Praise God for his demonstration of this fruit, and ask him to develop it in your life.

2

More Obstacles

Can You Hear Me Now, Lord?

guy recently called our church and asked to speak with me. He explained to my assistant that he had a favor to ask. If I remember correctly, he was heading off on a missions trip and was looking for some financial support. I recognized the caller's name and was a bit surprised to hear about his request. He had stopped attending our church a while back due to a disagreement he had with a decision made by our elders.

Actually, to say that he stopped attending is to put it rather mildly. It was more like he stomped off. And on his way out the door he said some rather nasty things to a number of people about our elders, me included. I had hoped that I would hear from him again—some day—with an apology.

But now he was on the phone to ask for a favor. As a British friend of mine would say, that was a bit "cheeky" of him. Even if he felt no remorse over his past behavior, I would expect him to try and mend fences before approaching me for financial support. I honestly harbor no resentment toward him, but it seems he was rather clueless about the way in which his past offense had disrupted our fellowship.

This encounter caused me to reflect on the fact that I sometimes pull a similar stunt with God. Ignoring the way in which my sins have offended him, I march into his presence with my latest list of requests. Doesn't it occur to me that God is waiting for me to repair my fellowship with him before I ask him for more favors? This introduces us to a fourth prayer buster.

No Purity

Sin disrupts our relationship with God. And God is not inclined to hear our prayers until we have confessed and been cleansed of our sins. The prophet Isaiah put it this way: "Surely the arm of the LORD is not too short to save, nor his ear too dull to hear. But your iniquities have separated you from your God; your sins have hidden his face from you, so that he will not hear" (Isa. 59:1–2).

Isaiah's readers were in the habit of complaining that prayer was useless. Why pray when God seemed to be deaf to their requests? Isaiah explained that the problem was not that God was hard of hearing. He was intentionally refusing to listen to their prayers because of their unconfessed sins.

How often are our prayers thwarted (which discourages us from further praying) because of our sin-sullied hearts? We need to apply this promise: "If we confess our sins, he is faithful and just and will forgive us our sins and purify us from all unrighteousness" (1 John 1:9). Confession overcomes the "no purity" obstacle to prayer.

Unfortunately, a lot of our sin goes undetected. And it's pretty hard for us to confess sin that we don't even see. David recognized the problem of his blind spot when he prayed, "Who can discern his errors? Forgive my hidden faults" (Ps. 19:12).

How can we bring our hidden faults into the open so that we can deal with them? I believe that this requires a daily inventory of our lives in which we invite the Holy Spirit to bring to light anything that is breaking our fellowship with God. I have found the words to a contemporary chorus very helpful in initiating this time of soul searching. The lyrics go like this:

Holy Spirit, take control,
  take my body, mind and soul.
Put a finger on anything that doesn't please you,
  anything I do that grieves you.
Holy Spirit, take control.[1]

After praying these words . . . I wait. I have extended an invitation to the Holy Spirit, and so I wait for his response. In the quietness that ensues, he impresses upon me those offenses that have displeased and grieved God. This, in turn, gives me the opportunity to confess them and seek God's help in forsaking them.

One of the things that I've learned through this daily practice is that God and I are often on different pages when it comes to identifying those sins that are most endangering my fellowship with him. While I am keenly aware of (and frustrated by) certain habitual transgressions, the Holy Spirit frequently brings to my attention sins that I have overlooked or trivialized.

A case in point: God says, through the prophet Malachi, that one of his pet peeves (my expression, not God's) is people robbing him of tithes and offerings and then expecting him to answer their prayers (see Mal. 3:7–12). Who would have thought that our unfaithfulness in giving would be such a serious offense to God? Serious enough to close his ears to our prayers?

I know a pastor of a large church who really takes this Malachi passage to heart. A regular aspect of his Sunday services is a time of prayer for the needs of his congregation. While the congregation is standing he invites those with heavy burdens to take their seats. Then he instructs those around them to place hands on their shoulders and for someone in each group to pray out loud for the seated brother or sister. "But don't pray," this pastor concludes his directions, "if you are not tithing. Because the Lord will not listen to your prayers until you stop robbing him."

Wow! What a way to make a point! And it underscores what I have been trying to say. The sins that we are most prone to overlook may be the very ones that are keeping our prayers from being heard. It is critical that we give the Holy Spirit the opportunity to impress on us anything that is displeasing or grieving God so that we can confess these sins, be forgiven and cleansed of them, and open God's ears to our prayers.

In chapter 6 I will return to this topic in greater detail. We'll take a look at the practice of journaling—how to do it and why it's so helpful in bringing to light our insidious hidden faults.

No Peace

One of my least favorite Bible verses is the apostle Peter's exhortation to married men: "Husbands, in the same way be considerate as you live with your wives, and treat them with respect as the weaker partner and as heirs with you of the gracious gift of life, so that nothing will hinder your prayers" (1 Pet. 3:7). I have to admit that I chafe under the truth of this Scripture, namely, that conflict with my wife will undermine the effectiveness of my prayers!

When I have been inconsiderate with Sue, the Bible teaches, I might as well not bother praying until I have reconciled with her. This is a bitter pill for me to swallow. I would rather give her the silent treatment until she realizes the error of her ways and apologizes to me. Why does this seem to happen when I need God the most?

There have been occasions, for example, when I've marched out of the house on a Sunday morning after an argument with Sue. I've arrived at my church office to prepare for the day's services, bowed my head and prayed: "Lord, please use me today. Empower my preaching; give me wisdom for my interactions with people." That's about the time the Holy Spirit impresses upon me, "I'm not going to do a thing for you until you fix it with Sue."

I've tried arguing with God at this point: "But she started it. Don't you think that she ought to be fixing it with me?" I've tried bargaining with God: "I promise to make things right just as soon as we get home from church this afternoon." I've tried to ignore God and increase the intensity of my prayer: "I am totally dependent upon you, Lord. If you don't speak through me then lives won't be changed."

But none of these diversions works. God presses his point relentlessly. And I am soberly reminded that I have but two options: reconcile with Sue or forfeit God's intervention in my life and ministry. Realizing that it is useless to kick against a brick wall, I always relent. (The thought of standing to preach in front of several thousand people, without the Lord's blessing, terrifies me.) I call Sue and seek her forgiveness. And then I return to prayer.

I wish God wouldn't put me in such a bind. But it is impossible to dodge the truth of 1 Peter 3:7. If I am not pursuing peace in my marriage, I might as well save my breath when praying. God is not listening.

The same could be said about the other relationships in our lives. God is not interested in hearing from us while we allow conflicts with others to go unaddressed. Jesus taught, "If you are offering your gift at the altar and there remember that your brother has something against you, leave your gift there in front of the altar. First go and be reconciled to your brother; then come and offer your gift" (Matt. 5:23–24). No doubt this would apply to our squabbles with parents, friends, coworkers, clients, teachers, bosses, whomever.

We can't talk sweetly with God while we're growling at others. There's an inconsistency here that God wants us to deal with. To use one of James' metaphors, fresh water and salt water cannot both come from the same spring (James 3:9–11; James has much to say in his New Testament epistle about what comes out of our mouths).

When all three of my kids were teenagers, an occasional dinner table conversation would break out into an argument. In the heat of the moment it was not unusual for an older sister to ream out a younger brother (or vice versa) with harsh words. About that time the phone would ring, and the caller would be the sister's friend. The rest of us listened in amazement as the tone of her voice changed in mid-sentence, and her "Hello" dripped with honey. Gag!

But don't we all do this? Don't we speak contentiously with others, walk away, and a short time later bow our heads to pray about something? I'm sure that the Holy Spirit would want us to understand that that prayer is not going anywhere until we mend our broken relationship. (Yes, there will be times when reconciliation just can't be brokered, in spite of our best efforts to make peace. On those occasions we can take solace in the fact that God requires only that, "If it is possible, as far as it depends on you, live at peace with everyone" [Rom. 12:18].)

Don't allow unresolved conflict with others become an obstacle to effective praying.

No Passion

It's insightful to study the prayers that are recorded in the Bible. Most of them are marked by a significant intensity. Jacob literally wrestled with God for an entire night (Gen. 32:22–32). Hannah prayed with such great emotion at the place of worship that Eli, the local priest, thought she was drunk (1 Sam. 1:9–16)! Jesus sweat drops of blood as he prayed in the garden of Gethsemane (Luke 22:39–44). And when the early church concluded one of its prayer meetings, "the place where they were meeting was shaken" (Acts 4:31).

By way of contrast, it seems as if we pray somewhat casually. The intensity in our voices is no greater than when we leave a voicemail message on a friend's phone. Even our posture is often laid back when we are praying.

At times I've wondered if this cavalier approach to God isn't an American phenomenon. When I travel abroad and gather with foreign believers, I am frequently struck by their passion in prayer. The first time I worshiped with Romanian Christians we were packed into a small church with a standing-room-only group pressed against the walls. When we bowed our heads in prayer and someone began to lead out, his prayer was punctuated with unison "amens" from the rest of the congregation. Nobody was daydreaming!

How do we interject more intensity into our prayers if it is lacking? Won't our attempts to do so be artificial? We feel it or we don't . . . right? I believe there are a couple of simple things we can do—sincerely—in order to pray with greater passion. (See ch. 5 for more details on this subject.)

First, we need to pay attention to our posture. No slumping in our chairs or sitting with our legs crossed as we approach our awesome God. It is far more appropriate to lean forward on the edge of our seats, or to kneel, or to stand with arms raised, or to lie face down on the floor. One contemporary writer on prayer has described this last position as "eating rug." How fitting, especially when we're confessing sin or expressing our total dependence upon God, to be prostrate before him. If you've never eaten rug, I'd highly recommend it.

I have also found it helpful to pace as I pray. I am more attentive and energized as I walk the river where we live or cover the hallways (or campus) of our church or stroll from one room of our house to another. When I am physically alert my spirit follows suit.

A second prayer intensifier is to add passion to our tone of voice. This may feel contrived at first, but if it is done out of a sincere desire to pray passionately it works. I am reminded of a poster of the legendary tennis pro Arthur Ashe on my dorm room wall years ago. He was stretched out, tennis racket extended, body parallel to the ground, reaching for a ball. The caption read: "If you'll act enthusiastic, you'll be enthusiastic."

I have found this to be true in many areas of life. When I make myself act appropriately, even though I don't feel like doing so initially, a transformation takes place in me. In a short time the desired behavior becomes natural. If I want to pray more passionately, I must begin to give my words an edge as I speak with God. Make them sound as if they're an appeal, not an aside.

When was the last time you prayed passionately about something? When was the last time you prayed passionately for the salvation of a spiritually lost friend or loved one? When was the last time you cried out to God for the wisdom you desperately needed to make a critical decision? When was the last time you pleaded with him to deliver you from a sin which has plagued you for far too long? When was the last time you interceded with a broken heart for those who are victimized by the tragedies of famine, AIDS, terrorism, or natural disaster?

Casual praying is so out of place in situations like these. If we're more apt to yawn than to weep when we pray, something is definitely wrong. No passion is a prayer buster.

No Persistence

"Then Jesus told his disciples a parable to show them that they should always pray and not give up." So begins Luke 18. A story about persistence in prayer follows. The central character is a poor widow who is seeking justice from a local judge with regard to an adversary. The judge doesn't want to be bothered by her case but she refuses to let things go.

Ultimately, he decides to give her what she wants so that, he says, "she won't eventually wear me out with her coming!" (Luke 18:5). Jesus then applies this parable to prayer. He points out, by way of contrast, that God is nothing like the reluctant judge. He wholeheartedly wants to come to the aid of those who trust in him. This ought to encourage us to be even more determined in prayer than the persistent widow.

Sometimes we forget that God is for us. This is especially true when we don't get immediate answers to our prayers. Doesn't God care? More than we know! And that's why *we should always pray and not give up.*

This past December our church presented three nights of Christmas Eve services with the intention that these would make a great venue for introducing our spiritually lost friends to Christ. A month prior to the big outreach, we challenged our congregation to begin praying for the guests whom they planned to invite. We provided "12/25" cards to stimulate their intercession.

Of course 12/25 is the date of Christmas, but it also reminded our folks to stop at "12" noon each day and pray "2" minutes for "5" unbelieving friends: 12–2–5. The result of this prayer campaign was that we saw several thousand outside visitors at our Christmas Eve services! It seemed like everyone had a story to tell of how God had worked in the lives of those whom they had invited.

I heard one positive testimony after another until one guy announced to me rather dejectedly: "0–for–9!" Uncertain as to what he was referring to, I asked him to repeat himself. "0–for–9," he said again. "I prayed for nine friends every day—not just the recommended five. I invited every one of them to the Christmas Eve services. And not one of them came! Now what?"

I could feel his pain. Not because I'm a particularly empathetic person (I'm not). But because I have often been in his shoes. In fact, sometimes I've wondered if one way God keeps me humble is by having my invitations to our outreach events regularly turned down. It seems to happen to me a lot. I've even had friends say "yes" and then back out on the day of the program.

I shared this information with my 0–for–9 buddy. "So what do you do?" he asked me. "I keep on praying," I told him. In fact, I explained, I'd actually had a breakthrough with the Christmas Eve service. The fifth name on my list was a friend who had turned down every church-related event I'd invited him to over the previous two years. I can't say that I prayed for him in advance with a lot of faith. But I prayed.

Guess who showed up for the Christmas Eve service? Yup, number five on my prayer list. And his family! In fact, a few weeks later I received an invitation from him for a Saturday brunch at his house. Our conversation that morning revolved largely around spiritual matters.

God wants us to always pray and not give up. If we throw in the towel too soon, we'll miss the opportunity to see what God would've done had we persisted.

No Partner

When we did our quick survey of Jesus at prayer in the Gospel of Luke, several pages back, you may have noticed that Jesus frequently brought his closest friends with him when he got away to pray. Peter, James, and John accompanied him up the Mount of Transfiguration for a prayer retreat (Luke 9:28). The disciples' request, "Teach us to pray" (Luke 11:1), was prompted by the whole team having observed Jesus at prayer. They were even with him in the garden of Gethsemane—although his appeal that they, too, pray was met with snores instead of earnest intercession (Luke 22:39–46).

I am not suggesting that Jesus somehow needed the camaraderie of others as encouragement to pray. He would've carved out time to meet with his heavenly Father with or without the accompaniment of his buddies. Still, I believe he modeled for us that prayer is one of those activities that benefits from the participation of friends. Even Luke's observation, on one occasion, that Jesus was "praying in private" adds that "his disciples were with him" (Luke 9:18). Was it private prayer or group prayer, Luke? Both!

No doubt about it. We are more likely to stick with (and enjoy) an activity once we find others to do it with. It doesn't matter if that activity is a personal habit (such as exercising or dieting) or recreation (such as going to the symphony or golfing) or a spiritual discipline (such as studying the Bible or praying). If it's something that we'd like to make a practice of doing, we should find others who will do it with us.

Let me offer several suggestions for including others in your prayer life. These ideas may already have occurred to you, but perhaps my voicing them will prompt you to give them a try. The first is simply to add more prayer to any Bible study group that you may be part of. So often the prayer in these groups consists of little more than an opening and closing formality. Even when the leader fully intends to allow time at the end for group intercession, it's easy for the Bible study portion to go long, limiting time to pray.

Make sure that prayer happens in these settings. Choose an environment that is conducive to group prayer. If your early morning Bible study takes place in a local restaurant it may not inhibit the group discussion but it will often cause people to be reluctant to pray out loud. Better to switch to a different location (you can live without the pancakes) than to cheat yourselves of the opportunity to pray with each other.

Another deterrent to Bible study group prayer is the preliminary act of soliciting requests. How often have you been in group meetings where so much time was spent discussing what to pray about that the praying itself got cut short? The only way to keep this from happening is to repeatedly ask group members to describe their personal requests in as few words as possible so that there is plenty of time to actually pray.

Bible study groups can be a great context in which to find prayer partners. If you want to take it to the next level I would recommend recruiting a personal prayer partner. This is someone who will meet with you once a week (or at least, every other week) for the sole purpose of praying together. Scheduling a set time and place will ensure that it happens. An ability to keep confidences is an essential character trait to look for in this partner. Get-togethers don't have to take a lot of time (thirty minutes will do) and may take place before or after a Sunday service if you both attend the same church.

If you are married, I can't encourage you strongly enough to make prayer a regular habit with your spouse. I have found that a lot of husbands balk at this. For one thing, their wives are often further down the road, spiritually speaking, and this is embarrassingly obvious when they pray together. In addition, women seem to have an easier time expressing themselves verbally than guys do and so rattle off their prayers effortlessly.

But I tell guys that it's worth eating a little humble pie for the benefits that come from praying with our wives. Over the years Sue and I have found several spots that work well for praying: on early morning walks that we take alongside our local river (even in winter!), or on our knees beside our bed before retiring for the night, or on our cell phones as we head off in different directions at the beginning of the day. Choose a time and place that works best for you, catch each other up on personal and family concerns, and then pray.

One final way to make prayer happen with others is to initiate it on the spot with those to whom you've been speaking. Whether on the phone or in person many people talk about their troubles in the course of a conversation. Difficulty with a boss, tension in a marriage, anxiety over a health problem, confusion with regard to a big decision, bitterness toward an ex-friend—it's not unusual for topics like these to pop up.

I have found it quite natural to suggest at the conclusion of such a conversation, "Would you mind if I pray for you right now about this issue?" In all the times that I've asked for this permission, I've only been turned down once. (And I'll describe why that happened in a later chapter—there was a happy ending to the incident.) Christians and unbelievers alike seem genuinely appreciative that I care enough to pray for them. While they are not, strictly speaking, partnering with me in prayer on these occasions (i.e., I'm doing all the talking with God), my intercession is energized when it takes place in the company of others.

A by-product of introducing prayer into my conversations is that it forces me to be a better listener. In order to pray intelligently and empathetically with other people I must pay close attention to what they are saying. Try it!

Onto the Praying Field

1. Why would God close his ears to our prayers because of unconfessed sin in our lives? What are the two categories of sin David refers to in Psalm 19:1–2? What does each mean?

   If the Holy Spirit were to put his finger on a hidden fault in your life, what might that fault be? Take a moment, right now, to confess it to God and ask him to forgive you.

2. Are there any broken relationships in your life due to unresolved conflict? What impact does this have on your praying, according to God's Word? What have you done to resolve your conflict? What would God want you to do next?

3. Do you know someone who prays passionately? Describe what you've observed.

   On the Celsius temperature scale—where the boiling point is one hundred degrees—how hot are your prayers? What could you do to inject more passion into them?

   What is the usual posture in which you pray? This week try praying several times while walking, kneeling, or lying on your face before God. Was this helpful? Why or why not?

   List three or four things about which you *should* be praying passionately. Choose one of these and pray about it right now—as if it were a matter of life and death (which it very well may be).

4. Describe a prayer that God answered in your life after years of praying it.

   Is there anyone or anything that you have given up praying for? Why might God want you to persevere in praying for this matter?

5. If you're married, do you pray regularly (i.e. as opposed to sporadically) with your spouse? What would be the benefits of doing this? How could you begin?

   If you're in a small group, how big a role does praying play in the weekly agenda? What improvements could be made?

6. Make it your goal to conclude at least three conversations this week with an offer to pray for the person you have been talking with. Write their names and prayer requests here.

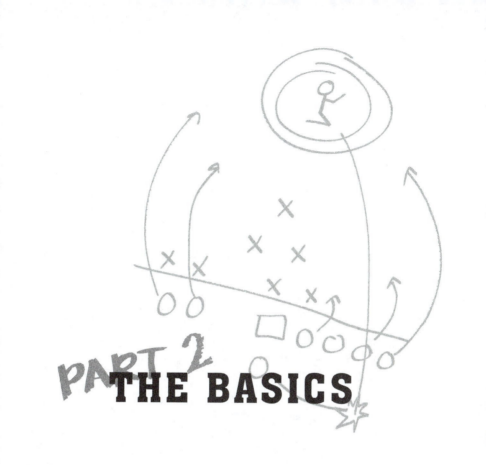

PART 2 THE BASICS

3

Patterns

Get into a Rut

I made three lunch appointments with three different people last week. Nothing unusual about that. But what may strike you as a bit odd is that I scheduled each of these lunches for the same time of day (1:00 p.m. on three successive days) and at the same restaurant (California Pizza Kitchen). In fact, I even ordered the same meal each day (you just gotta try the bacon and Gorgonzola chopped salad the next time you eat at CPK).

Am I stuck in a rut? You betcha! And it's by intention. The reason I schedule my lunch appointments, if possible, at the same time and place is because I never have to think twice about when and where I'm going. I just go. And as far as ordering the same meal is concerned, I do that—besides for the fact that I love Gorgonzola cheese—because it allows me to immediately begin a conversation with whomever I'm meeting (as opposed to being distracted for the first ten minutes as I scan a menu trying to decide what to eat).

Okay, maybe I'm a bit over-the-top when it comes to the use of routines. All I know is that routines help me avoid distractions and jump into whatever needs doing. The same holds true when I pray. Certain routines get me started. While there's nothing wrong with extemporaneous praying, I've discovered a few patterns that I return to again and again as prayer launchers. Here are a few you might find helpful.

The Believer's Armor

Not long ago I was attending a national conference for pastors when the event's organizer, a friend of mine, asked me if I would open the next session in prayer. I've never really liked this sort of an assignment because it has a tendency to reduce prayer to program filler. What can one say, on such an occasion, other than to ask God to "bless" the next speaker? That's when the idea occurred to me to lead these pastors in the praying on of the believer's armor. What better prayer for a group of soldiers serving in the trenches?

This is a pattern of prayer (see ch. 1) that I use on an almost daily basis. So I'm quite familiar with the half dozen pieces of armor that Paul describes (Eph. 6:13–17). As I began to lead these pastors through the belt of truth, the breastplate of righteousness, and so on, I could feel my own enthusiasm mounting. It didn't hurt that the audience included a good number of Hispanic and African-American pastors who spurred me on by punctuating my prayer with their interjections of "Yes, Lord!" and "Thank you, Jesus!" (What a welcome change from the response I'm used to getting from my mostly white, suburban congregation.)

By the time I finished my prayer, the atmosphere in that auditorium was spiritually supercharged. I felt like a football coach who had just finished his pre-game locker room rant and was sending his team onto the field to kick major butt. The vocalist who took the platform after me to present some special music said, "Wow! What a prayer!" How could I be flattered—after all, I had just borrowed Paul's outline.

I can think of no better way to begin a day than by praying on the believer's armor. Every day we're engaged in a spiritual war—whether we're aware of it or not. Our enemy stalks us relentlessly, like a roaring lion, hoping to devour us (1 Pet. 5:8). If we are not prepared for such a foe we will end up becoming his lunch. That's why I've taught my kids—and the men whom I disciple in an early morning small group—how to pray on the armor.

There are six pieces of armor described in Ephesians 6. Each article consists of two parts: belt/truth; breastplate/righteousness; shoes/gospel; shield/faith; helmet/salvation; sword/Word of God. Both parts must be considered in order to understand how to pray on each piece of armor.

Let's begin with the belt of truth. When a Roman soldier went into battle he would tuck his loose-hanging outer garment into his belt so as not to trip on it as he advanced against the enemy. God has given us a belt to wear. Our belt is truth. If we want to avoid getting tripped up and falling on our faces, spiritually speaking, we must pray that God helps us to be honest, free-from-deceit people of integrity throughout the course of our day.

The breastplate, the next piece of armor, was intended to cover a soldier's most vital organs. Without his breastplate in place he was dead meat. If we want to protect our spiritual lives we must cover our hearts with the righteousness of Christ. This righteousness, in terms of its practical outworking, is a reflection of Christ's character. So we pray on the breastplate of righteousness by asking God to make us more like his Son—more loving, holy, patient, faithful, merciful, and so on.

A soldier's shoes, in Paul's day, had cleats on the bottom. This allowed him to move forward without slipping and sliding. (As the dad of a soccer-playing son, I've had many opportunities to watch players whose shoes failed to grab wet turf. It's an amusing sight—until somebody gets hurt in a collision or from a pulled groin muscle.) Our shoes help us to advance Christ's kingdom. That's why Paul refers to them as "gospel" shoes. We need to pray that God will give us both the courage and the right words to share the good news of Christ with others—to move forward into these situations instead of retreating from them.

Don't think of a Roman soldier's shield as being the size and shape of a garbage can lid. The shield that Paul had in mind was almost as tall as the man, protecting him head to toe when he was crouched behind it. It was made of numerous layers of leather that had been soaked in water. All incendiary missiles would be extinguished upon contact. The believer's shield is faith. Not just saving faith, but a daily confidence in God. We must pray for God to give us an optimistic spirit when the arrows of discouragement, criticism, hardship, stress, and dilemma are shot at us.

A helmet, of course, covered a soldier's head. A believer's head—mind, thoughts, attitudes—is to be protected by salvation. What is included in this concept of salvation? Well, what has happened to us as a result of being saved? The Holy Spirit has taken up residence in our lives. Our sins have been forgiven. We have become citizens of an eternal kingdom. There is an unimaginable inheritance awaiting us in heaven. We pray on the helmet of salvation by asking God to fill our minds with these realities. We invite God, for example, to give us a greater preoccupation with the thought of his being our Father (by virtue of salvation) than with our usual thoughts: worrying about buying a new lawnmower, or noticing the good-looking girl who just walked by, or lamenting the raise we didn't get, or growling at the terrible traffic.

Finally, no soldier is fully equipped without a sword in hand. This is the only offensive piece of armor. It enables one to take it to the enemy. Our sword is God's Word. Jesus showed us how to use it when he turned the tables on Satan's temptations in the wilderness. Jesus responded to each attack with a Scripture quotation. (Notice that all the verses Jesus used came from the Old Testament book of Deuteronomy. How many of us could defend ourselves against our spiritual enemy—and go on the offensive—by quoting from Deuteronomy?) We pray on the sword by asking God to give us the time and discipline and insight to study his Word. And the ability to put it into practice.

Attributes of God

A few Christmases ago, I bought our family a pool table. I found it through an ad in the newspaper. When I called the private number, a friendly guy picked up the phone. He not only offered me a great deal on his used pool table, he also volunteered to deliver it to my home in his pickup truck—and then helped me set it up!

As we were assembling things in my basement he discovered that I'm a pastor. "There's something I've always wanted to ask a pastor," he called from under the pool table where he was attaching a leg. Uh-oh, I thought. Here comes the theological question that has stumped Bible scholars for centuries. But he surprised me as he continued. "I lead a men's small group in my church. Occasionally I'll wrap up our meetings by suggesting, 'Why don't we just take a few minutes to praise God in prayer?' Do you know what happens next?" he asked me. I didn't.

"Nothing. Absolutely nothing. It gets real quiet. Nobody knows what to say. How can I teach the guys in my group to offer up prayers of praise?" Great question. I began my answer by introducing him to the A to Z list of God's names and attributes (mentioned in ch. 1). I explained the importance of expanding his understanding of who God is, by increasing his prayer vocabulary with words that Scripture uses to describe God.

Of course, just knowing the attributes on this list will not necessarily make one a better God praiser. It takes practice to learn how to use these descriptors in an expanded way. Otherwise we'll find ourselves saying nothing more than, "Lord, I praise you for being *faithful*. Lord, I praise you for being *familiar with suffering*. Lord, I praise you for being a *Father*. Lord, I praise you for being a *fire*. Lord, I praise you for being the *firstborn* among many brothers. Lord, I praise you for being a *fortress*." (Can you tell that I'm in the *f*'s?) This doesn't feel like I'm praising God. It feels like I'm reciting a page out of a dictionary.

What can we do with one of God's attributes or names that will turn it into heartfelt praise? Let me answer that question, I hope not irreverently, by recalling a game you may have played. Are you familiar with the "word association" game? One person begins by announcing a word, any word. The next player says the first related word that comes to his or her mind. On and on it goes.

I remember a fishing trip to Canada, with my son and a few of his buddies, when boredom during a long van ride was relieved by the word association game. It went something like this: "pizza" (how else would a teenage boy begin?) . . . "Chicago" (where you'll find the best deep dish) . . . "Cubs" (Chicago's favorite team) . . . "heartbreak" (do I need to explain?) . . . "cancer" (a form of heartbreak) . . . "doctor" . . . "dentist" . . . "cavity" . . . "candy" . . . "trick or treat" . . . "pumpkins" . . . "orange" . . . "apple" . . . "Adam and Eve" . . . "garden" . . . "weeds" . . . "work."

What does this have to do with praising God according to his attributes? Each attribute is like the first word in the word association game. But instead of coming up with just one word that relates to this attribute, our goal is to try to think of as many associated words (or expressions or phrases) as possible. Let me give a few examples. We'll go back to the attributes beginning with the letter *f* which were mentioned a moment ago. Here are some ideas that I would associate with:

Faithful: dependable . . . never changes . . . always there when I call . . . keeps his promises . . . so unlike my up-and-down, hot-and-cold behavior . . . consistent . . . loyal . . . a characteristic that God demonstrates in a fresh way each day, even though I've not exhausted the previous day's allotment (see Lam. 3:22–23).

Familiar with suffering: Christ took on humanity . . . could've been spared the pain had he stayed in heaven . . . it was my sin for which he suffered . . . just resisting temptation, never giving in to it, brought about suffering for him (Heb. 2:18) . . . empathetic, understands my hurts . . . endured the Father's wrath.

Father: has compassion on me, remembering that I'm dust (Ps. 103:13–14) . . . an intimate relationship with me . . . knows me thoroughly . . . protects . . . provides . . . cares . . . has adopted me . . . disciplines me for my good . . . calls me by name.

Fire: purges sin from my life . . . refines me as gold . . . not to be trifled with (remember Nadab and Abihu, Lev. 10:1–3?) . . . will one day destroy all evil . . . a mark of the zeal that the Holy Spirit produces in me.

Firstborn among many brothers: rose from the dead . . . triumphed over sin and death . . . guarantees my resurrection . . . others, who had been previously raised from the dead, eventually re-died—but he was raised to live forever . . . one day the trumpet will sound and something incredible will happen.

Fortress: protects me from my enemies . . . nothing can penetrate his walls . . . gives a sense of security . . . allows a reprieve from battle . . . provides insulation from the world's constant press.

Each morning I choose three or four attributes or titles of God like these and pray them back to him by voicing everything that they bring to mind and giving him thanks for such. It's a great way to begin my day.

The Fruit of the Spirit

John Goldingay is an Old Testament professor at Fuller Seminary (California) and the past president of an Anglican seminary in England. He has written a wonderfully insightful and heart-warming book about the challenges he's faced in caring for a wife with multiple sclerosis for more than thirty years. With a humble openness, Goldingay tells of a friend's candid remarks. His friend said that the fruit of God's Spirit was evident in Goldingay's life—with the exception of joy!

Goldingay chalked up this deficiency to a temperament weakness, coupled with his burden of round-the-clock caregiving. But after reflecting on the friend's feedback a bit, he decided to pray and ask God for joy. To his surprise God gave it to him! Then negative circumstances came along and crowded the freshly received joy out of his life. So he prayed for joy a second time, hardly expecting a positive response. But God gave it to him again . . . and again . . . and again. Each time he asked for it.

By this time Goldingay realized: "If joy is a gift, a fruit of the Spirit's presence, there is no reason why God should not give it at any moment. It is not dependent on my persistence or failure but on God's giving. Not that I did nothing: I did sing praise songs on two or three occasions. But that would have gotten me nowhere without God's giving. And perhaps that is true for anyone, with joy or with whatever gift or fruit we would like. If we believe these things are God's gifts and not dependent on us, we might even ask God to give them to us."[1]

We can't ask God, however, to give us the fruits of his Spirit unless we know what they are. They are love; joy; peace; patience; kindness; goodness; faithfulness; gentleness; and self-control (Gal. 5:22–23). Nine fruits in all. (Someone with a background in New Testament Greek will want to point out that Paul uses the singular "fruit" to describe these nine characteristics. But this collective singular should not discourage us from considering the nine traits individually.) I did not have to turn in my Bible, just now, to type this list because I memorized it some time ago. If you are going to use it as a pattern for prayer it would be a good idea to write the nine fruits on a three-by-five-inch card and review them until you know them by heart.

I don't usually pray through this entire list. I just choose the fruit that seems most needful in my life at the moment and ask God to produce it in me. Sometimes I pray this prayer when I'm by myself. Sometimes I use it to stimulate prayer when I'm with one of my kids or wrapping up a small group meeting. "Let's pray the fruit of the Spirit," I'll suggest. "I'll take one and pray it through and then you take one and do the same." (No matter how often I do this, it always seems as if I ought to begin with *patience.* Ugh!)

When praying for a particular fruit of the Spirit there are two sides of it that I like to mention. First, as a matter of praise, I note how I see this fruit manifested in the life of Christ. With patience, for example, it is easy to identify a variety of ways in which Jesus has demonstrated a gracious forbearance toward me. As the psalmist points out, the Lord has been slow to anger, not treating me as my sins deserve nor rewarding me according to my iniquities (Ps. 103:8, 10). I praise God for how he models patience.

The flip side of this prayer is to ask God to manifest this same patience in me. I try to be specific about situations in my life that presently call for it: interruptions to my day's agenda; overly-cautious (or overly-aggressive) drivers; balls that others drop and I am expected to pick up; long meetings—made longer by the rabbit trail someone takes us down.

You get the idea. Choose a fruit that you need. Praise the Lord for the way in which he models that fruit. Ask him to produce the fruit in you—and be specific.

Body Parts

Although I often use this pattern of prayer in private, I have much more fun with it when I introduce it to a group of people—because I insist that it be accompanied by body motions (always a challenge with guys). "'Body parts' prayer!" I'll announce, for example, on a Sunday morning to our congregation.

This will be followed by the declaration: "Lord, we give you our eyes." As soon as this is said, we all put our hands on our eyes while I continue. "Our eyes have been used for sinful purposes this week—to look at people and things in a way that made us covet, or lust, or boast. But now we offer you these eyes and ask you to help us see others as you see them."

"And, Lord, we give you our feet." Now, we begin to stamp or shuffle our feet. "These feet have taken us to some places where we shouldn't have gone. But now we ask you to use them to carry us into situations where we can serve others or share Christ."

"And, Lord, we give you our tongues. Stick them out and grab them if you'd like!" (I'm not kidding.) A quick confession ensues of all the ways in which we've used our mouths sinfully, followed by an entreaty that we might use our words in a way that pleases God and blesses others.

"And, Lord, we give you our hands." We lift them high over our heads and shake them. (All charisphobics are now freaking out.) "Our hands have been used," we acknowledge, "to hoard stuff and to strike our kids in anger and to gesture (profanely) at drivers who cut us off in traffic. But we want our hands to be employed," we tell God, "in serving others and in communicating squeezes of encouragement."

"And, Lord, we give you our hearts." We place our hands over hearts like we're reciting the Pledge of Allegiance. Our hearts represent our desires and affections. What have we been wrongfully setting them on? What would God want us to have hearts for?

Do you see how this "body parts" pattern of prayer works? After each part is mentioned and identified by some motion, we pray for it along two lines. First, we repent of the ways in which we have used that member of our bodies to sin. Second, we offer God that very same member to use in his service.

If this sounds at all familiar, it is because it's nothing more than a literal application of Paul's counsel to us: "Do not offer the parts of your body to sin, as instruments of wickedness, but rather offer yourselves to God, as those who have been brought from death to life; and offer the parts of your body to him as instruments of righteousness" (Rom. 6:13). And just in case we missed it the first time he said it, Paul repeats these same instructions (v. 19).

This is a prayer pattern that you can teach your kids. And it comes in handy when you've got just a few minutes with them in the car on the way to school, or to a soccer game, or to a friend's house. You start with a body part of your choice. (I always began with the mouth since that seemed to be the member that was most likely to get my kids into trouble.)

"Lord, we give you our mouths." (Use plural pronouns as you pray since you're interceding for both yourself and anyone else who's participating.) "These mouths have been used to say some pretty bad stuff—lies, put-downs, profanity, gossip, complaints. We feel like Isaiah, who asked you to touch his lips with a burning coal to purify him. We want you to use our mouths to communicate words of praise, encouragement, salvation, wise counsel."

Now, somebody else gets to choose a body part and pray for all of you. Round and round it goes. Try to say something different each time you use this prayer pattern so that it stays fresh and you avoid rote repetition.

A Few Friends

Do you know anyone who prays for you on a regular basis? Wouldn't you love to have an intercessor in your corner like Paul? Paul was always praying for his friends. He wrote to:

- the Romans (Rom. 1:9–10): "God . . . is my witness how constantly I remember you in my prayers at all times."
- the Ephesians (Eph. 1:15–16): "Ever since I heard about your faith . . . I have not stopped giving thanks for you, remembering you in my prayers."
- the Philippians (Phil. 1:4): "In all my prayers for all of you, I always pray with joy."
- the Colossians (Col. 1:9): "Since the day we heard about you, we have not stopped praying for you."
- the Thessalonians (1 Thess. 1:2–3): "We always thank God for all of you, mentioning you in our prayers. We continually remember before our God and Father your work."
- Timothy (2 Tim. 1:3): "I thank God . . . as night and day I constantly remember you in my prayers."

I am so grateful for a mom and a dad and a mother-in-law who pray for me like Paul prayed for his friends. But it's dawned upon me recently that as these senior citizens (all in their 80s) eventually pass from the scene, I am going to lose the benefit of their regular intercession for me.

I know that I don't begin to realize and appreciate what a difference their prayers have made in my life. What dangers have I been protected from, what temptations have lost their hold on me, how much love has been infused into my marriage, how many of my decisions have been made wisely, how have my kids' lives been impacted, how many successes have I enjoyed in ministry because these folks have constantly remembered me in their prayers?

The examples of a praying Paul and praying parents make me want to be that kind of a faithful intercessor on behalf of others.

Unfortunately, my tendency in the past has been to pray only for family and friends if there was an urgent need in their lives—if someone had lost a job, or been hospitalized, or was struggling at work or in a marriage, or was facing a financial crisis. It was strictly the squeaky wheel that used to get the grease of my prayers.

Some time ago I realized that I should be much more systematic in my praying for others. This squeaky wheel approach was too hit-and-miss. (And, to be honest, it was more "miss" than "hit.") The first thing I did—and I would recommend this same initial step to you—was to make a list of all the people for whom I thought I ought to be praying. It was helpful, at this stage, to think in terms of a few basic categories: extended family members (the ones I'm close to), Christian leaders (in my church and around the world), good friends, work associates, and those who need Christ.

My list had over 100 names on it! No way could I pray for all those people every day. (I know that some would-be intercessors settle for praying a one-line, "Bless So-and-so," for each person on their lists. It's quick. But it's nothing more than a roll call. Real intercession requires addressing specific concerns.) I resolved my problem—or so I thought—by dividing up my list of names among the seven days of the week.

Have you ever done this? Ever created a massive prayer list and then broken it down for each day of the week? If you have, you've probably discovered, as I did, that this approach works well—at producing guilt! Here's what happens. The first day you miss your prayer time (because you slept through your alarm and are now running late for work), you decide to double up your prayer lists the next day so that no name gets skipped. But this is pretty unrealistic since it requires that you pray tomorrow for a boatload of people. You might do this once or twice. But, eventually, you'll let dropped days stay dropped—and then feel guilty about all those people for whom you failed to pray.

Let me offer you a simpler approach. A guilt-free approach. An approach that recognizes the fact that some days you're going to miss your prayer time. I keep an A to Z list of friends on one page, front and back, in my "quiet time" journal (a spiral bound notebook in which I record my daily insights from Scripture). I stick a little Post-it note under the person's name I last prayed for on a previous day. Some days I have the time to pray for five or six people, so I move the note down accordingly. Other days I'm in a hurry and may get to only one or two names.

And occasionally I miss interceding for others altogether. But I don't beat myself up over this lapse. I don't do penance by making myself pray for twice as many people the next day. I just pick up where I left off and continue on down my list, moving my Post-it note as I go. It may take me a few weeks to cover everyone I've determined to pray for, but there's a steady thoroughness to this approach that gives me a sense of deep satisfaction.

One of my favorite times to pray for others is on my early morning jog. I'll take a quick look at the next few names on my A to Z list as I'm stretching my muscles (the older I get, the longer it takes to get ready to run), and then I'll head out to exercise and intercede at the same time. Other venues for this kind of praying are while washing dishes, running errands, walking the dog, or standing in lines.

There's a more extemporaneous version of this routine that I also employ quite regularly. Instead of taking several names off my list (which I may not have handy at the time), I'll invite the Lord to bring someone to mind spontaneously. Just one person. As soon as a name pops into my mind, I'll pray for that individual. When I'm finished, I'll ask the Lord, "Who's next?" And I'll continue to pray for people, one by one, as God puts them on my heart and until I run out of time.

I've found that this make-it-up-as-you-go method works great when I'm traveling in the car with one of my kids. "Let's pray for some people," I'll suggest, "whoever God brings to our minds. I'll go first." Then I'll pray for somebody. Then they'll pray for somebody. Then it's my turn again. Then it's their turn. And so it goes.

Maybe you're wondering at this point: "What do I pray for others if there's no crisis in their lives right now?" I have to admit that it is easier to intercede for my friends when I'm aware of some urgent need they're faced with. But that's not typically the case when I'm just working my way through my A to Z list.

However, I've concluded that most of those for whom I pray would benefit from my bringing to God the same sorts of concerns that are common to everyone. If they're married, I pray that they will love each other, resolve conflicts, resist sexual temptation, and so on. If they are parents, I pray for wisdom in raising their kids. If they're believers, I pray for their roots to go down into God's Word, and for them to boldly share Christ at work. Pray for the usual stuff.

A side benefit I've discovered, in becoming a more consistent intercessor for others, is that I'm learning to listen more attentively during conversations. I want to detect and remember any prayer-worthy concerns that are expressed. This will give me something specific to talk to God about the next time I'm praying for those I've spoken with.

I also experience great joy when friends mention in passing something that God has recently done in their lives—and it's the very thing I've been praying for them! There's almost a secret exchange that takes place between God and me when this happens. "Little do they know," I tell God, "that my prayers made a huge contribution to this outcome." (And God usually responds, "Let's just keep that between the two of us.")

Have you made your list of friends yet? That's where you need to begin. Do it now. If you're a perfectionist, no need to wait until you can draw up a comprehensive list that doesn't miss a soul. (Perfectionism always leads to procrastination.) Consider this a rough draft. You can always add names down the road. And don't feel guilty about subtracting names in the future when certain people are no longer a regular part of your life. (You're not "pulling the plug" on them!)

Take out a piece of paper, make five columns for the five categories I described above (extended family, Christian leaders, good friends, co-workers, and those who need Christ), and add names to each column. Next, take all those names and make one, big, A to Z master list. The only thing left to do is to stick a Post-it note to your list. Oh . . . and don't forget to pray.

Thank-You's

Thanksgiving was one of my favorite holidays as a boy. There were a few personal rituals that I looked forward to celebrating each year on this special day. For starters, my sister Debbie and I would get up early, climb on our bikes, and go for a long, adventuresome ride. The air would be crisp, the roads would be empty, and we would wander to places we never told our parents about. (One time we ended up at an old railroad yard and climbed aboard abandoned boxcars).

We would usually arrive home about the time the parades began on TV. And as we watched the floats and bands move across the screen we would each compose an annual Thanksgiving list. We did our creative best to include everything that we could possibly thank God for on that piece of paper.

I miss Thanksgiving. Somehow the commercialization of Christmas has edged out this late November holiday. Captain John Smith, Pocahontas, and a turkey dinner have been replaced by the ever-earlier appearing of Santa Claus, Frosty the Snowman, and a reindeer-powered sleigh of presents. It seems that we're more interested in *getting* stuff than in *giving* thanks—an imbalance that can also be detected in our prayers throughout the year.

We don't have to wait until Thanksgiving to make our "thank-you" lists. This is a wonderful pattern of prayer to practice on a regular basis. Whether you're by yourself, or with a friend, family members, or a small group, simply announce, "It's 'thank-you' prayer time." Then start thanking God for whatever he brings to mind—one item at a time.

I've found it helpful to do this by category (otherwise I forget entire classes of things to thank God for). I'll start out with the most obvious type of blessings: physical. This would include my health, my job, my home, my cars (both of which have over 150,000 miles on them and are still going strong), vacation getaways (right now, as I'm writing, I'm looking at Lake Michigan from the beach house of a friend who's made it available to me), music (from Bach to Bono), and so on.

Spiritual blessings are my next category. I thank God for (in no particular order): the forgiveness of sins, the indwelling Holy Spirit, the counsel of his Word, an eternal home in heaven, the life-mission of advancing Christ's kingdom, and the peace of God's presence.

The people in my life—relational blessings—follow. I thank God for my wife of thirty years. I could spend my entire "thank-you" prayer time on Sue (which would be healthy for my marriage—especially if she's within earshot). I thank God for my three kids (to balance out all the times I've spent wringing my hands over how they'll turn out). I thank God for my co-workers, the guys in my small group, my accountability partner (being especially grateful for the way he keeps confidences). If you're in sales, thank God for your customers. Are you a doctor? Thank God for your patients (but stop short of thanking him for the illnesses that bring you their business).

One final category of blessings: trials. All of chapter 9 is devoted to trials, so I won't say much more at this point. Thanking God for our trials is an art. And the better we get at it the more of God's peace (Phil. 4:6–7) and joy (James 1:2–3) we experience in our lives. Start practicing this pattern today. Go for a long walk, scroll through every hardship you're currently facing, and find something to thank God for in each situation.

Persecuted Brothers and Sisters

One Sunday morning after the service a member of our church approached me and asked me to pray for her brother. He is a missionary in Uzbekistan (actually, he's an "undercover" missionary since the country does not officially allow foreign missionaries within its borders). His house had recently burned to the ground, possibly as a result of arson. He and his wife and their three kids had barely made it out, with nothing more than the clothes on their backs.

As this woman was recounting the tragedy to me, I was struck by the thought: *She's not talking about just any missionary—she's talking about her brother. No wonder she's so urgently asking me to pray.* No sooner had this thought occurred to me than the Holy

Spirit seemed to add: *He's your brother, too. Pray for him like he's a member of your family—because he is.*

Imagine that your brother or sister had been in one of the Twin Towers on 9/11. Wouldn't you have viewed that calamity in an entirely different way? Watching scores of people lose their lives on that day was horrible—just think of how much worse it would've been if you had lost a family member.

As Christ followers, we have brothers and sisters around the world who are enduring persecution—right now—because of their faith. They have lost their jobs, their kids have been denied schooling, they have little to eat, they have been socially harassed and physically abused, they are in prison or in hiding—all because they love Jesus and aren't afraid to say so. More individuals have lost their lives for Christ in the past century than in all previous nineteen centuries combined! Members of our family.

I confess that it has taken me far too long to become concerned about these "relatives" of mine. But over the past couple of years God has been expanding my heart for persecuted brothers and sisters by making them an object of my prayers. God used Hebrews 13:3 to first get my attention on this score: "Remember those in prison as if you were their fellow prisoners, and those who are mistreated as if you yourselves were suffering."

I had heard ministries in local jails and state penitentiaries use this verse to support their work. But on inspecting the context more closely, I realized that the writer of Hebrews is not referring to those who are guilty of genuine crimes. He's talking about those for whom imprisonment is a mistreatment—their faith in Christ has landed them in jail.

How does one "remember" these people? By praying. And I will personally vouch for the fact that a love for these brothers and sisters doesn't lead to praying so much as praying leads to a love for these brothers and sisters. Isn't that the way it often works in matters of obedience? As we do the right thing, God transforms our hearts. But when we put off obeying until we "feel like it," we seldom get around to the right behaviors.

I have been especially helped in learning to pray intelligently for persecuted family members by Voice of the Martyrs (VOM). This ministry was begun years ago by Richard Wurmbrandt, a Romanian pastor who spent considerable time in communist prisons because of his faith in Christ. VOM produces a monthly newsmagazine that will often focus on a particular country where persecution is rife (e.g., North Korea, Columbia, or Ethiopia) or on a group of people who are suffering for Christ (e.g., the Hmong in Viet Nam, the "untouchables" in India, or widows of martyrs who are left to raise their families alone). In addition to this monthly resource, VOM has a website (www.persecution.com) that gives weekly reports covering four or five recent cases of persecution (click on "Prayer Update").

What does all this have to do with patterns of prayer? Simply this. I've made it my habit, for some time now, to pray for my persecuted brothers and sisters every weekend. I'll read an excerpt from VOM's magazine or Web site, stop and pray for those it describes, then move on to the next account and pray some more. Little by little I've found myself becoming more of a world Christian. And I can't begin to tell you how this practice has prepared me to worship each week at my cushioned-theatre-seats-in-a-beautiful-auditorium setting.

Your family is in trouble. Brothers and sisters around the world are counting on you to uphold them in prayer. Will you do it? Regularly? Having a pattern will make it a habit.

I've described seven different patterns in this chapter, each of which could launch you into prayer:

- believer's armor
- attributes of God
- fruits of the Spirit
- body parts
- a few friends
- thank-you's
- persecuted brothers and sisters

You don't need to start using them all today, just one or two of them. Experiment. Try them out as you go for a jog or drive to work or stand in line at the grocery store—or as you're waiting for your bacon and Gorgonzola chopped salad to arrive at CPK.

Onto the Praying Field

1. List the six pieces of armor that Paul mentions in Ephesians 6:13–17. What topics for prayer does each suggest? (For example, the *belt of truth* prompts me to pray that I'd be honest in conversations; I wouldn't engage in hidden sins; I would accept correction from others.)

   _____ of truth:

   breastplate of _____:

   _____ of _____ shoes:

   shield of _____:

   _____ of salvation:

   sword of the Spirit which is the _____ of _____:

   Try praying on these six pieces of armor right now.

2. Choose three "B" titles or names of God from the appendix. What does each tell you about God? (List a few associated words or phrases for each title or name.) Make your brief lists into prayers of praise.

   B_____:
   B_____:
   B_____:

3. Name four body parts and describe ways in which each

could be used to serve sin or God. Then offer these body parts to God in prayer.

To serve sin:				
To serve God:				

4. Who prays for you on a regular basis? How does that make you feel?

   Make a list of people to systematically pray for in each of the following categories. Pray for two or three of these people each day this week.

   Extended family members:
   Christian leaders:
   Friends:
   Work associates:
   Those who need Christ:

5. Have a spontaneous "thank-you" prayer time with another Christ follower. Go back and forth for several minutes, expressing your gratitude to God for specific items.

6. Visit the Voice of the Martyrs Web site at www.persecution. com and/or begin a free subscription to Voice of the Martyrs monthly newsletter. Choose one situation in which Christ followers are being persecuted and pray for them.

4

Promptings

Pray When the Spirit Says Pray

Now that we have learned some formulaic ways to pray, we are ready to discover how to respond to the more spontaneous promptings of the Holy Spirit when it comes to prayer.

Our lives are filled with prompters, reminding us to attend to important tasks. The battery that runs my basement sump pump sounds an alarm when it needs to be recharged. My cell phone beeps when I've been away from it and missed a call. My last dog (who is now in heaven, I'm sure) used to sit by the kitchen cabinet where her treats were kept so that I wouldn't forget to feed her. Sometimes the prompters in my life are even self-initiated—I often turn my watch around on my wrist to remind me to do something later (although I occasionally can't remember what that something is).

In a similar fashion, the Holy Spirit often uses promptings to draw us to the important task of praying. We need to learn how to identify these signals so that we will be alerted: *It's time to pray.* The life situations covered in this chapter that call us to prayer include those times when we're anxious, joyful, tempted, concerned, or angry.

When We're Anxious

My all-time favorite Scripture on prayer is Philippians 4:6–7: "Do not be anxious about anything, but in everything, by prayer and petition, with thanksgiving, present your requests to God. And the peace of God, which transcends all understanding, will guard your hearts and your minds in Christ Jesus." We'll focus an entire upcoming chapter on this text, but for now I just want to note the prayer prompter it identifies: anxiety.

Whenever we find ourselves worrying about something a little alarm should go off in our minds. "Time to pray! Time to pray! Time to pray!" This is so basic. It's so basic that I get embarrassed when I find myself fretting and suddenly realize that I haven't prayed about my concern. ("And you're a pastor!" my conscience scolds me.)

At the end of a recent missions trip to Haiti with a team from my church, we were returning home via a stopover in Miami. In Miami we were supposed to claim our luggage, go through customs, recheck all bags and hustle to the gate for our next departure. Whoever had made our reservations had failed to take all of this into account because we had very little time between flights to get everything done. And to make matters worse, the first leg of our journey had been delayed. We'd arrived in Miami later than scheduled.

While I was waiting for my suitcase to appear on the conveyor belt, I could feel my anxiety level rising. All around me I could hear the grumbling of other passengers who were also in danger of missing connecting flights. It was then that my leadership gift kicked in. I started mentally strategizing how to meet our challenge. *Maybe* (the gears of my thinking were now whirring) *we should send someone ahead to the departure gate and ask the ticket agent to hold the next flight. Maybe we should put our biggest guys up at the conveyor belt to grab our bags first. Maybe we should bribe the customs official to give our luggage a quick pass.* (I'd been in corruption-prone Haiti for too long.)

Suddenly it dawned on me: *Maybe I should pray!* (Duh! How often do I come up with *plans* when God wants me to come up with *prayers*?) Without bothering to bow my head or close my eyes I began to mumble a petition to God. I told him that if he wanted us to spend an extra few hours in Miami—or even an overnight—we would do so with cheerful hearts and with the expectation that he had something to accomplish in or through us as we waited. But I quickly added that it sure would be nice to get home on time, having just worked our tails off for 10 days in a third-world country.

I was still praying when an airlines official showed up and announced to the crowd: "If you're headed to Chicago, don't worry about making your connecting flight. It's been delayed by an hour." Coincidence? I don't think so. I started high-fiving the other members of my team. My only regret was that I hadn't announced to others my intention to pray so that I could now claim credit for the answer to prayer. (What a sicko!)

Whenever I preach on Philippians 4:6–7 someone is bound to come up to me afterward and ask: "How big does my anxiety have to be before I pray about it?" I know the thinking that goes on behind a question like that. We assume that God is awfully busy and prefers not to be bothered with our concerns unless they're significant enough to warrant interrupting him, right? But this text certainly doesn't encourage that sort of thinking. This Scripture plainly teaches that if something is big enough to worry about, it's big enough to pray about. (Note the *anything* and *everything* of v. 6.)

What are you anxious about? Pray about it. And, if you're like me, don't wait to pray until you've strategized every other possible way to address your concern. Begin with prayer. I can't remember who said it, but it's worth repeating: "You can do all sorts of things *after* you've prayed. But you can do nothing of significance *until* you've prayed."

I need to put that quote someplace where I can see it. Because I'm too quick to problem-solve and too slow to pray. How many illustrations of this tendency would you like to hear? Okay, one more. Last year Sue's parents were traveling from their winter home in Florida to their summer residence in Ohio. Somewhere along the way they got lost. Or to put it more accurately, we lost them. They were supposed to stop, en route, at Sue's sister's house and they didn't show up.

When Char called us to report, "No Mom and Dad," we were all immediately concerned. My parents-in-law are in their mid-eighties and their driving reflexes aren't what they used to be. We put together list of things to do. Call the highway patrol for each state they were to pass through. Check. Contact their Florida neighbors to see what time they'd left for Ohio. Check. Get in touch with other family members to find out if anyone had heard from them. Check.

When we went to bed that night we still had no idea where Mom and Dad were. And we'd done everything we could have done to locate them. All that was left to do was to pray. What an incriminating statement. All that was *left* to do. Why had prayer been *left*? (Note: We had done some praying throughout the ordeal. Mostly "quickie" prayers rather than concerted praying.) Long story short, we went to bed earnestly praying (finally!) and got up the next morning to learn that Sue's parents were just fine. Bad traffic had slowed them down the previous day so they'd decided to check into a hotel. (No, they haven't discovered telephones yet.)

If something is big enough to worry about, it's big enough to pray about. Immediately. Don't wait. Anxiety is a prompting from the Holy Spirit to pray. Are you worried about the traffic that's keeping you from getting to work on time? Pray. (God may not part the sea of cars but I guarantee that something good will come of your praying.) Are you worried about finances? Pray. Are you worried about the funny noise that your dishwasher is making? Pray. (I mean it.) Are you worried about not understanding calculus? Pray. (You might want to throw some fasting in for that one.)

I've discovered that I sometimes worry without even realizing that I'm worrying. I'm like the duck that appears to be floating along serenely while below the waterline it's paddling desperately. Impatience or irritability are usually the tip-off that some invisible anxiety is gnawing away at me. I actually have to go to God on these occasions and ask, "Lord, would you help me define what I'm worried about?" Only then am I able to pray about my anxiety.

Our worries are a sign of our helplessness. Something is out of our control. Something is wrong and we can't fix it. Something is confusing and we can't figure it out. Something needs to happen and we are powerless to make it happen. Helplessness. Do you feel it? Then pray. I read a definition for prayer some time ago that I really liked: *Prayer is helplessness plus faith.* Yes!

Although we'll be returning to Philippians 4:6–7 in a later chapter, there is one more insight from this text that I want to note now as it relates to anxiety. There is a two-word phrase in these verses that must not be neglected, or we will sabotage all attempts to put our worries to flight by praying. The phrase I'm referring to is *with thanksgiving.*

It is quite possible to be more worried when you've finished praying for something than you were before you began. Leave thanksgiving out of your anxiety-prompted prayer and it will probably end up as hand-wringing. Ever have that happen to you? You decided to talk to God about some concern and as you did so—giving him all the gruesome details, of course—your problem got bigger and bigger. You weren't relieved when you said "amen." You were all worked up.

Let's say that you heard a knock in your car's engine—and as soon as you realized that this strange noise was making you anxious you prayed about it. Good move! You began your prayer: "Lord, I don't know what's causing my car to make that sound. But you do. Please heal my engine or direct me to a mechanic who can do the job." So far, so good.

Unfortunately, you continued: "You know I can't afford a new vehicle, Lord. We're saving money for our kids' college fund. Of course, they'll probably never get into college considering their current grades. And how can they bring up their grades until they learn how to focus, Lord? But focusing isn't going to happen because they're so easily swayed by peer pressure and the friends who are leading them astray. And speaking of their friends. . . . " Wow! You're on a roll. A negative roll.

Thanksgiving keeps that from happening. Thanksgiving reminds us that God is in control and that he has a long track record of resolving crises like ours. This is why it is so important to think of anything and everything we can thank God for when we're bringing him our concerns. "I don't know where the money is going to come from for a car repair, Lord. But thanks for always providing in the past. Thanks, too, for the 100,000 miles I've already gotten out of this car. And thank you for an honest mechanic and the opportunity this will give us to build a relationship." (I'm serious.) More about this to come.

When We're Joyful

Who do you tell when you've got something to celebrate? On many such occasions I still call my college roommate, John. We've been best friends for over thirty years, in spite of the fact that we live a thousand miles apart and are fortunate if we see each other once a year. But if I've got good news that I want to share with somebody, John will often be that somebody. And I'm his somebody.

Just recently John called me to say that the church he pastors had over six hundred people show up for Sunday services. I knew that when he had taken the leadership of this struggling congregation, just over a year earlier, there were barely sixty people showing up each week. I was ecstatic to hear how God had been growing John's ministry. I felt privileged that I was the one he was calling with this good news.

Of course, I also had to remind John of a previous time he'd called me to celebrate his church's attendance—the Christmas Eve when he'd nearly burned his building down. No exaggeration. His candlelit service had been packed. So much so that John could barely squeeze around the crowd to get onto the platform. As he did so he knocked over one of the candles and its flame set the straw in the manger scene ablaze. One of his elders ran for a fire extinguisher as the auditorium filled with smoke. It wasn't funny at the time but John and I laughed long and hard when he recounted the incident to me on the phone.

I'm so glad that I was the one he chose to call with both the attendance figure and the torched manger story. Joys shared, they say, are doubled. Does it ever occur to us that God wants us to share our moments of celebration with him? Consider two pithy exhortations that Paul puts side by side: "Be joyful always; pray continually" (1 Thess. 5:16–17). Is Paul telling us that joy and prayer are to go hand in hand? That seems to be his point.

Occasions of joy are the Holy Spirit's promptings to pray. God desires that we share our good news with him. When you close a big deal that you've been working on for months, take a few minutes for a "Yeah, God!" before you pick up the phone to call your boss. When your son climbs into the car after winning his soccer game, turn to him and say, "Let's tell God how much we enjoyed that victory and everything that went into it." When you see a spectacular sunset, don't just *feel* awed. Share the experience with the One who painted that sky.

Several times a week it's been my practice to head out the door for a run first thing in the morning. Before I cover my first block I have already begun to express my joy to God. Joy over the fact that my body still allows me this activity. Joy over the new day, the new sunrise. Joy over the privilege of living in a country where a peaceful run is possibile. Interestingly, I recently messed up my knee and am now waiting to find out just how much running I can return to. But God has freed me from any angst over the possible loss of this activity because I have never treated it as an expectation—as something I deserve. No, every run has been a gift. My habit of expressing joy for such has underscored that fact.

"Is anyone happy?" James asks in his epistle (James 5:13). He continues with this word of instruction to the joy-filled person: "Let him sing songs of praise." "Songs of praise" are just prayers of joy that have been set to music. Happiness should not go unexpressed. It must be given voice. And the One to whom we address these outbursts, first and foremost, should be God.

We see God's people doing this on a regular basis throughout Scripture. Moses and company, for example, cross the Red Sea on dry ground after which their enemies are drowned by returning waves. What do they do next? Sister Miriam picks up a tambourine, brother Aaron plugs his electric guitar into an amp, the rest of the band starts jamming, and all the people sing a song of joy to the Lord (see Exodus 15).

Nehemiah finishes the daunting task of rebuilding a wall around vulnerable Jerusalem. God's enemies, who have done everything possible to stop the project, are left grinding their teeth while God's people are crazy with joy. What do they do with their joy? They express it to its Source: God. "At the dedication of the wall of Jerusalem, the Levites . . . were brought to Jerusalem to celebrate joyfully the dedication with songs of thanksgiving and with the music of cymbals, harps and lyres" (Neh. 12:27). A blowout worship party follows.

The apostle Peter has the opportunity to explain the good news of Christ to Cornelius, a Gentile centurion, who is amazingly converted. Then Peter tries to explain to the suspicious Jewish leaders of the church what he's been doing in the home of an unclean Gentile. The explanation is well received. Everyone is elated. Who do they tell about this incredible breakthrough? Scripture records that they "praised God, saying, 'So then, God has granted even the Gentiles repentance unto life'" (Acts 11:18).

The pattern is obvious. When God's people have something to celebrate they are quick to communicate their joy to him. Let occasions of joy prompt you to pray. Pray while your emotions are still bubbling—not after they've lost their carbonation.

When We're Tempted

The writer of Hebrews tells us that Jesus "has been tempted in every way, just as we are" (Heb. 4:15). Initially, this encourages me with the thought that Jesus will be able to empathize with me. He knows how hard it is for me to resist the sins that are dangled in front of my nose because they've been dangled in front of his nose. But then the verse continues, and I lose all hope of Jesus understanding my battle with temptation. Jesus "has been tempted in every way, just as we are—yet was without sin."

Yet was without sin. He never slipped? No. He never gave in to a fleshly impulse? Not once. He always resisted sin's pull? Every time. Then how can he possibly understand *my* predicament? He's obviously not had to undergo the struggles that *I've* experienced. I imagine that's got something to do with his being the Son of God. No doubt temptation was nothing more than a minor irritation to him. He just turned a supernatural eye toward it and it withered.

Whoa! Not so fast. Why do we assume, because Jesus never yielded to temptation, that temptation was not as big a challenge to him as it is to us? In an earlier chapter of Hebrews this misperception is put to flight. We're told Jesus "suffered when he was tempted" (Heb. 2:18). Suffered? How so? Bible scholars point out a couple of reasons for Jesus' suffering in the face of temptation. First, because he was going toe-to-toe with Satan himself. And Satan was holding nothing back. Second—and don't miss this—Jesus suffered from temptation because he never gave in to it.

Think about it. How do we often find release from the pressure of temptation? We give in to it, right? Someone aggravates us and we're tempted to give him or her a piece of our mind. As long as we hold our tongue the pressure to let the person have it builds and builds. Finally, we can stand it no longer. A torrent of hot lava spews from our lips. Sweet relief! We couldn't have held it in a second longer.

It works the same way with other sorts of temptations. We're in an acquiring mood (which the Bible calls "coveting" and prohibits in the tenth commandment of God's "Big Ten"). At first we resist the urge to splurge, but it grows until we just have to go out and buy something. Something we don't need—but something that relieves the pressure.

And then there's lust (a temptation I know only from a guy's perspective). We feel a sexual craving. What do we do with it? Some seek release from it by turning to a pornographic Web site (and possibly by masturbating to the images they view). Sure, there's a weight of guilt that will eventually overwhelm the conscience. But initially the yielding to temptation brings relief.

71

Now recall the fact that Jesus never yielded to temptation. Never. The pressure to say "yes" to it just kept mounting. But Jesus always said "no." Do you understand why Hebrews tells us that Jesus "suffered when he was tempted"? That same verse (Heb. 2:18) goes on to explain that this is why "he is able to help those who are being tempted." Far from being unable to empathize with our struggle because he breezed through similar struggles himself, Jesus understands exactly what we're facing—and far worse.

The writer of Hebrews now draws an application from this truth: "Let us then approach the throne of grace with confidence, so that we may receive mercy and find grace to help us in our time of need" (Heb. 4:16). Temptation should prompt us to pray! Why? Because Jesus understands our predicament, because he has successfully fought—and won—similar battles, and because he has explicitly invited us to approach him in prayer when cornered by temptation.

Let me offer one other good reason to pray when tempted. Every temptation is a solicitation to illicitly fulfill a desire that God wants to satisfy in a good and wholesome way. Listen to what James has to say on this score. First, he defines temptation as the product of our runaway desires: "Each one is tempted when, by his own evil desire, he is dragged away and enticed" (James 1:14). Next, James tells us not to be fooled by this process: "Don't be deceived, my dear brothers" (v. 16). In what sense are we likely to be fooled? And what is the truth that will deliver us from this deception? James spells it out: "Every good and perfect gift is from above, coming down from the Father of the heavenly lights . . ." (v. 17).

In summary, James would tell us to remind ourselves, when tempted, that the very desires which are pulling us toward sin can be met in a much better way—by presenting them to the Giver of all good gifts, by asking the Giver to satisfy us. Have you ever prayed along these lines in the midst of temptation? Try it. Open your mouth and say, "Lord, I'm feeling the tug of sin. Would you please satisfy the desire that sin is promising to fulfill?" It may help you to identify what that desire is. But even if you can't put your finger on it, cry out to the Giver with the simple entreaty, "Lord, satisfy me."

David could've used this prayer when he was tempted by his desire for Bathsheba. In fact, the very accusation that Nathan the prophet leveled at David after the affair was that David had failed to allow God to meet his desires. Hadn't God proven to David, again and again, that he was the Giver of all good gifts? Nathan speaks for God with these words of rebuke: "I anointed you king over Israel, and I delivered you from the hand of Saul. I gave your master's house to you, and your master's wives into your arms. I gave you the house of Israel and Judah. And if all this had been too little, I would have given you even more. Why did you despise the word of the LORD by doing what is evil in his eyes?" (2 Sam. 12:7–9).

"I would have given you even more!" What a statement. God can satisfy us in a way that sin cannot—despite its promises to the contrary. This is why we must pray when tempted. Not just for Jesus-like strength to resist the pressure, but also for a wholesome satisfying of the desire that will eliminate that pressure.

And while we're at it, let me throw in one more item to include in our temptation-prompted prayer. Pray for somebody else who may be undergoing a similar temptation. This is a bit of wisdom that I picked up from Bill Thrasher in *A Journey to Victorious Praying*.[1] Thrasher suggests that we ask God to give us a "prayer burden" when we're tempted. This is a deep concern to intercede for another person. For whom? Ask God for a name, if nobody immediately comes to mind.

Thrasher points out that by using a temptation to do wrong as a motivation to do right—to pray—we turn the tables on our enemy, which often results in his leaving us alone. I've tried this and it works. When I'm struggling, for example, with wandering eyes (the kind that latch on to any possible object of lust), I have found relief in praying for a particular friend (it's hard to choose just one) whom I know is also facing this temptation. What's that line from William Cowper's poem? "And Satan trembles, when he sees/The weakest saint upon his knees."[2] That's what happens when we begin to treat temptation as a prompting to pray.

When We're Concerned

The concerns being referred to, at this point, are not the variety of personal anxieties that we covered in the opening section of this chapter (which are to be prayed for along the lines of Phil. 4:6–7). I now have in mind the concerns of others. Concerns that they bring to our attention in casual (or not-so-casual) conversation. We must cultivate the habit of immediately interceding for those who have just unburdened themselves on us.

Their concerns should be recognized as a prompting to pray. Not eventually. Right now. Because we all know the guilt of forgetting to pray for those to whom we made that simple promise, "I'll be praying for you." The guilt only intensifies when these folks see us a few days later and say, "Thanks so much for praying for me—God has really turned things around." We smile and say, "Oh, it was nothing." And it *was* nothing. Truth be known, we had neglected to pray for them as we had promised we would.

Friends of mine who are into antiquing (shopping for furniture that's old, used, and beat up) tell me, "The time to buy an antique is when you see it." What's *that* supposed to mean? Well, if you see something that will fit perfectly in the corner of your dining room but you decide to look around a bit longer—it probably won't be there when you return. You missed your opportunity. You should have bought it on the spot.

I don't know if that's really true for buying antiques. But I know it applies to praying for others' concerns. When we don't intercede as soon as we encounter these needs there's a good chance that we'll never get around to doing so.

This is not to minimize what I said earlier about the importance of scheduling time to systematically pray through your A to Z list of friends. Remember all those references from Paul's epistles about his habit of interceding for those to whom he was writing? Paul couldn't possibly pray for all those friends, with the regularity that he claimed, without setting aside a chunk of time in his daily schedule to do so.

But that's not the sort of praying that I'm talking about now. Our present topic is prayer promptings, those spontaneous urges to jump right in—praying for others, in this case, on the spot because of concerns they have just divulged to us. Our key verse for such a practice is Ephesians 6:18: "And pray in the Spirit on all occasions with all kinds of prayers and requests. With this in mind, be alert and always keep on praying for all the saints." You can't miss the three "all's" and one "always" in this verse. Paul is encouraging us to pray for others at the drop of a hat. Or, as we're prompted, at the drop of a concern.

When a friend confides in you that he and his wife have been doing quite a bit of arguing lately, don't just offer him the latest Christian book on marriage. Volunteer to pray for him. When your neighbor whispers to you that she's headed to the doctor tomorrow because of a suspicious lump in her breast, don't just say, "I hope it turns out okay." Offer to pray for her. When a work associate complains about being stressed out by everything that's got to get done, don't just commiserate by reciting your own "to do" list. Pose the question: "Would you mind if I pray for you? I've found that asking God for help does wonders for me. Let me pray for you."

Ninety-nine percent of the times that I offer to pray for people (which I'm doing more and more these days), they give me the green light to go ahead. Christians and unbelievers alike! I would have said 100 percent of the times, but I recently got rebuffed and that dropped my batting average. But let me tell you about what happened after I received that "no."

Sherry (not her real name) manages the shop where I have my car repairs done. She's a single mom, raising four kids who are young adults and lean heavily upon her for support. One of her daughters has had a baby out of wedlock—a grandson that Sherry would die for. Another daughter battles depression and suicidal tendencies. I have become Sherry's friend over the years (which says something about how often my aging cars need a mechanic). So it was not unusual for me to volunteer to pray for her on a recent occasion after she'd told me about her latest struggles.

"No, thank you!" was her immediate response. "Prayer doesn't seem to work for me. To be honest with you, I don't really feel like God cares about my situation." What does one say to a rebuff like that? Especially when it takes place in a busy auto shop with customers waiting in line? This was no time to affirm the benefits of prayer or to defend the character of God or to correct Sherry's perspective on life. I just mumbled a quiet, "I'm really sorry," and I left.

Later that afternoon my cell phone rang and the caller I.D. indicated the call came from the repair shop. I assumed a mechanic was calling to give me an estimate on the work my car needed. But it was Sherry calling to apologize. She felt that she had been rude to me and wanted to thank me for my offer of prayer. The point of my story? Even when people turn down our proposal to pray for them, be assured that God is working on their hearts. Deep down they sense the genuine concern that's behind our, "Would you mind if I pray for you?"

More and more I'm discovering that there's hardly a phone conversation that wouldn't benefit from interjecting prayer into it. So it's not unusual for me to conclude one of these interchanges with: "Hey, before we hang up, let me take a minute to pray about. . . ." I end that sentence with one or two concerns that were voiced during the previous minutes. (Men's phone calls are rarely longer than minutes. We get in. We get out.) And then I pray. If it's a believer on the other end of the line, often my "Amen" will be followed by their, "Now, let me pray for you." I can't tell you how much prayer seems to raise the value of my phone conversations.

The same thing is true of my interchanges with people before and after church services. As a preacher, I'm always eager to ask my wife during Sunday lunch, "How did my message go?" As a people-lover, she's always eager to ask me, "Did you have any good contacts?" After thirty years of being married to this woman she has finally begun to rub off on me. These days I think that I'm enjoying my Sunday contacts with others even more than I enjoy speaking to the crowd. And this is due, in large measure, to the prayer I've been throwing into these conversations. I try not to let people get away without praying for them about something.

Please understand. I don't do this because I'm a pastor. I do it because I'm a pray-er. I'm excited about the opportunities that talking with others gives me to pray for them. I'm regularly challenging the thousands of non-pastors who show up at my church each week to do the same thing. "Don't leave here today," I'll say, "without praying for somebody." And there's nothing that warms my heart more than to see, in an emptying auditorium or a bustling lobby, a guy with his arm around a buddy's shoulder, both heads bowed, praying.

When We're Angry

Ask any unbeliever unacquainted with the Bible to summarize the basic principles that Jesus taught and "love your enemies" is sure to make the short list. Everybody knows that this is something that Christ followers are supposed to do. And most of us feel like we *do* do it. That's because we've reduced Jesus' words to mean: tolerate your enemies, or ignore your enemies, or don't do anything bad to your enemies. We respond to Jesus' command with passivity.

But when we look at this command in its context, we see that Jesus will not settle for a passive response. He expects us to take action. What action? Let's read it for ourselves: "Love your enemies, do good to those who hate you, bless those who curse you, pray for those who mistreat you" (Luke 6:27–28). Loving our enemies includes doing good to them, blessing them, and praying for them.

We've just identified another prayer prompter. When we become aware of a personal enemy we are to pray for that individual. This is, quite frankly, a bit difficult for me to apply because I don't tend to see myself as having *enemies*. At least not the capital E kind of enemies. I'm a relatively nice guy. People don't go around hating me. So I could easily fail to sense a prompting of this sort to prayer.

But what if I don't define *enemies* quite so strictly? What if I include in this category, not only real enemies, but people who honk me off in general? Everybody has enemies of this kind. The guy who cut you off in traffic. The teacher who crushed your child's self-esteem. The mechanic who "fixed" your brakes three times in the last week—and they still squeak. The politician who got elected on a platform that you oppose. The business competitor who wooed away your best customer.

I could justifiably add to this list the entire New York Yankees baseball team (does anybody outside of New York City like those guys?). Seriously, the minute we redefine *enemies* as "those who get under our skin," we have a lot more people to pray for. And every time that someone does something that really makes us angry the prayer-prompter bell ought to go off in our heads.

I had to pray for my son's soccer coach along these lines. Andrew had a starting position on the varsity team for a couple of years at a public high school. I know I'm not the most objective person in making this judgment, but I'd still say that Andrew was *gooooood!* He was a defender on a team that set records for its defense. He gave 100 percent on the field. He was known as a friendly guy who didn't swear or drink. A coach's dream. Well, for whatever reason, I never felt as if this coach liked my son. *What's not to like?* I wondered.

Then one day it came to a boil in the locker room after a heartbreaking loss. The coach was in a foul mood. The players were glum as they stripped off sweat-soaked jerseys and tossed soccer balls into the bin. Andrew kicked a ball in the direction of that bin just as the coach walked in front of it. Bonk! He got nailed in the head. Whipping around, he yelled, "I don't know who the —— hit me with the —— ball but he better run for his —— life or I'm going to kill him!"

As Andrew was telling me this story that evening, I interrupted him at this point and asked, "What did you do?" "I ran for my —— life." While I chuckle at this scene in retrospect, at the time I was furious with the coach. Nobody treats my son that way. I wanted to bounce more than a soccer ball off his head!

Pray for your enemies. God's Spirit convicted me that this was a prompting to pray. And I did. No, I didn't pray the plagues of Egypt down on him. I prayed, among other things, that he would see the damage that his outburst had done and be sorry for his behavior. I prayed for my son, too. I prayed that Andrew would learn whatever God wanted to teach him from this situation.

Shortly after this, Andrew told me that his coach had apologized (sort of) to him. And Andrew admitted to the coach that kicking the ball toward the bin had not been the smartest way to put it away. My prayer was answered beyond expectation. (And I didn't end up in jail for a felony against the coach.) When we're angry with someone we can be certain that the Spirit is prompting us to pray.

Prayer is always a great first-response when we're
anxious,
joyful,
tempted,
concerned, or
angry.

Onto the Praying Field

1. Why do we sometimes (perhaps often) miss the Holy Spirit's promptings to pray? How could we develop a greater sensitivity to these leadings?

2. What are your top three anxieties at present? What two or three things could you *thank* God for in each of these situations? Take a moment to do that now.

3. Why would God want to hear from us when we have something to celebrate? Describe one of your current joys. Pray this joy back to God, giving him credit for his role in it.

4. In what way (just one) are you frequently tempted? How has God, the Giver of every good gift, provided for your needs to be met in this area? Thank God for this, and pray for someone you know who struggles with the same temptation.

5. Who is one of your enemies (whether capital "E" or small "e")? Why? What blessings could you pray for this person? Do so now.

6. In order to recognize the Holy Spirit's promptings to pray, keep your eyes and ears open this week to situations in which you are
anxious:

joyful:

tempted:

concerned (for others):

angry (with enemies):

Describe a time when you spontaneously prayed this week because of that prompting.

Passion

Say It Like You Mean It

I am deeply indebted to Bill Gothard for crystallizing my thoughts on the importance of praying with passion through *The Power of Crying Out*.[1] Less than a hundred pages long, this book is packed with insights. Sue and I read it out loud to each other. Then I bought seventy copies to give away (okay, I resold them at a greatly discounted rate) to men in my church who are committed to praying for me on a regular basis.

The book's thesis is pretty well summed up in its title. There is more power to our prayers when they are delivered with some oomph. (Don't ask me to define *oomph*. Just the sound one makes when saying it should communicate its meaning.) We can pray. Or, we can PRAY. What's the difference? PRAYING (as compared to praying) is marked by greater volume, determination, and passion.

Gothard claims to see a pattern in Scripture. There are times, he notes, when God allows difficult circumstances in the lives of his people. We pray for help. But nothing happens. God refuses to get involved until we "cry out"—and not a second sooner. This crying out demonstrates an earnestness in our praying. It's a bit like kneeling down or fasting, two other physical acts that underscore the fact that we mean business.

Our crying out stirs the heart of God. Psalm 18 paints a vivid picture of God's response to a passionately prayed prayer. "In my distress," the psalmist recounts, "I called to the LORD; I cried to my God for help. From his temple he heard my voice; my cry came before him, into his ears" (Ps. 18:6). King David didn't just pray. He called and cried to the Lord.

What happened next, as described in Psalm 18, was so thrilling that I once read this passage to my congregation on a Sunday morning with the "William Tell Overture" (also known as "The Lone Ranger Theme Song") playing in the background. It was so cool! Our sound technician just cranked up the music (go ahead and hum along) as I read these words:

> The earth trembled and quaked,
>   and the foundations of the mountains shook;
>   they trembled because he was angry.
>
> Smoke rose from his nostrils;
>   consuming fire came from his mouth,
>   burning coals blazed out of it.
>
> He parted the heavens and came down;
>   dark clouds were under his feet.
>
> He mounted the cherubim and flew;
>   he soared on the wings of the wind.
>
> He made darkness his covering, his canopy around him—
>   the dark rain clouds of the sky.
>
> Out of the brightness of his presence clouds advanced,
>   with hailstones and bolts of lightning.
>
> The LORD thundered from heaven;
>   the voice of the Most High resounded.

He shot his arrows and scattered the enemies,
>   great bolts of lightning and routed them.

The valleys of the sea were exposed
>   and the foundations of the earth laid bare at your re-
>   buke, O LORD,
>   at the blast of breath from your nostrils.

He reached down from on high and took hold of me;
>   he drew me out of deep waters.

He rescued me from my powerful enemy,
>   from my foes, who were too strong for me. (Ps. 18:7–17)

Now that's an answer to prayer! Would you like to see God intervene in your life with that kind of flair? Ain't gonna happen as long as you're praying ho-hum prayers. Don't forget what launched God on this spectacular search and rescue mission. David had filled his lungs with air and then let loose with a loud cry to the Lord. That's exactly what Heaven had been waiting to hear. "I'm on my way!" God responded.

A passionate prayer is definite. A passionate prayer is desperate. A passionate prayer is dependent. And these are characteristics that invite God to fly to our rescue.

A Definite Prayer

Crying out gives definition to our prayers. Clarity. Allow me to illustrate how this works. Some time ago, Sue and I were out shopping for new patio furniture. A local store was running its annual sale on lawn supplies so we dropped by to see how good a deal we could get. I was all about saving money. Sue was all about the visual appeal of our purchase. (Can you see the conflict coming?)

Surprisingly, we quickly agreed on the table and chairs we wanted. We even liked the same decorative chair cushions and the same umbrella. There was only one decision left to make. Which of two possible umbrella stands would we go with? Option one was a simple, plastic, sand-filled device. Option two was a more attractive, wrought iron piece. But option one was only a third of the price of option two. A no-brainer for me. We'd go with option one.

As I began to give our information to the saleswoman who was waiting on us, I heard Sue mumble something about option one looking kind of lumpy. When I ignored this remark and continued to place our order, Sue said a bit more loudly: "And it's not the right shade of green." Still getting no response from me, she now raised her voice to a level that other customers could hear. "My birthday's coming up real soon. I'd love the right ensemble on our patio." When she saw that I had not received a single one of her subtle messages, my wife finally blurted out: "I want the nicer umbrella stand!"

Why didn't she just say so the first time? In all seriousness, the more volume Sue used, the more definite and unambiguous her appeal became. Similarly, our prayers gain clarity as we cry out to the Lord. We stop meandering aimlessly and express what's truly on our hearts. This is what God is waiting to hear from us: an unambiguous petition.

Jesus once asked a guy, point-blank, to stop beating around the bush and just say what he wanted. An invalid for thirty-eight years, the man spent his days lying by a pool called Bethesda, which was thought to have curative powers. Some Bible scholars speculate that he had probably given up all hope of ever getting better and had settled for a life of begging. Maybe he still occasionally prayed for God's healing—but it was a prayer that lacked conviction. It was a halfhearted plea.

Then Jesus arrived on the scene. "When Jesus saw him lying there and learned that he had been in this condition for a long time, he asked him, 'Do you want to get well?'" (John 5:6). Do you want to get well? This was either a very stupid or a very astute question. If we surmise that an invalid of thirty-eight years would certainly want to be healed, then the question was stupid. But given that the inquirer was Jesus, it is probably best not to conclude: "Dumb question!" In what sense, then, was it astute? In the sense that it exposed the guy's wishy-washiness about being healed.

Jesus wanted to hear, in no uncertain terms: "I want to get well." This would be a risky declaration. Risky, because it would open the man up to the possibility of disappointment in the event that Jesus did not heal him. But it would also be an expression of faith. And Jesus loves it when we trust him with our requests.

Perhaps our prayers lack definition because our hearts lack faith. If we stop short of being really specific about what we want from God then we won't be let down when he doesn't deliver. I have a feeling that a lot of "your-will-be-done" praying falls into this category. If we use this expression to communicate our surrender to whatever God deems best, that's fine. But more often, I suspect, we throw that line into our prayers to let God (and ourselves) off the hook if he doesn't seem to answer us. "It must not have been God's will," we sigh.

When we cry out to God with clarity, on the other hand, we're putting it all on the line. We're taking a step of faith. We're declaring our confidence in God's ability to do exactly what we're asking of him. This is what he's waiting to hear from us.

On another occasion, Jesus encountered a boy who was tyrannized by an evil spirit. The demon seemed intent on killing him by throwing him into the fire or the water. The boy's dad was deeply distraught and approached Jesus with the plea: "But if you can do anything, take pity on us and help us" (Mark 9:22). The man immediately regretted the doubt that his opening words expressed, because Jesus shot back at him: "If you can? . . . Everything is possible for him who believes" (v. 23).

To the dad's credit, he got Jesus' point right away and humbly responded: "I do believe; help me overcome my unbelief" (v. 24). Jesus welcomes that sort of honesty. He much prefers that we ask him for help with believing as opposed to covering up our lack of faith with prayers that are timid or vague.

James, in his New Testament epistle, goes so far as to say that if we allow doubt to creep into our prayers we might as well not pray. Just save our breath. He offers this counsel to those who are asking God for wisdom:

> If any of you lacks wisdom, he should ask God, who gives generously to all without finding fault, and it will be given to him. But when he asks, he must believe and not doubt, because he who doubts is like a wave of the sea, blown and tossed by the wind. That man should not think he will receive anything from the Lord . . . (James 1:5–7).

Do you want to drive doubt out of your prayers? Cry out to the Lord! Tell God, passionately, that you need him to heal your body, or give you victory over some sin, or restore your marriage, or provide a job, or help you understand algebra, or embolden you to share Christ with your friends. Passionate prayers are definite prayers. And definite prayers get answered.

A few years ago I was browsing through a knick-knack shop in rural Wisconsin with Sue. I typically wouldn't be caught dead in such a place, but there was an ice cream counter in this one. As I licked away at my two scoops, I walked up and down the aisles of cutesy country crud. That's when I spotted it. Something I just had to purchase. A small clay jug, cork in the top, with the words *Answered Prayers* emblazoned on its side. It was even the color of our kitchen (something my wife was amazed that I noticed).

We took that jug home and instructed our kids that when we experienced answers to prayer we were to write them out on slips of paper and deposit them in our new piece of crockery. Periodically, we would empty its contents, read the answered prayers out loud, and praise God for his faithfulness. I have to admit that we were not as consistent in using our jug as I would've liked us to be. But for a while (before the dog knocked it over and it shattered), it reminded us to clearly articulate our prayers and their answers.

A passionate prayer is a definite prayer.

A Desperate Prayer

A passionate prayer is a desperate prayer. Sherman Jackson prayed this kind of a prayer with astonishing results. His story was recorded, not too long ago, in the *Dallas Morning News.*[2] Here's what I remember of it. Sherm was on his way to church with his seven-year-old daughter, Alexa, when he decided to stop for gas. A young man, standing idly by, asked for help in jump-starting his car. He said it was parked down the road.

After hopping into Sherm's vehicle, the guy pulled out a gun, shoved it into Sherm's ribs, and asked for all his money. Sherm gave him a money clip stuffed with bills. But when the thief turned around and looked into the back seat, he saw a stack of Gideon Bibles next to Alexa. A dollar bill was tucked into the cover of each Bible. Sherm was planning to give these to homeless people as part of a ministry he was involved in.

"You held out on me!" the young man accused Sherm menacingly. It was getting ugly. That's when Sherm decided it was time to cry out to God. He did so right out loud (crying out *silently* being hard to do). There was desperation to his prayer. Immediately, his assailant demanded that Sherm turn the car around and head back to the gas station.

On the return trip Sherm felt a growing confidence. He declared, "My Jesus is stronger than your gun!" and explained the forgiveness that God offers those who will repent of their sins and put their trust in the Savior. When his captor jumped out of the car, in front of the gas station, Sherm even had the nerve to demand: "I want my money clip back." And the guy gave it to him!

Not everybody believed this tale when it first appeared in the *Dallas Morning News.* But a few days later police apprehended the thief and confirmed Sherm's story. The newspaper reported that Sherm was making regular visits to the local jail, continuing a relationship that had begun at gunpoint in his car.

Crying out to God gives our prayers an edge of desperation. C. H. Spurgeon, the famous late-nineteenth-century London preacher, said, "He who prays without fervency does not pray at all!"[3]

Spurgeon's "fervency" is just another word for the desperation I'm recommending. Other synonyms would include enthusiasm, zeal, intensity, earnestness—and, of course, passion. Are our prayers marked by these qualities? We're not really praying, Chuck Spurgeon would say, until they are.

I was recently invited to participate in a roundtable discussion with twenty senior pastors from around the country. To launch the conversation our moderator asked us each to identify the top two or three strengths of our churches. The first thing that came to my mind was prayer. I recalled something that one of our newer hires had said to me that very week about the advice he'd received his first day on the job. Another staff member had approached him in the hall with the warning: "Get ready to pray—'cause we do a lot of it around here!"

And that's the truth. Our pastoral staff (about thirty people) gathers twice a week, an hour each time, for some intense intercession for ministry concerns. Those who lead meetings are encouraged to weave prayer throughout their agendas—not just use it as an opening and closing formality. It is not unusual for us to interrupt the worship portion of our services by asking the entire congregation to get on its knees as we bring an important matter before God. We have rotating bands of Prayer Partners—almost a hundred men in all—who pray as I preach on Sunday mornings. After each service Prayer Counselors are available at the front of the auditorium. We have a team of Prayer Warriors whose job is to cover all the prayer requests that are turned in on weekly welcome cards.

There's more. One Sunday last month we created a huge Prayer Wall in our atrium lobby. During our announcements that day we described what happens at Jerusalem's famous Wailing Wall. This stone structure, which is part of the foundation that supported Solomon's temple, is a gathering place for those who wish to pray. Many write out their petitions on little slips of paper that they then tuck into the cracks between the stones. We invited our attenders, in a similar fashion, to write out any urgent requests they had on three-by-five-inch cards and pin them to our Prayer Wall. Over 1,300 cards went up that day! And all those requests were prayed for, individually, by staff and prayer team members that week.

So I was all ready to tell that round-table group of senior pastors that prayer is one of my congregation's greatest strengths. But then I balked. I hesitated because that Charlie Spurgeon quote was rattling around in the back of my mind: "It ain't prayin' if it ain't fervent" (or something like that). I wondered: *How much praying around our church is really, really fervent? Really desperate? Really enthusiastic-zealous-intense-earnest-passionate?* I'm not sure. I can vouch for the *time* we spend praying but not for the *temperature* of that praying.

What about you? Is there any heat to your prayers? Allow me to repeat a series of questions that I barraged you with in chapter 1, when I warned you about praying with no passion: "When was the last time you cried out to God for the wisdom you desperately needed to make a critical decision? When was the last time you pleaded with him to deliver you from a sin which has plagued you for far too long? When was the last time you interceded with a broken heart for those who are victimized by the tragedies of famine, AIDS, terrorism, or natural disaster? When was the last time you prayed for a spiritually lost friend as if you believed his eternal destiny was at stake?"

Would it help if I gave you some biblical examples of people who prayed in desperation? In Exodus we learn that the "Israelites groaned in their slavery and cried out, and their cry for help because of their slavery went up to God. God heard their groaning" (Ex. 2:23–24). God not only heard them, he sent them a deliverer by the name of Moses who led them out of Egypt.

The same thing happened, and happened repeatedly, during the era of the Judges. God's people would periodically get themselves in a mess (i.e., oppression at the hands of a foreign power). Each time they cried out to God (never just prayed but always "cried out"—see Judg. 3:9, 15; 4:3; 6:7; 10:10). And God would raise up a hero to rescue them. Guys with names like Othniel, Ehud, Gideon, Jephthah, Samson, and Deborah (okay, they weren't all guys).

89

Or what about the reluctant prophet, Jonah? The guy who was stuck in the belly of a giant fish? That would certainly make a desperately praying man out of me! "From inside the fish [Scripture records] Jonah prayed to the LORD his God." What? He just *prayed*? Is that all the passion Jonah mustered? Keep reading: "He said: 'In my distress I called to the LORD, and he answered me. From the depths of the grave I called for help, and you listened to my cry'" (Jonah 2:1–2). That's two "called's" and one "cry." The needle on the intensity meter was far right.

Let's not forget Peter's quickie prayer on the Sea of Galilee. At Jesus' invitation, Peter had stepped from his fishing boat to walk on the water toward the Savior. But then he saw the wind and the waves (which meant he'd taken his eyes off the Lord) and he began to sink. Not much time for extended prayer when you're busy drowning. But that's no problem. Desperate prayers come in quickie versions. "Peter *cried out,* 'Lord, save me!'" (Matt. 14:30). And Jesus did. *Immediately,* Scripture says.

One last reference. When James selects a role model for passionate praying, it's Elijah he holds up to us. Talk about a desperate guy! Elijah lived during the reign of wicked Ahab and Jezebel—the Old Testament Bonnie and Clyde, notorious for their murderous ways. And Elijah's job, as God's prophet, was to get in their faces and tell them—and the nation of Israel—to repent of their idolatry and other sins. It would take a miracle for God's people to turn back to him with leaders like Ahab and Jezebel. So Elijah prayed for a miracle (see 1 Kings 17 and 18).

I'll let James give you the *Reader's Digest* version of what happened next: "Elijah was a man just like us. He prayed earnestly that it would not rain, and it did not rain on the land for three and a half years. Again he prayed, and the heavens gave rain, and the earth produced its crops" (James 5:17–18). Just note two things from this summary. First, there was nothing special about Elijah. He was a man *just like us.* So how did he get such an incredible answer to his prayer? That's the second thing I want you to note. He prayed *earnestly.*

Desperate prayers invite God to show up. As you pray, do your posture and tone of voice and intense focus all say, "I really mean this"? You aren't praying until they do.

A Dependent Prayer

The passion with which we pray communicates our dependence upon God. As Bill Gothard puts it, "The need to 'cry out' is a humbling reminder of our total inability to accomplish anything significant for God. And the result of 'crying out' is a wonderful demonstration of God's supernatural power to achieve all that is needed."[4] This is dependence in a nutshell.

This brings to mind Jesus' familiar line from his "I am the Vine, you are the branches" speech (John 15): "Apart from me," Jesus stated emphatically, "you can do nothing" (v. 5). Say it out loud a few times: "I can accomplish nothing of significance apart from Jesus." Go ahead and try it. Say it again—and louder this time.

Please note that the practical expression of this dependence is prayer. Two verses after Jesus points out that we can do nothing apart from him, he says: "If you remain in me and my words remain in you, ask whatever you wish, and it will be given you" (v. 7). We demonstrate our total dependence upon Jesus by bringing him our heartfelt needs and desires in prayer. Praying is asking Jesus to do what only he can do, what we could never do on our own.

Here's an illustration of what I'm talking about. I have a friend named Abby. Abby is a beautiful young woman from India. Her parents run a Christian school in a small village near the border with Nepal. I have a special interest in that school because my missionary grandfather started it many years ago. When I first met Abby she was a high school senior in India.

As we talked about colleges, she expressed a strong interest in coming to the United States for a degree. Not only would that give her the opportunity to choose from a wide selection of Christian schools, it would also solve a personal problem Abby was facing. She was being stalked at home by a young man from the local village whose behavior was becoming more and more threatening. College in the States would give her a reprieve from this troubling situation.

It just so happens that there is a fine Christian college within minutes of where I live. Abby applied to that school and soon had a scholarship offer from it. Everything seemed to be falling into place until she applied for a student visa. She was turned down, for no apparent reason. (Reasons are not required when dealing with Indian bureaucracy.)

As Abby prepared to formally challenge this ruling, she was told that if her appeal failed she would have to wait for three years to apply again for a visa. In other words, she had one shot—and only one shot—at an appeal. As her friends, we did what any red-blooded Americans would do in such a situation. We contacted people who might have some pull in getting Abby a visa. We solicited letters of reference for her from the college president and from the U.S. Congressman from our district (who happens to be a Christian).

Yet, in spite of the heavyweights Abby had in her corner, there was a sense that a miracle was needed. Most people who were familiar with the visa system in India gave us little hope for success. Some minor official reviewing Abby's appeal, they reminded us, could dismiss her VIP letters with a wave of his hand. We all felt pretty helpless, considering the circumstances.

But do you remember that definition for prayer that I cited pages ago? *Prayer is helplessness plus faith.* Helplessness. Apart from Jesus we can do nothing. Our prayers are cries of dependence. "Please do," we call out, "what only you can do." That's how we prayed in Abby's case. And we got everyone we could muster praying along the same lines. We all knew that only God could deliver that visa.

When Abby went for her appeal she was armed with her letters of reference. But, more importantly, she was armed with prayers of dependence. The letters we had worked so hard to collect (I love this part) turned out to be worthless. The visa official didn't even look at them. Nope. He didn't need to. He just handed Abby a visa. In less than five minutes. It was a "God thing."

God loves doing God things. Things that nobody else can do. God loves being the Go-to Guy (no irreverence intended) who, alone, can get the job done. "Call upon me in the day of trouble," God says through the psalmist, "I will deliver you, and you will honor me" (Ps. 50:15). It's almost as if God relishes opportunities to show us his stuff. He's not bothered by our appeals for help. He's honored by them.

Maybe it's a poor analogy, but I have to admit that it flatters me when my wife or one of my kids asks me to do something for them that is beyond their capacity to do. (We'll call it a guy thing, definitely *not* a God thing.) Sue may be fixing dinner when she hands me a jar of spaghetti sauce and says: "Honey, would you open this? I couldn't get it." No problem. I take that jar in my vise-like grip, flex my bulging biceps a few times (don't ask me what biceps have to do with it), and give the lid a twist. Off it comes with ease. "I need you," she smiles at me. And I think to myself, "You sure do."

Okay, I overplayed the analogy. But you get the point: God is honored by prayers of dependence. He loves to hear us acknowledge that we need him. When we pray without passion it's almost as if we're saying: "I could probably do this without you, but if you want to take a swing at it, go ahead." What kind of an invitation is that to the God who created the universe?

One more story. Bill Gothard writes about a plumber friend who left his truck idling while he ran into a convenience store to pick something up. When he got back out to the parking lot the truck was gone—and all his tools (read "livelihood") with it.

The police came by to fill out a report. They told the plumber he'd done something stupid. (Like he didn't know?) They estimated that if the truck were not located within the hour he could kiss his tools good-bye, because they would all be sold as "hot" items by then. What could the guy do? Nothing—except pray. He prayed with passion. He cried out to the Lord. He expressed his utter dependence on God.

Two days later the police called and told him to come and pick up his truck. They'd recovered it in one piece. In fact, his job orders were still neatly stacked on the front seat. What about his tools?

Some of them were missing—but only for a short time. Less than a week later he just "happened" to see them at a flea market and they were immediately returned to him. And in the meantime (this is the best part) the widow of another plumber had heard about his plight and given him all of her deceased husband's tools. Now he had two of everything![5]

Sometimes God is such a show-off! But he only does that for people who declare their dependence on him by praying with passion. So, put some energy into your prayers. Go find a place where you can kneel, or prostrate yourself, or march about. Raise the volume of your voice until it reaches a "call" or "cry" level. Tell God that if he doesn't intervene you have no "plan B." Then watch what happens!

Onto the Praying Field

1. Why does God often wait for us to pray passionately before granting our requests? What keeps you from praying with greater intensity? How could you remove these obstacles?

2. What are your three top prayer requests at present? Make these requests more definite by listing several specific things to pray about for each of them.

   a.

   b.

   c.

3. What is one of the most desperate situations in your life or in the life of someone you know? Have you prayed for this situation with a passion equal to its level of desperation? If not, why not?

How could you add intensity to your prayers? (Or, what evidences of passion would you like to see more of in your praying?)

Find an isolated place where you can go and pray passionately about a particular desperate situation. Pray out loud—in fact, pray as loudly as possible. (Cry out!) Punctuate your prayer with hand motions.

4. For what problem have you been depending upon yourself or circumstances to take care of—instead of praying about it? Pray about it now.

In what ways does your praying about this problem bring honor to God?

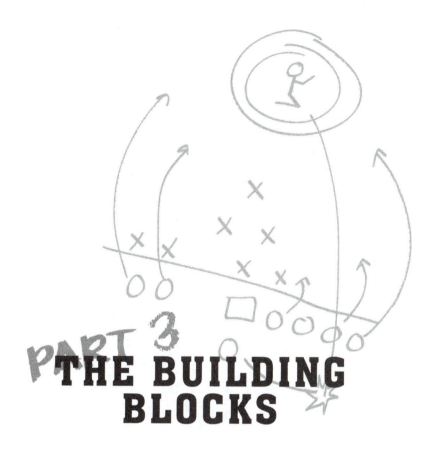

PART 3
THE BUILDING BLOCKS

6

Confess

Pull Sin up by the Roots

S
everal years ago my church completed a multimillion-dollar
auditorium that gave us the technological ability to clearly
communicate God's truth to a large group of people—the
best in sound, lighting, and media. Well ... almost. "Clearly
communicate" was a bit of a problem, at first.

Our sound system wasn't quite balanced, with the result that
musical presentations were marred by a booming bass. I've always
been a big fan of lots of bass in my music—but not to the extent
that it hurts the ears and drowns out the other parts. We eventually
got the problem fixed.

Is there a booming-bass imbalance to your praying? Most
often our prayers are heavily weighted in the direction of personal
requests. We're always asking for this or for that. While God certainly welcomes these petitions, it must be hard on his ears when
they comprise the bulk of our praying.

How can we bring balance to our prayers? By praying in four-
part harmony. The four aspects of prayer have sometimes been
represented by the acronym ACTS. *A* stands for adoration, *C* for

confession, *T* for thanksgiving, and *S* for supplication. Balanced praying requires that we give equal time and attention to each of these ingredients.

Although ACTS has been a helpful tool for me to use over the years, I've often felt that this acronym could be improved upon. For starters, who even knows what *supplication* means anymore? Let's replace that with a better word. Next, there are times when I just can't begin my praying with *adoration* because I'm feeling dirtied by my sin and distant from God. But if I deal with this problem by launching my prayer with *confession*, this would change the acronym to CATS. As a dog lover, I just can't go there.

Finally, ACTS, as a word, has nothing to do with prayer. Let me suggest a new acronym that does: CHAT. When it's time to talk (i.e., chat) with God, I am reminded to balance my prayer with four emphases (stated as verbs here to give them a sense of action). Confess. Honor (for *adoration*). Ask (beats *supplication* any day). Thank.

This chapter and the next three are devoted to spelling out, in greater detail, what is meant by each of these words and how we can pray accordingly. We'll begin with *confess*. And that's not just because CHAT begins with a *C*. It's because we want to ensure a good connection before we start talking to God.

Cell phone companies are fond of promoting their services by promising that we will never be outside the range of a good connection. Certainly there is nothing more frustrating in this age of "unrestrained reachability" than to discover that we have lost our phone signal.

Maybe you've seen the commercial about the support group for deeply troubled cell phone users. They're sitting in a circle on the beach. One by one they stand, share their personal testimonies of losing their signal, and then hurl their cell phones into the ocean. I've been there. Haven't you? It always seems to happen right when I'm in the middle of a very important call.

When the person we lose communication with is God, we have a much bigger problem. But that's exactly what sin does to our connection. And until we confess that sin we will not have a signal. No bars on our prayer phone.

If you think that I am exaggerating the extent to which un-confessed sin hampers our getting through to God, let me repeat a Scripture that we looked at when we were considering obstacles to prayer: "Surely the arm of the LORD is not too short to save, nor his ear too dull to hear. But your iniquities have separated you from your God; your sins have hidden his face from you, so that he will not hear" (Isa. 59:1–2). The psalmist said much the same thing: "If I had cherished sin in my heart, the Lord would not have listened" (Ps. 66:18).

It should be obvious to us, from these verses, that if we want to connect with God in prayer we must make a habit of regularly confessing our sin. And the best place to go in Scripture to learn how to effectively do that is Psalm 51. This is the prayer that King David composed after his affair with Bathsheba.

I have an easy time locating Psalm 51 in my Bible. When I look at the gold edging around the pages, there's a dark line that runs down the middle of it. The dark line is the result of the gold having been rubbed off and replaced with smudges. That's because I've turned to this particular chapter of God's Word again and again and again. About as often as I've needed to do some thorough confessing of sin. King David has been my mentor in this regard. His psalm teaches us five aspects of confession.

The Review

After an initial plea for God to show him mercy and forgiveness ("Blot out my transgressions. Wash away all my iniquity and cleanse me from my sin"), David adds: "For I know my transgressions, and my sin is always before me" (Ps. 51:1–3). David was well aware of what he'd done wrong. He had his buddy, Nathan the prophet, to thank for that.

Nathan was an in-your-face kind of guy. But when the Lord sent him to David to expose the king's sin, Nathan knew that he'd

better do it with finesse. If the king took offense at his confrontation, Nathan might lose more than his job as court counselor. He
might lose his head! Better be subtle. Begin with a story—everybody
likes a good story.

Nathan's story was about a rich man who owned a large flock
of sheep. But when a guest arrived for dinner, instead of serving his
own mutton he took his poor neighbor's pet lamb and made it into
stew. Nathan was such a scintillating storyteller that when he got to
this point in the tale David jumped to his feet in anger and shouted,
"The man who did this deserves to die!" (2 Sam. 12:5). Nathan looked
the king in the eye and said, "You are the man!" (v. 7).

Gotcha! David was busted. Nathan's punch line is even more
poignant in the original text because "You are the man!" is only two
words in Hebrew. With two words, Nathan forced David to take a
good look at his sin. And David couldn't get what he saw out of his
mind. "I know my transgressions, and my sin is always before me"
(Ps. 51:3).

Unfortunately, very few of us have a friend like Nathan. Someone who knows our secret sins and is willing to address them with
both courage and genuine concern. We're pretty much on our own
when it comes to detecting our transgressions. And, the truth is, we
don't do a very good job of it. Our tendency is to ignore our sins—or
excuse them, or rationalize them, or redefine them as something
other than sin, or blame them on somebody else.

In his book *Why Sin Matters*, Mark McMinn says that the
popular doctrine of self-esteem hinders our ability to recognize
personal sin: "One of the unexamined assumptions of contemporary
society is that we should strain to see the best in ourselves. . . . We
are depressed and anxious and stressed, we are told, because we
are not nice enough to ourselves. So we learn to use positive self-
talk, to affirm ourselves, to see how others have hurt us without
considering how we have hurt others. We trade the language of sin
for the inert dialect of self-help books. . . . Part of our mess is not
knowing we are a mess."[1]

Part of our mess is not knowing we are a mess! Well stated.
David expressed the same sentiment in the form of a question in

another of his psalms: "Who can discern his errors? Forgive my hidden faults" (Ps. 19:12). We're just not very astute at detecting our own sins. They remain hidden to us. And that creates a big problem. Assuming that undetected sins will go unconfessed, they will chronically cut off our prayer signal. Our communication with God will be in a constant state of disconnection.

The only way I know to keep this from happening is by doing a thorough review of my life, every day, with the Holy Spirit's help. One of the first things I pray each morning is that God's Spirit would put his finger on anything in my life that grieves—or even mildly displeases—him. And then I confess whatever he brings to mind.

Sometimes this process just takes place orally. But a couple of times a week I have to conduct this review with pen and paper in hand. Otherwise my oral evaluations have a tendency to become superficial. Kind of like the way my kids cleaned their rooms when they were teenagers. A clean room was a house rule. But that didn't mean that the job was always done well. My kids would do just enough to get by. So their mom would periodically give those rooms a thorough cleaning herself (the "white tornado" treatment, I called it).

A regular stem-to-stern cleaning of our hearts is a similar necessity. This doesn't seem to happen—at least, not in my life—unless I do it in writing. Some people refer to this as journaling. I'm a bit hesitant to use that term, however, because I know that just the sound of it scares would-be confessors away. But let me describe to you how I approach journaling. I hope you'll find it more inviting.

First, I don't require it of myself every day. If I did, it would feel more like a diary to me—and I've never been very good at keeping a diary. In fact, I used to have a shelf of diaries that I'd begun at various points in the past. Not a single one made it beyond fifteen or twenty pages before going blank. (Not even the ones with the nice leather covers.)

I don't treat my journal as a daily diary. I write in it only twice a week (Monday and Friday)—just often enough to keep me in the habit of confessing sin thoroughly. And that habit of thoroughness, developed by writing things out, prepares me to do a better job of confessing sin orally on my non-journaling days. It's much like my experience with public speaking. Because I've practiced for years the discipline of crafting full manuscripts from which to preach, I can now communicate effectively when called upon to do so extemporaneously.

Here's a second feature of my journaling that has ensured its consistency. I never fill up more than one side of a page. Never. Even if I am tempted to keep on writing, I force myself to wrap up my summary and put down my pen. Why? Because I don't want to burn out on this spiritual discipline. And that happens whenever I keep raising the bar of what I expect from myself. If I journal three pages worth of stuff today, then I'll feel like I should fill at least three pages the next time around. And I'll consider myself a slacker if I stop at a page and a half. (Anybody else wired this way?) Eventually, I'd conclude that I can't keep up this pace, and I'd quit journaling altogether.

So I stick with a one-page summary of my previous three days. Period. My objective is not to record everything that happened in my life during that time. I'm just trying to identify those "hidden faults" that need to be exposed and confessed. I won't, for example, record that I went to the Dairy Queen—unless I sense that I made a pig out of myself there and need to confess my gluttony. I won't write down that I talked over the backyard fence with my neighbor— unless I need to confess that I squelched the Holy Spirit's prompting to bring up Christ in that conversation.

A third way that I've simplified the discipline of journaling is by not requiring myself to write in complete sentences or with creative flair. This is not a work for publication. (It better not be! If my journal were ever published it would be terribly incriminating.) Occasionally, I hear people talking about rereading their old journals so as to reminisce about where they were "at" during certain periods of their lives. I've never done that. I am not compiling my memoirs. I am not collecting material for a future autobiography. I am just helping myself confess sin on a given day.

Here's something else that goes along with this point about my truncated writing style. I use a wide variety of code words and abbreviations when I journal. If I'm confessing a previous day's lustful leering at a pretty girl, you are not going to read about it as lustful leering at a pretty girl. Hopefully, you're not going to read about it at all. But should my journal ever get lost and you find it and open it up to read it (just to identify who it belongs to, of course), you would not be able to decipher exactly what it is that I'm confessing. Code words and abbreviations are what you'll encounter.

A fourth technique that has enhanced my journaling review process is the creation of plus/minus lists. Whenever I'm evaluating a situation in which I found myself, it helps me to note both the positive and negative aspects of those circumstances. Let's say that my in-laws had been visiting for a few days. As I journal about this experience, I will first make a bullet-point list of four or five good things that came out of that visit. This gives me something to thank God for—and thanksgiving is how I avoid the sins of ingratitude and discontent. On the other hand, I'll also make a list of several sinful behaviors or attitudes that I engaged in while my out-of-town relatives were around (e.g., not being a good listener, grabbing the biggest piece of chicken at dinner, allowing others' quirks to drive me nuts).

Thinking in lists forces me to be specific and exhaustive when reviewing my life for sin. I may compile a plus/minus list to evaluate a staff meeting, or an extended phone conversation, or a date with Sue, or a confrontation with one of my kids, or a purchase I made. What did I do, say, or feel that was God-honoring? What did I do, say, or feel that grieved God's Spirit?

Finally, when I'm done filling up a page in my journal, I'm ready to pray. I don't consider the writing itself as praying. It just helps me identify everything I need to confess. Now the confessing begins. I pray through that page, elaborating on anything that seems to deserve more attention. Sometimes that expansion takes the form of getting even more specific about the sin. Sometimes it involves expressing deeper regret for having offended God.

Let's review reviewing. Confess sin via journaling a couple of times a week. Keep your entries to a single page. Write in a condensed style that sums up your transgressions. Make bullet-point lists when evaluating what went right/wrong in certain situations. Pray.

Sound too tedious? It's really not. Get yourself a spiral-bound notebook and begin today. Don't take an hour per entry or you'll quickly give it up. Concentrate on completing each review in twenty minutes. (I'm not trying to rush you. Feel free to take more time on occasion. But keep the bar set at a level that will encourage you to practice this discipline over the long haul.)

The Results

After Nathan exposed David's sin, he spelled out the repercussions of that sin (see 2 Sam. 12:10–14). It wasn't a pretty picture. The God who had given David so much had been dishonored. God's enemies now had reason to gloat. Violent military opposition, as well as tragic upheaval in David's immediate family, could be expected. And the son that Bathsheba carried would die.

Ouch! I once heard an African-American preacher describe the results of sin with these colorful words (and with a cadence to his voice): "Sin will take you where you didn't plan to go. It will keep you there longer than you planned to stay. And it will cost you more than you intended to pay." I'm sure that David would agree with this assessment.

When we confess our sins to God it is a good idea to acknowledge the results of our transgressions, to own up to the mess we've made. This will keep us from trivializing our wrongdoing or cheapening the grace that forgiveness requires. And let's not miss the major repercussions by focusing too much attention on the lesser damages brought on by our sin. We are prone to choke on gnats, as the saying goes, while being oblivious to the camels we've swallowed.

Allow me to illustrate. When I was in junior high my most prized possession was my ten-speed bike. One day I was racing to school, zigzagging down the street as if I were on a giant slalom course. On one of my zigs I turned the handlebars too abruptly, causing the bike's front end to stop dead and the bike's rear end to catapult me onto the street. After sliding on my face for a number of yards, I came to a halt, got to my feet, and assessed the damages. To my horror I saw that I had ripped a hole in the knee of my pants. My new pants.

When my mom arrived on the scene—called by a neighbor who had witnessed my acrobatics—I immediately started apologizing for the torn pants. I was sure that I was in big trouble for ruining them. But my mom was looking at my face—and the front tooth that I'd broken off. That tooth turned out to be a far more expensive, time-consuming, and painful repercussion of the bike accident than the torn pants were. In my immaturity, I didn't realize that at the time.

Often when we're surveying the results of our sin, we're more preoccupied with torn pants than with broken teeth. But David cuts right to the chase by identifying the worst effect of his affair with Bathsheba. It was the fact that he had offended the Lord. "Against you, you only, have I sinned and done what is evil in your sight" (Ps. 51:4).

We are tempted to object to this assessment of the damages on David's part. How can he say that God is the "only" one he's sinned against? After all, he has sexually exploited Bathsheba, he has conspired to kill Uriah (her husband), he has betrayed the people whom he was responsible to lead, he has thrown his family into turmoil, and he has lied to everyone to cover things up.

In what sense, then, has God been the only one against whom David has sinned? In the sense that God has been the principal party offended. As horrible as his actions have been against everyone else, David's sin against God has been many times worse. Martin Luther, the great reformer, pointed out that all commandments are wrapped up in the first one (i.e., requiring us to honor God as God), in the sense that every sin is contempt of God. Whatever commandment we break, we have also broken the first.

Do we understand this about our own sins? The damage that they do to our relationship with God is worse than the hurt that they inflict on anyone else (not to minimize that hurt in the least).

That's why even "minor" sins are so serious. They're an affront to God and drive a wedge between God and us.

Diabolical Uncle Screwtape is well aware of this. Screwtape is a fictional character created by famed author C. S. Lewis. He's a demon of some stature who corresponds extensively with his nephew, Wormwood, giving instructions on how to harass Christians. One of Screwtape's recommended strategies is to tempt believers with small, seemingly innocuous sins:

> You will say that these are very small sins; and doubtless, like all young tempters, you are anxious to be able to report spectacular wickedness. But do remember, the only thing that matters is the extent to which you separate the man from the Enemy [God]. It does not matter how small the sins are provided that their cumulative effect is to edge the man away from the Light and out into the Nothing.[2]

Our sins—even the smallest of them—are an offense to a holy God and they do serious damage to our relationship with him. This must be acknowledged when we are confessing them. For example, let me use the sin that I mentioned when I was giving tips on journaling. "Lustful leering at a pretty girl," I said, is something that I would confess in code. Okay, suppose that I am guilty of just such a sin. What does it mean to acknowledge its results in a way that recognizes it is against God (not Sue), first and foremost, that I have sinned?

My confession would go something like this: "Lord, please forgive me for these lustful thoughts. I've brought filthy fantasies into the temple where your Holy Spirit lives. While your Spirit's job is to make me more like Christ, I have been working against him. When he said, 'Don't stare!' I deliberately disobeyed. I was willing to trade a sense of your presence for my moment of lust, since, as Jesus said, only 'the pure in heart . . . will see God.' And how it must offend you when I'm unfaithful, like this, to the wife you've given me. Forgive my ingratitude."

My intent is to demonstrate how important it is for you to confess your sin as an offense against God. Certainly there will be collateral damage to others that must be prayerfully acknowledged as well. You will want to express remorse for those you have hurt with your anger, selfishness, dishonesty, bitterness, or indifference. But don't forget to start with God. Confess your sin in terms of how it has grieved him.

The Roots

A few years ago I had two cats and a dog. Since that time all three have died. In each case, their dying was a lengthy process, accompanied by a lot of throwing up. It's amazing what a pet owner will put up with out of love for a pooch or a kitty. (Are we whacked out or what?) Almost every day I was cleaning up piles of pet puke from some new area of carpet. I started buying spray bottles of carpet cleaner in bulk. The worst part of it was that the dye in pet chow (whose idea was that?) always left behind the shadow of a stain.

After a while these residual shadows made our carpets look like a connect-the-dots picture from a child's coloring book. That's when we brought in the pros, the guys with the steam cleaner. Their equipment reached down deep into our carpets and pulled up the stains by the roots.

This is the sort of treatment that our sins require. Superficial spot cleaning won't do. We've got to get to the roots of our transgressions.

David prayed, "Surely you desire truth in the inner parts; you teach me wisdom in the inmost place" (Ps. 51:6). David knew that God wants us to be people of integrity down to the very core of our being. Our *inner parts,* our *inmost place* must be cleansed of sin. We need to deal with the underlying cause of each sinful behavior. We need to get at the sin behind the sin.

Let me give you a couple of examples of what I'm talking about. Paul identifies anger as a source of other sinful symptoms. "In your anger do not sin," Paul warns us (by quoting a familiar dictum from

109

Ps. 4:4). Then he adds: "Do not let the sun go down while you are still angry, and do not give the devil a foothold" (Eph. 4:26–27). Do you follow the sequence that's implied here? Deep-seated anger gives the devil a foot in the door of our lives. And once that door has been cracked by his size 666s, other sins can squeeze through the opening.

I don't know about you, but I have found that this is definitely the case in my life. Anger leads to other sins. And sometimes these other sins will get confessed, because they're more obvious, while the anger goes undetected. A familiar scenario might look like this: I'm bugged by an argument that takes place in a staff meeting at work. I brood about this conflict the rest of the day, and I'm still brooding about it over dinner. When Sue asks what's bothering me I say, "Nothing," because I don't want to talk about it. Instead, I go into the family room, turn on the TV, and flip through a variety of channels until my anger is anesthetized by all the junk I've watched.

The next day I'm feeling guilty about the previous night's media contamination. So I confess to the Lord the lust that was stimulated by what I watched on TV. But I might miss entirely, in my confession, the real culprit in this scenario. I might fail to identify and deal with the anger that set me up for my excursion into lust. See how this works?

Here's a second example of a sin behind the sin. I can quite easily recognize impatience when it pops up in my life. And it pops up a lot. I get impatient with telemarketers, with slow-moving drivers, with doctors who are behind schedule, with long lines at the store, with employees who don't correct problems we've talked about, and with my microwave oven (believe it or not). I've always known that I should keep short accounts with God when it comes to my impatience.

But one day I read something about impatience that really troubled me. Some author (I can't remember who) noted that the root cause of impatience is grandiosity. I'd never heard it put that way before. Okay, truth is I'd never heard the word *grandiosity* used in a sentence. I looked it up and discovered that it's just a fancy way of talking about pride. But I like grandiosity better because it captures that sense of being too big for one's britches. I'm such hot stuff that I shouldn't have to wait for telemarketers or doctors or drivers or long lines or employees or microwave ovens.

So, these days when I confess my impatience to God, I also own up to the pride that's behind it. *Forgive my grandiosity*, I pray. This is steam cleaning. This is getting to a deeper level of dirt. This is dealing with the roots of my sin.

As you prayerfully review your life (with the help of journaling or not), ask the Lord to reveal to you what was behind each sin that you confess. What was behind your sarcastic retort? What was behind your flirtation at the watercooler? What was behind your missed time in God's Word? What was behind your overeating?

Sometimes when I'm journaling, I'll jot down some sin I need to confess (in code, of course) and immediately after it I'll write, "Lord?" This reminds me to ask the Lord, when I'm praying through my page of journaling, to put his finger on what prompted that sin. And after I ask, I listen with my heart for God's response.

The Request

Some of my favorite verses in the entire Bible come from the middle of Psalm 51. After David has reviewed his life, acknowledged the results of his sin, and stressed the importance of being sin-free down to his roots, he finally gets around to asking God for forgiveness. And this is his request: "Cleanse me with hyssop, and I will be clean; wash me, and I will be whiter than snow. . . . Hide your face from my sins and blot out all my iniquity. Create in me a pure heart, O God, and renew a steadfast spirit within me" (Ps. 51:7–8, 10).

What is this hyssop that David refers to? Hyssop is a plant that has a straight stalk and a head of bushy leaves. It looks like a giant paintbrush. And that's one of the ways it was used in Bible times. The first time that hyssop pops up in Scripture is in the account of Israel's deliverance from slavery in Egypt. Pharaoh, as you may recall, needed some convincing before he was willing to let God's people go. So God sent ten plagues, the final one being the slaying of all firstborn humans and animals.

In order for God's people to protect themselves from this ultimate plague, it was necessary for them to take the blood of sacrificed goats or sheep and apply it to the door frames of their houses. The Lord promised to pass over these blood-covered homes when he visited death on the rest of Egypt. With what was the blood applied? It was painted on the doorframes with bunches of hyssop (Ex. 12:22).

So hyssop became associated with sacrifices and blood and protection from the judgment of God. When David requested that God cleanse him with hyssop he was asking, no doubt, that his sacrifices might be found acceptable. That the blood of the animals he offered might cover his sins and deliver him from God's condemnation.

Fast-forward to the gospel account of Jesus' death on the cross. Interestingly, this is where we come across another one of the handful of appearances of hyssop in Scripture. When near his death Jesus called out "I am thirsty," a sponge was soaked in wine vinegar and lifted to his lips at the end of a stalk of hyssop. He then declared, "It is finished," and died (John 19:29–30). Is it coincidental that hyssop appears in this context of sacrifice, blood, and the appeasement of God's wrath against sin? I don't think so.

When I confess my sins to God, using David's Psalm 51 prayer, I am appealing to Christ's saving work on the cross as I plead: "Cleanse me with hyssop, and I will be clean." I am asking God to apply Jesus' purifying blood to my sullied heart. The result is that I am washed *whiter than snow*!

A New Testament verse sums up in a nutshell this passage from Psalm 51: "If we confess our sins, he is faithful and just and will forgive us our sins and purify us from all unrighteousness" (1 John 1:9). I encourage new Christ followers to memorize this verse as soon as they can. Like Psalm 51, it comes in handy whenever there is sin in our lives that needs to be confessed (i.e., every day).

I have often meditated on the two attributes of God that John links to God's forgiveness in this verse. John promises us that God will respond favorably to our confession of sin because he is *faith-*

ful and just. Not the two attributes that I would've associated with forgiveness. God forgives sins because—the first two words that come to my mind—he's *loving and gracious.* Right? Why does John choose *faithful and just* over my combo (other than the fact that he's Spirit-inspired and I'm not)? Because John is explaining to us the grounds, not the motivation, for God's forgiveness.

The reason that God forgives our sins is, first of all, because he is *faithful.* Faithful to what? Faithful to his promises (see Heb. 10:23). If God says that he's going to do something—he does it! And one of the things that God says he's going to do for his people is forgive their sins. The prophet Jeremiah records God's promise: "I will forgive their wickedness and will remember their sins no more" (Jer. 31:34). If God didn't forgive me when I confess my sins, he wouldn't be faithful. Fortunately for us, he's a God of his word.

But in what sense is God's forgiveness dependent on the fact that he is also *just*? Paul answers that question in Romans 3:21–26. The gist of this passage is that Christ has fully paid the penalty for our sin upon the cross. Therefore, it would be unjust of God to demand further payment from those of us who have put our faith in his Son. Every time that we confess our sin we are implicitly appealing to Christ's blood ("Cleanse me with hyssop") that purchased our forgiveness. And because God is *just,* he must forgive us ("and I will be clean").

Faithful and just are a fantastic duo. Now I understand why the apostle John chose to highlight this pair of God's attributes in 1 John 1:9. There's another twosome in this verse that I would also like to mention. A pair of God's actions. Because God is *faithful and just,* John says, he *forgives and purifies.* What a combination of verbs!

Forgives tells us that God cancels our sin's debt (i.e., because Christ has picked up the tab for us). *Purifies* tells us that God removes our sin's stain—that residual sense that, even though we've been forgiven, we're still dirty or hopeless or unusable or a huge disappointment to God. Are you hearing Psalm 51 playing in the background of 1 John 1:9? After David asked God to forgive him—"Cleanse me with hyssop, and I will be clean"—he asked God to purify him—"Wash me, and I will be whiter than snow." When we request God to do this for us, our sin's debt and stain are history! Instantly.

Is this wonderful news or what! Doesn't it make you want to burst out in song? Do you know some good lyrics with which to celebrate what we've been digging out of Psalm 51 and 1 John 1:9? As much as I love many contemporary worship songs, I'm always drawn back to the old hymns when it comes time to praise God for the way in which he *forgives and purifies* me.

> What can wash away my sins? Nothing but the blood of
>   Jesus.
> What can make me whole again? Nothing but the blood
>   of Jesus.
> Oh, precious is the flow, that makes me white as snow.
> No other fount I know. Nothing but the blood of Jesus.[3]

Or:
> Jesus paid it all.
> All to him I owe.
> Sin had left a crimson stain.
> He washed it white as snow.[4]

Recently I was talking to a friend who doesn't have a relationship with Christ. What's more, he doesn't see his need for one. I decided to tell him why I need Christ. "I don't know what I'd do with my sin, otherwise," I acknowledged to him. "I couldn't live with a sense that, day after day, I am compiling a longer and longer list of moral failures. I'd be ashamed of my track record, burdened by my guilt. But Christ has taken care of all that for me. I begin each day with a clean slate and a light heart." He wasn't convinced, but it got him thinking.

The Responsiveness

When David finished confessing his sin, he characterized his prayer as an offering of brokenness to God. "You do not delight in sacrifice, or I would bring it; you do not take pleasure in burnt offerings. The sacrifices of God are a broken spirit; a broken and contrite heart, O God, you will not despise" (Ps. 51:16–17). God receives our confessions as gifts of brokenness.

Isn't this strange? Who would've thought that being *broken* is a good thing? We usually use the word to describe something that's been damaged or destroyed. Broken dishes can no longer be used. A broken arm has to be set in a cast and given time to heal. Broken promises undermine the trust that's foundational to a relationship. Broken is bad, isn't it?

Not always. When I played baseball as a boy, I had to occasionally break in a new mitt. Remember, you ex-Little Leaguers, how stiff those mitts were when you first brought them home from the store? They weren't much use in that condition. They wouldn't close around a pop fly or a hot grounder. To break in my new mitt I'd rub it with oil, tuck a baseball into its web, and wrap it tight with rubber bands. A week or so of this treatment would produce a baseball glove that was well formed, pliable, and ready to be used. Broken.

When we confess sin on a regular basis, we keep ourselves in a state of brokenness—in the best sense of that word. Our character is being conformed to the image of Christ. Our spirit is supple and responsive to God's leadings. God can use us. On the contrary, when we are not confessing sin as a daily habit, we are living in a state of unbrokenness. Telltale signs of this include pride, irritability, impatience, insensitivity, and resentment in relation to others—as well as indifference toward God.

It's somewhat embarrassing to admit, but I used to find myself especially prone to this unbrokenness when I was on vacation with my family. It's easy to diagnose why this happened. My daily routine of meeting with God first thing in the morning was often thrown off as my wife and kids and I jam-packed our days with fun activities, went to bed late, and then woke up mid-morning in a crowded (and not-so-private) hotel room. Prayer time slid. Confession was neglected. Hardness began to set in. Family members noticed.

I can remember a trip that we took to the east coast when we decided to stop in Washington, D.C., for a day. What sort of a fool tries to see the nation's capital in a single day? That would be me. We raced from buildings to monuments to museums. My family was longing for the sun to go down so that we could call it quits. But I wasn't about to be stopped by darkness. I pointed out that many of D.C.'s attractions are illuminated at night. So we kept piling in and out of our van in an endless succession of stops.

Along the way, my wife and kids occasionally suggested that maybe we had had enough. I accused them of being wimps and party poopers (maybe not in those exact words—I may have used stronger expressions). At one point, as I was trying to herd everyone back into the van for another jog, Andrew called out: "Quick! Form a giant X!" We had no idea what he was talking about until he explained that these were the instructions he'd been given in grade school to avoid being abducted into a stranger's car. Stretch out those arms and legs. My entire family—with the exception of me—immediately assumed the X position, a sign that they were refusing to get into the van one more time. They thought they were hilarious. I barked at them to quit screwing around and pile in.

Unbroken people don't demonstrate a whole lot of grace toward others. And that's because they aren't experiencing grace themselves. By way of contrast, when we are in the habit of confessing sin and throwing ourselves on the mercy of God, he pours out so much grace on us that it spills over into the lives of others. Broken people are a blessing to be around.

Are you a broken person? Do you set aside time each day to review your life and confess your sins? Do you acknowledge the Spirit-grieving results of your wrongful behaviors, words, and attitudes? Do you get to their roots—the sins behind the sins? Do you request that God, by virtue of Christ's sacrifice on the cross, forgive and purify you? Do you seek a responsiveness in your heart toward him, a perpetually broken spirit?

Onto the Praying Field

1. Practice journaling two times this week. Take out a piece of paper (or, if you're ready to make this a regular habit, open up a new spiral-bound notebook). Ask the Holy Spirit to put his finger on anything in your life that is displeasing or grieving him. Then review the previous twenty-four hours, recalling all major activities, conversations, and attitudes for evidences of sin.

2. Take apart any situation about which you feel uneasy (and may not know why)—a phone call, the ballgame you watched on TV, your shopping excursion, a meeting with co-workers. What were the pluses and minuses of that experience?

   Pluses:

   Minuses:

3. Select one of the sins that the Holy Spirit brings to your attention from this past week. In what way(s) is that sin, most significantly, a sin against God? Who else is impacted by that sin? How?

   Express all this in prayer to God and acknowledge Christ's blood-bought forgiveness for this very transgression. Thank God for washing you white as snow.

4. Trace this sin back to its roots. What prompted it? How could a sinful response be avoided in a similar situation in the future?

5. Use the CHAT formula for prayer each day this week.

6. Write out Psalm 51:7–12 on a 3 x 5 card and carry it around with you until you've memorized it.

Honor

Enter His Courts with Praise

ack in 1788, when our country elected George Washington, one of the first items on Congress' agenda was to decide how to address the man. Those who were sick and tired of kings opted for a simple "George" or "Mr. Washington." Others, who were concerned for the dignity of the office, suggested "His Highness the President of the United States of America and Protector of the Rights of the Same." (Imagine trying to fit that latter title on a business card!) This debate over what to call our first, fearless leader was so heated that it nearly came to blows in the Senate.

We face a similar dilemma when approaching God in prayer. How do we balance intimacy and reverence as we address the One who is both heavenly Father and Creator of the Universe? Is there a biblical protocol for how we are to begin our prayers? Psalm 100 instructs us to enter "his courts with praise" (v. 4). That's helpful advice. Is this how you typically greet God?

Do you open your prayers with words that communicate adoration, worship, awe . . . honor? Honor is the *H* of our CHAT acronym. The only reason that we're considering honor *after* confess, as explained earlier, is that sometimes it seems necessary to deal with nasty sins before we can feel like praising God. But on other occasions, it's entirely appropriate to put our sins on hold until after we have properly exalted God. As often as possible when you pray, let the first words out of your mouth be words of praise. Honor God.

Why is this so easy to talk about and yet so difficult to do? Why is praise often the weakest aspect of our prayers? Why is there always so much more to say to God when we confess, ask, or thank than when we honor? Interestingly, this is not the case with many of the prayers that are recorded in the Bible. They often major in praise, whether it's Hezekiah's prayer as he pleads with God to deliver Jerusalem from enemy siege (2 Kings 19:15–16), or Paul's prayer as he intercedes for the pain-in-the-neck Corinthians (2 Cor. 1:3–5), or Jesus' prayer as he teaches his disciples to follow his pattern (Matt. 6:9–10). God is thoroughly honored in these prayers before they turn their attention to other matters.

Tired of praiseless praying? Look with me at Psalm 100 to discover four things you'll need in order to have something to say when you enter the Lord's courts.

The Hunger

Psalm 100 begins with an attitude. A disposition. A spirit with which one approaches Almighty God. "Shout for joy to the LORD, all the earth. Worship the LORD with gladness; come before him with joyful songs" (vv. 1–2). Hard to miss the theme of these opening verses. Joy! When the psalmist began to pray his heart would swell with delight.

Would you describe yourself as joyful when you enter God's presence? I can think of other words that would characterize how I often feel when I launch into prayer: tired, dutiful, distracted, needy, guilty, rushed, stressed. Not joyful. In fact, I frequently find myself borrowing the words of Psalm 51:12 as I address God: "Restore to me the joy of your salvation."

Why am I not pumped up at the prospect of spending a few moments talking to the King of all Kings? It's certainly not a matter of temperament. I'm an excitable guy who can become quite animated when a conversation lands on certain topics. Most of my male friends are wired the same way. If you mention, for example, the Chicago Cubs, they will light up and start talking a mile a minute. You won't be able to shut them up as they tell you about the last game they saw at Wrigley Field, the heartache of watching the Cubbies throw away the play-offs back in '69, or the batting averages of current players.

Isn't that amazing? I know Christian men who haven't memorized a Bible verse in months (or longer), but they can reel off the batting averages of their favorite team's players. Or the Dow Jones averages for countless stocks. Or the par for every hole at the local golf course. Or the Internet addresses for a dozen interesting Web sites. Or the stats on a sports car they're considering.

Where is that same exuberant joy when we begin to talk to God about God? Why can't we rattle off long lists of things that just blow us away about him? Because we're not hungry. Our appetite for joy has been satiated by so many other things that we are not excited by the prospect of feasting upon God.

The good news is that we can get the hunger back. Let me explain what I'm getting at with the help of an analogy. Steve Arterburn has written *Every Man's Battle,* an excellent book for guys who are struggling for purity in their lives (i.e., all guys).[1] I've given away enough copies of his book to fill a library. One of the problems that Steve addresses is the loss of sexual desire which married men often experience toward their wives. This, in turn, leaves them open to outside temptations. To listen to the guys talk about the problem, you'd think it was their wives' fault. These women have lost their sex appeal, the husbands' theory goes, because they're not staying in shape or dressing attractively.

"Baloney!" Arterburn counters. (He doesn't actually say, "Baloney!" This is my paraphrased summary of his insights—which you ought to read for yourself sometime.) The reason that men lose their appetite for their wives is because they snack all day on the visual stimulation of other women. They're nibbling away at images of good-looking co-workers, models in lingerie ads, actresses in movies, porn stars on the Internet, cheerleaders at sports events, bikini-clad girls at the beach, and flirtatious friends. Nibbling, nibbling, nibbling. Then, when they go home for "dinner"—surprise—they're not hungry for their wives.

There's no surprise to it, is there? What's the solution to the problem? Simple. Stop the snacking. Starve your eyes, husbands, all day long (i.e., train them to look away). And you'll be amazed at how delicious your wife appears when you walk in the door of your home. Steve Arterburn has letters from guys who put this advice into practice and are astounded at how quickly they became sexually attracted to their wives again.

By now you're probably wondering what in the world this analogy is intended to teach in a book on prayer. Stay with me. I'm not coming from as far out in left field as you may think. My contention is that we lose our appetite for God, our delight at the prospect of entering his presence, because we snack on junk-food joy all day long. We're stuffing ourselves with transient excitements that lack ultimate substance and significance.

Like what? Like tickets to a big game, or dinner at a great restaurant, or a 50-percent-off sale at Gap, or a new sofa for the living room, or a cell phone that acts as a blender (why not, they can do everything else these days), or a three-day getaway, or our favorite movie coming out on DVD, or a promotion at work, or a good workout at the club, or you fill in the blank. There's nothing morally wrong with anything I've just mentioned. It's just that, as a source of joy, each of them is inadequate. They're about as nourishing to our spirits as junk food is to our bodies.

But they *will* fill you up. You'll be so full that you won't be very hungry for God. So, if you want an appetite for God to return—don't miss this—you must fast from some of these bite-sized joys. That's right. You figure out what you've been snacking on (a TV show you never miss, daily lattes at Starbucks, shopping for a new car?) and you deliberately cut it out of your diet. I'm not kidding.

And if you've got kids, it's time to stop and think about their diet. If their lives are crammed full of video games, traveling sports competitions, shopping trips to the mall, movies with multimillion-dollar special effects, sleepovers at friends' homes, ballet recitals, and ski weekends, how can they be excited about God? Can reading the Bible together as a family compete with all that? Can the church's youth group or your Sunday morning service? Can volunteering to serve meals at the local homeless shelter? Can leading a friend to Christ? Are your kids hungry for the truly good stuff or has their appetite for God-food been lost to other fare?

We've got to recover a hunger for God. Otherwise there will be no genuine gladness and joy when we come before him in prayer. Honoring him with praise will just be a mechanical exercise, a lifeless spiritual discipline. The key to a restored appetite for God is to deliberately cut back on everything else we've been feeding ourselves. The biblical word for this self-imposed restraint is fasting, a practice that can be applied not only to food but also to anything that keeps us from God-hunger.

The Humility

One of my favorite contemporary worship bands is . . . Oops! I almost gave you their name. But it's best that they remain anonymous because I'm about to diss the lyrics of one of their latest songs. My intention is not to cast these brothers in Christ in a negative light, but to point out how misdirected the words of worship music can sometimes be.

The song that I have in mind begins innocently enough. It expresses a desire to praise God but confesses an inability to find adequate words with which to do so. This is a bummer, the songwriter continues, because he desperately wants his praise to be like an ocean breeze, a summer sun, a gentle rain, a fragrant rose, a soaring eagle. It's a worship song about worship. All the colorful metaphors describe the attributes of really hot praise.

The composer even goes so far as to say that he just wants to give God whatever God needs from him. Excuse me? God doesn't need anything from him. Or from you and me. Praise is not about what we bring to the table. It's about God and what he brings to the table. Songs in praise of praise need to be replaced by songs in praise of who God is.

This point is underscored as Psalm 100 continues: "Know that the LORD is God. It is he who made us, and we are his; we are his people, the sheep of his pasture" (v. 3). God is our creator, our owner, our shepherd. He is not dependent upon us for anything—least of all, for our praise. Let's approach him with humility. May our honoring of him in prayer remind us that he is God, and we are not.

I recently read a biography of John Adams, patriot and second U.S. president. During the Revolutionary War, Adams, along with Ben Franklin and Thomas Jefferson, served as an ambassador to France. In later years, he sent his son, John Quincy Adams, back to France for an education. Johnny Q. wrote frequent letters home to mom and dad describing his experiences in this foreign country.

On one occasion, he witnessed the baptism of King Louis XVI's infant in Notre Dame Cathedral. Everyone paid homage to the king as he made his solemn way to the front of the church. But when he reached the altar, he dropped to his knees. And for the next half hour a massive choir sang songs of worship to God. J. Q. wrote to his folks: "What a sight. An absolute king of one of the most powerful empires on earth, and perhaps a thousand of the first personages of that empire, adoring the Divinity—the God who created them. And acknowledging that he can, in a moment, reduce them to the dust from which they spring."[2]

Even kings are nothing before the King of Kings. As Louis XVI dropped to his knees before the Lord, so should we. I have previously made a case for this posture as a means of interjecting passion (instead of lethargy) into our prayers. But let me now say a word about our body language as it pertains to humility. How should we approach the One who is not only our heavenly Father but also the God of the universe?

The psalmist answers this question in Psalm 95. After reminding us that "the Lord is the great God, the great King above all gods," he then encourages us to assume an appropriate position before God: "Come, let us bow down in worship, let us kneel before the LORD our Maker; for he is our God and we are the people of his pasture, the flock under his care" (vv. 3, 6–7). Bowing and kneeling express our humility as we draw near to God's throne.

I'm not going to suggest that we should always kneel when we pray. Certainly, we find people in Scripture praying in other postures as well. But I would like to recommend that we drop our habit of approaching God in a cavalier fashion, lounging in chairs with our legs crossed, as if we were sipping coffee with a pal. I must confess that this is a pet peeve of mine. Whenever I'm circled up with a group that is about to pray I'm tempted to say something to those who look a bit too relaxed. So far I've managed to resist the urge—but I haven't been as reticent with my kids. They've heard me instruct, on more than one occasion, "Sit up, now—we're talking to the King!"

This is the God whom angels worship. Angels! Do you know what we would do if we ever encountered an angel? I'll tell you what the apostle John did. John was given a vision of the future Wedding Supper of the Lamb, which will take place in heaven. And when a magnificent angel instructed John to write down what he'd seen, he was so awestruck at the angel that he fell at its feet to worship.

Wrong move! The angel rebuked John, saying: "Do not do it! I am a fellow servant with you . . . Worship God!" (Rev. 19:9–10). While John's worship was misdirected, it was also quite understandable. Evidently the mere sight of an angel is enough to drop a guy to his knees. What should be our reflex action, then, upon entering the presence of Almighty God—the One who is incessantly worshiped by these awe-inspiring angels? Doesn't it make sense to get low before him?

Humility. We lift God up as we lower ourselves down. Our words and our posture communicate his greatness. This is not groveling. And this is not something that God demands from us so as to flatter himself or to stroke his ego. C. S. Lewis, in *Reflections on the Psalms*, confesses that he once had such a twisted view of praise. He wondered if God needed our worship in order to feel good about himself.

But one day an analogy came to Lewis' mind that helped him understand that God's demand for praise is for our own good. Lewis noted that a magnificent work of art simply must be appreciated. "Admiration is the correct, adequate or appropriate response to it . . . if we do not admire we shall be stupid, insensible, and great losers, we shall have missed something."

Lewis then relates this insight to the topic of praise: "I had never noticed that all enjoyment spontaneously overflows into praise. . . . I had not noticed how the humblest, and at the same time most balanced and capacious minds, praised most, while the cranks, misfits and malcontents praised least. I think we delight to praise what we enjoy because the praise not merely expresses but completes the enjoyment."[3]

Our praise of God enables us to take full pleasure in him. Making much of God as we humble ourselves before him is not, as I said a moment ago, an act of groveling. It's an expression of delight that completes our enjoyment of God.

The "Hello"

I have a friend who is a brilliant New Testament scholar. He has been a mentor of mine ever since I sat in his classroom years ago. I keep his phone number near at hand because he is my go-to guy whenever I'm wrestling with the interpretation of a biblical text or with some theological issue. He's a very busy man and so I rarely catch him in. I usually just leave my big questions on his voicemail, knowing that he'll get back to me at his earliest convenience.

Like my scholarly friend, I am also often difficult to reach by phone. So he typically leaves his responses on my voicemail. And this is the part that amuses me. He almost never begins with a greeting (other than, occasionally, identifying himself as the caller). He just launches right into his reply: "Regarding the issue that you raised, . . ." Those are the very first words out of his mouth. I immediately know who the caller is. I smile at my telephone and sarcastically say, "Hello to you, too."

Do we do this with God? Do we bop into his presence with our latest list of requests, failing to offer even a simple, "Hello"? Let's remind ourselves again of what a "hello" should include, according to Psalm 100: "Enter his gates with thanksgiving and his courts with praise; give thanks to him and praise his name" (v. 4).

Think of praise and thanksgiving as being like the phrase that initiates a call on your voice-activated cell phone. Somebody recently tried to show me how this works, using his own new toy. "Suppose I want to call So-and-so," he began. "All I have to do is say . . ." and he spoke to his cell phone. Only trouble was, he'd forgotten the right line to use and so nothing happened. He tried various other lines. Still nothing. Finally, he gave up. Praise and thanksgiving are what activate our connection with God. This is how our conversations with him are to begin.

When we fail to enter God's gates with thanksgiving and his courts with praise, we are just being plain rude. And this is a discourtesy of great magnitude because we are dealing with royalty. Ever read about the deference with which Nehemiah approached King Artaxerxes? King A was the ruler of Persia, the superpower of the day. And while Nehemiah had a close relationship with the king (he was the king's cupbearer—he both tasted the king's food for poison and served as an informal advisor), he did not just waltz into the throne room without the proper decorum.

What was that decorum? Well, I can tell you what it wasn't. One day Nehemiah approached the king with a long face. He was brooding over a recent report he'd received from his homeland, describing the capitol city of Jerusalem as being in ruins. When King A asked Nehemiah, "Why does your face look so sad?" Nehemiah's knee-jerk reaction was fear: "I was very much afraid" (Neh. 2:2). Why was Nehemiah afraid? Because he suddenly realized that he'd violated a very important protocol. One didn't approach a king (especially the king of the world's superpower) in whatever way one pleased. Certain etiquette was called for.

If that is true when coming before an earthly king, how much more should we pay attention to the way in which we enter the presence of our heavenly King? It is easier, however, to nod in agreement with this point than it is to put it into practice. It makes good sense to enter God's courts with praise—but will we take the time to do that the next opportunity we have to pray? Or will we start *asking* before we've done any *honoring*?

My wife and I do some of our best praying together as we walk beside the river that winds its way through our town. There are paved bike paths on both sides of this waterway. So we saunter (I want to saunter, Sue wants to "power walk") for two miles in one direction, cross a picturesque wooden bridge, then return along the other bank to where we began. We do it for the exercise. We do it for the pleasure of being out in nature. We do it for the contribution it makes to our marriage. But most of all we do it for the opportunity it gives us to pray.

And most of what we pray about has to do with our kids. They're now young adults, the two oldest are married. I used to think that our days of parenting would be over when we reached this point. Boy, was I wrong! The challenges they face have just gotten bigger! And so our responsibility to pray for them has increased exponentially. It is so tempting, when we start down that river path, to jump right in to interceding for our kids. There's not a minute to lose. We can fill an entire four-mile stroll praying for them.

But we don't. That's no way to treat our God. He is so majestic, so awesome, so wonderful. Before we can start talking *about* Emily, Rachel, and Andrew, we've got to talk *up* God. We praise him for who he is (citing specific attributes) and thank him for what he's done. This is how we approach his throne. This is how we say "hello" to our King.

How do you say "hello" to God?

The Habit

I've already touched twice on the practice that I'm about to describe in greater detail—once when I alerted you to the "No Praise" obstacle to prayer and second when I covered the pattern of praying God's attributes. I make no apologies for the repetition. I figure you're a lot like me—I never catch on to anything until the third time. Besides, I've got something more to say about this topic each time I bring it up.

Take a look at the closing verse of Psalm 100: "For the LORD is good and his love endures forever; his faithfulness continues through all generations" (v. 5). Can you spot the three attributes of God that the psalmist throws into his conclusion? He mentions God's goodness, love, and faithfulness.

We can learn a lot about God by meditating on his attributes as we come across them in Scripture. The same is true of his titles. What titles of God surface in Psalm 100? He is referred to as LORD. (Whenever this title appears in small caps it's a translation of the Hebrew "Yahweh." And "Yahweh" is the "I AM" handle—same root—by which God revealed himself to Moses. There are all sorts of lessons to be learned about God from the title, LORD.)

In Psalm 100 God is also addressed as God (not surprisingly, but worth some pondering), as Creator and Owner (both implied in the line: "It is he who made us, and we are his"), as Shepherd (since we're "the sheep of his pasture"), and as King (since he has "courts" that we are to "enter with praise").

If you want to get good at honoring God in prayer you must make a habit of observing the attributes and titles and names by which he goes in Scripture. These, specifically, are what you will be praying back to him—as opposed to offering him that lame, catch-all line of, "I just praise you for who you are." Ugh! What a nonstatement.

Dr. Louis Agassiz, a nineteenth-century naturalist who taught in the biology department at Harvard, was especially known for his ability to teach students the discipline of observation. At the beginning of each semester, students would gather around lab tables and Dr. Agassiz would pass out samples of dead fish. Then he would instruct his learners to write down everything they could observe about these specimens.

After about ten minutes, most students would tire of this exercise and would look up to find that Dr. Agassiz had left the classroom. And he didn't return for the rest of the period. The next day their teacher was back, but he merely repeated the previous day's assignment. Everybody observed dead fish while the professor disappeared. This happened, class after class, for two weeks. By then most students had caught on to what Agassiz was trying to teach them about persevering at observation. And they were making more and more discoveries about their dead fish.

The unfortunate truth is that most of us are not very observant when it comes to our knowledge of God. We're aware of a few basic attributes and titles of his—which we use over and over again in our prayers and worship songs. But there's so much about God that we miss, so little of who he is that ever gets meditated upon. Why, for example, does the prophet Isaiah call him "a trap and a snare" (Isa. 8:14)? Try turning that one into something to praise God for!

What does it mean, that God is "zealous" (Ezek. 39:25), or "my song" (Ps. 118:14), or "a carpenter" (Mark 6:3), or "obedient" (Heb. 5:8), or "an eagle" (Deut. 32:11), or "despised" (Isa. 53:3)? Can you squeeze some truth out of each of these that can be prayed back to God?

We've got to train ourselves to be more observant. It's my theory that guys are weaker at this activity, in general, than women. We just don't see what we see. Sue and I were eating out a couple of weeks ago, and she said to me: "Did you see that waitress's eyes? She had one brown and one blue." No, I'd missed that. Now, I was reasonably certain that the waitress had eyes. I'd picked up on that. But it had escaped me that they were two different colors. My wife notices things like that. What do we notice when we look at God?

Let me suggest three tools for helping you observe God in greater detail. First, there's the book of Psalms. While God's attributes, titles, and names are scattered throughout the pages of Scripture, there is a greater concentration of them in this Old Testament book than anywhere else in the Bible. Maybe that's why many Christians read through Psalms every month. One hundred and fifty psalms break down into five per day. But don't just zip through them. Stop every time God is referred to as merciful, or as a rock, or as the One who restores your soul. And tell God why this truth about who he is means so much to you.

A second tool is a good hymnbook. Find an old one that you can cut up, and save pages of your best hymns to put in your journal. Or stick two or three pages of them at a time inside the cover of your Bible to be used during the week. As much as I love rocking out to contemporary praise songs (yes, I think I can justify rocking out on biblical grounds), the old hymns give me so much more food for thought in terms of who God is.

A third and final tool is the A to Z list that I've included as an appendix to this book. Here are all the attributes and titles and names of God that I've been able to find in Scripture. Some of them are inferred from the text. Many of them are linked to one specific member of the Trinity. But this list makes a great journal companion for use in your daily meetings with God.

Before you leave this chapter behind, why don't you practice what you've learned? Take those three attributes of God that are mentioned in the closing verse of Psalm 100—*goodness, love, faithfulness*—and use them to praise him. Let's do the first one together. Goodness. What do you know about the goodness of God from Scripture? In what sense is God good?

We can get no further than the opening chapter of the Bible before we run into the word "good." And it's repeated seven times over, so we can't miss it. After God speaks into being each aspect of creation, we read that "God saw that it was good." So as you reflect upon his goodness, you will want to praise him for his artistry in creation. "Lord, you are a *good* painter, splashing the colors of a sunset on the canvas of an evening sky. You are a *good* architect, designing the Rocky Mountains." Keep going. How else do you see God's goodness portrayed in creation?

Finished? No, you've only just begun. (Remember Dr. Agassiz' exercise?) What about goodness as a moral quality? Think of the tree of the knowledge of good and evil located in the middle of the garden of Eden! Good and evil are regularly contrasted in

Scripture. Paul exhorts us to "Hate what is evil; cling to what is good" (Rom. 12:9).

So the Lord's goodness is a reflection of his moral perfection, his wholesomeness. "Good and upright is the LORD," the psalmist says. But he doesn't stop there. He goes on to tell us that this morally good God "instructs sinners in his ways. He guides the humble in what is right" (Ps. 25:8–9). Aren't you glad that, in this morally gray world, God's standards are black and white? Praise God for his goodness in giving you a clear sense of right and wrong.

But don't stop. There's still more to God's goodness. God is a giver of good gifts. Jesus taught this in his Sermon on the Mount (Matt. 7:11). King David describes God as the One "who satisfies your desires with good things" (Ps. 103:5). What good things have you received from the hand of God? Praise him for these displays of his goodness. Tell him that you have, indeed, tasted and found him to be good (Ps. 34:8).

You're just getting warmed up. If you wanted to keep going, you could extol God for the uniqueness of his goodness. Jesus said: "There is only One who is good" (Matt. 19:17). You could thank him for bringing you the message of salvation, his good news (Rom. 10:15). You could recognize goodness as one of the fruits that his Spirit wants to produce in you (Gal. 5:22). You could honor him as your good Shepherd (John 10:11) who laid down his life for you.

Believe it or not, you still have not covered everything that God's Word has to say about his goodness. Do you see, now, why it's so lame to limit your praise to one-liners like, "Lord, I praise you for being good"? *Honoring* God in prayer takes time. Time to choose one of his attributes, titles, or names. Time to trace that quality in a Bible concordance. Time to meditate on its various facets. Time to craft your insights into praise.

Onto the Praying Field

1. What two or three subjects get you so excited that you could talk enthusiastically about them for hours? Why is it

often easier to go on and on about these subjects than about God's greatness?

2. What activities in your life do you "snack" on so continually that they possibly diminish your appetite for God? How could you fast from (i.e. limit) these activities so that your hunger for God returns?

3. In what ways could you demonstrate humility as you come before God in prayer?

4. C. S. Lewis makes it clear that God does not *need* our praise—but we have a need to praise God. Why is that? What will you miss if your prayers are praise-less?

5. Take three or four titles or attributes of God from the A to Z list in the appendix. Choose several that you are unfamiliar with. Go for a long walk (preferably outdoors) and pray these back to God. Come up with as many things as you can say about each (at least a half dozen associated ideas).

6. Dig up or purchase a hymnal. Every day this week read the words of a hymn to God—slowly and meditatively—as a prayer of praise.

Ask

Value the Relationship over the Request

I gave my son-in-law, Jameson, a pretty rough time the day he asked for my daughter's hand in marriage. When he called me on the phone and asked if we could get together and talk, I had a feeling he was going to ask if he could marry Rachel.

I was headed to my son's soccer game that afternoon. So, I volunteered to Jameson: "Why don't you come to Andrew's game with me, and we can talk in the car?" He quickly agreed. The soccer match was in a neighboring town, so we had about a fifteen-minute drive to get there. Jameson spent the first fourteen minutes or so just working up to the big question.

At last, he spit it out—the very question I had anticipated—just as we were pulling into the school's parking lot where the game was to be played. But instead of acknowledging his request, I jumped out of the car and shouted: "Looks like the game has already started. We'd better hurry up!" And I headed off, at a jog, toward the soccer field.

I'm sure that the next hour and a half was pure misery to Jameson. He'd asked me for something of great importance—but I

133

hadn't responded. And it didn't look like I was likely to respond any time soon. He could see that I was temporarily preoccupied with other things. I had to watch my son play soccer. I had to converse with all my parent friends. I even had to process a tragedy—while we were watching the game, a horse barn across the field caught on fire and all sorts of emergency vehicles were arriving on the scene.

Finally, at the conclusion of the game, Jameson and I were walking back to the car when it dawned on me that I had never answered his big request. (Had I forgotten or was I just messin' with him? What do *you* think?) So, I turned to him and stated the obvious: "I suppose you want an answer to that question you asked me just before the game." Then I paused. (Definitely messin' with him now.) "The answer is 'yes.'"

I don't know if Jameson wanted to hug me or slug me at that point.

A lot of people find the *asking* part of prayer—the A of CHAT—to be equally frustrating. Oftentimes, it seems as if God doesn't answer our prayers—at least, not in a timely fashion. Maybe we write off that lack of response (as Jameson did with me) as owing to the fact that God is temporarily preoccupied with other stuff. Urgent stuff.

God's got a universe (not just a soccer game) to watch over, he's got millions of people (not just a few friends) trying to talk to him at one time, and he's got plenty of emergencies (not just burning horse barns) to deal with. We're not surprised—even though we are disappointed—when God seemingly puts our requests on hold, so that he can attend to wars and famines and who wins this year's World Series.

So, what's the secret of snagging God's attention? How can we get him to respond to our requests? How does the *asking* part of prayer work? Jesus addressed this issue in John 15:7, when he told his disciples: "If you remain in me and my words remain in you, ask whatever you wish, and it will be given you." Three important principles in this brief verse must be considered when we arrive at the A portion of our CHAT with God.

134

Prioritize the Relationship

At first glance, John 15:7 seems to be a carte blanche promise from Jesus to give us anything we ask for in prayer. But please note that the verse opens with a conditional clause. That means that we don't get what's promised in the second half of the verse unless we meet the condition that's spelled out in the first half of the verse.

If we meet the condition, *then* Jesus will give us whatever we ask for in prayer. What's the condition? "If you remain in me and my words remain in you, . . ." There are actually two parts to this condition.

(1) We've got to remain in Jesus. How do we do that? Centuries ago, one writer described it as "practicing the presence of God." We keep a running dialogue going with Jesus throughout the course of the day. We make communing with Jesus our top priority. We carefully avoid any behavior or attitude that would disrupt our fellowship with him.

(2) Jesus' words have to remain in us. We must become people of God's Book. We must faithfully read and study and digest and meditate on and apply and obey the Bible.

Do we want Jesus to respond to our prayers? He'd love to—*if* (read this last word out loud for emphasis) we'll remain in him and see to it that his words remain in us. The bottom line of this condition is that Jesus wants a relationship with us.

Earlier in John 15, Jesus described that relationship as being like the connection between a grapevine and its branches. If the branches remain in the grapevine, according to Jesus, they'll draw nourishment and produce much fruit (v. 4). But if the branches become detached, they'll whither and die (v. 6).

Jesus wants us to stay connected to him—for our own good. That's why, when it comes to prayer, he requires that we *relate* before we *request.* He requires that we get more *of* him before we can get more *from* him.

I love the way that George MacDonald, a Christian novelist of a century ago, expressed the purpose of prayer: "What if the main object of God's idea of prayer be the supplying of our great, our endless need—the need of himself. Hunger may drive the runaway child home, and he may or may not be fed at once—but he needs his mother more than he needs his dinner."[1]

Jesus knows that we need him—even more than we need the things that we ask for in prayer. So, Jesus puts a condition on responding to our prayers. A condition that moves us in the direction of a deeper relationship with him. We must remain in him and his words must remain in us.

If Jesus didn't put this condition on answering us, we might treat him like a giant vending machine. What do you need? Go to Jesus, put in a few prayer coins, pull the lever, and out comes your preferred selection. Or maybe a better analogy would be—since prayer involves some verbal communication—treating Jesus like a teller at the drive-thru window of a fast-food restaurant. Jesus asks: "What would you like?" And we respond: "I'll take a double promotion at work, a happy marriage, and a cottage on a lake. No, let's supersize that lake cottage and make it an ocean condo." Now, all we have to do is pull up to the window and pick up what we ordered.

Is that what praying looks like in our lives? Maybe our requests are more legit than an ocean condo. But is our expectation the same—that Jesus should give us whatever (within reason) we ask for? Jesus won't stand for that! He's not going to answer our prayers until we start to value our *relationship* more than our *requests*, until we want more *of* him than we want *from* him.

Jesus took me to school, with regard to this lesson, several months ago. I got a call on a Wednesday evening from my doctor. My doctor happens to be a good buddy of mine, so I just assumed that he was calling for some friendly banter. But it turned out that he had some potentially bad news for me. My latest blood test had shown a spike in the PSA count. The elevated number could possibly indicate prostate cancer.

I had to schedule a biopsy with a specialist. The earliest opening was a week away. And then it took them eight days to get the results. So, for more than two weeks I was left wondering if I would soon be fighting cancer.

Even though prostate cancer is not as lethal as some other types of the disease, I thought it was rather ominous that one day during this waiting period my executive associate announced to me: "The trustees need some information from you." (The trustees are the ones who manage all the financial affairs of our church.) What did they want? "They said that we don't have an emergency succession plan, in case something should ever happen to you. You know, if you should *die* or something."

Gotta love those trustees! (And I sincerely do.) They didn't know about my medical testing but were just covering their bases. And they weren't the only ones who were rattling my cage. I also just "happened" to be reading a book on prayer, *The Papa Prayer* by Larry Crabb, and this simple yet profound book was shaking me up.[2]

Dr. Crabb's basic thesis is the point that I've been driving home from John 15:7: when we pray, God wants us to put a greater priority on our *relationship* with him than on our *requests*. In fact, Crabb says if we truly want more *of* God than *from* God, then we should be willing to accept whatever answers to our prayers draw us closer to him—even if those answers are not the ones we'd hoped for.

Wow! I knew that Crabb was right. Now, that didn't mean—as I waited for the report from my prostate biopsy—I shouldn't pray for a clean bill of health. I did! But I also adjusted my overall prayer perspective, so that my greatest desire was for a closer fellowship with God, good health or not.

In the end, the biopsy detected no signs of cancer. Believe me, I rejoiced in that good news. But I was also glad for the way in which my new approach to prayer had deepened my relationship with God.

I'd like to add an anecdote taken from Crabb's preface. A friend of his was headed off on a personal two-day retreat. Crabb asked him what he planned to do with himself for forty-eight-plus hours. "I hope to spend some time praying," was the reply. Crabb pressed him further. "What do you get out of an experience like that?" The friend's response sums up what I've been trying to say over the last few pages. "I've never thought about what I get out of it. I just figure God likes it when I show up." God likes it when we show up in prayer, friends. And he likes it when we accept from his hand whatever draws us closer to him.

Present the Requests

Look again at John 15:7. What does Jesus tell us to do, once we have met his condition—prioritize the relationship—for prayer? "Ask whatever you wish." Ask! Don't just think about presenting requests to God. Do it.

I love the bluntness with which James makes this same point in his New Testament epistle: "You do not have, because you do not ask God" (James 4:2). How many times have we blamed God for not meeting our needs, when the truth is that we haven't presented those needs to him in prayer?

What are we waiting for? We are way too frugal in our praying. We use our prayers like they were lifelines on that popular TV show, *Who Wants to Be a Millionaire?* Remember how the game is played? If you, as a contestant, are stuck with a question that you can't answer, you're allowed to call somebody on the outside. But you have to use these lifelines sparingly because you only get a limited number of them. And once they're gone, they're gone.

Prayer isn't like that! You don't have to save your praying for something really, really big.

You may have heard the story about the guy who found a bottle on the beach, rubbed it, and a genie appeared. (Who *hasn't* heard a story that begins this way?) The genie said: "I'll give you one wish—but only one."

The guy thought about it for a moment, and then replied: "I'd like a highway between California and Hawaii. I've always wanted to go to Hawaii, but I'm afraid of flying. If there was a highway bridge, then I could drive there." The genie was a bit taken back by such an enormous request, and so she countered: "That's a pretty tall order. I'm not sure I can pull it off. Isn't there something else you'd rather have?"

Shrugging his shoulders, the guy offered: "Well, I've never been able to figure out women. Can you make it so I understand my wife?" The genie quickly shot back: "Would you like that highway to be two lanes or four lanes?"

Jesus doesn't limit us to just one wish. He welcomes us to "ask whatever you wish." This, of course, assumes that we have met the prayer condition. That we are remaining in him and his word is remaining in us. That we are wanting, more than anything else, for the answer to our prayer to result in a more intimate relationship with God.

If we are truly prioritizing this relationship, then we are ready to present our requests. And God is eager to respond to them. Any how-tos to keep in mind as we do this?

Back in chapter 5, we considered the importance of praying with passion because passion causes us to be more definite about what we desire from God. Let me reiterate that principle here. When we are presenting our requests to God, we should be as specific as we possibly can. (Admitting, of course, that there will be times—according to Rom. 8:26—when: "We do not know what we ought to pray for, but the Spirit himself intercedes for us with groans that words cannot express.")

Matthew's Gospel tells the story of two blind men who were seated by the side of the road, begging, outside the city of Jericho. One day Jesus passed their way. And when they learned that the Miracle Worker was within earshot, they began to call out, "Jesus! Jesus!!"

People in the crowd tried to get the blind guys to shut up. But that just made them cry out even louder, "Jesus! Jesus!" So, Jesus went over to them and asked them a question. Jesus was always asking questions—like a doctor diagnosing his patients. Sometimes, like on this occasion, his questions were a bit startling. Jesus asked them, "What would you like me to do for you?" (Matt. 20:29–32).

What would you like me to do for you? Wasn't it obvious what they would like Jesus to do for them? They were blind. They wanted to see. Hello!

None of this was lost on Jesus. He was just waiting for them to frame their request with actual words. I'm reminded of the times when my kids were younger and they'd approach their mother with a question, or a concern, or some bit of extraordinary news—but they'd be too worked up to spit it out. Sue would patiently say: "Use your words." That's what Jesus was waiting for these two sightless guys to do. To use their words. To ask him, specifically, for the ability to see.

Don't assume that just because Jesus already knows what you need that there's no reason to state the particulars in prayer. "You do not have," James shakes his head at us, "because you do not ask God" (James 4:2).

Sometimes our failure to pray specifically is just plain laziness on our part. It takes too much energy. Other times we pray in vague generalities because we're busy—in too much of a hurry to elaborate on our requests. So, we speak to God in broad brush strokes: "Please, Lord, cause someone to look at my résumé and offer me a job." Or "Please, Lord, give us a safe trip." Or "Please, Lord, direct me as I make this big decision."

Nothing wrong with one-liners—as long as they're just the opening line to more extended, detailed prayers. Be specific.

At our church we've recently been asking God for a new middle school pastor. I don't know how others are praying for this need, but I can tell you that when I raise this request to God, I roll out the particulars. I'm not going to settle for just any ole middle school pastor. I've been praying: "Lord, bring us somebody who loves sixth through eighth graders, spends time in your Word (and can apply it to kids' lives), has a strong marriage, will fit well with the rest of our youth ministry team, can endure 'All Night Riots,' is aggressive in recruiting volunteer leaders, and has a track record of introducing young people to Christ."

Maybe I won't get everything I ask for. But it won't be because I didn't ask! What are you praying for these days, in vague generalities, that you need to express in more specific terms to God?

Are you a mom or dad who starts each day by praying: "Lord, please bless my kids today"? Just what does that mean? Is the heavenly Father supposed to sprinkle your kids with fairy dust at that point? Exactly what do your kids need? Do they need some positive-influence friends, or help in understanding chemistry, or a stronger interest in spiritual values, or better control of their temper? Then pray for such things. Be specific.

Are you a salesperson who heads off to work praying a quickie: "Lord, please help me close a deal or two"? What's behind that one-liner? Unpack it in prayer. Do you need more leads, or greater confidence when you close, or more tech support, or a greater sense that you're representing Christ—as well as your company, or grace for dealing with your competition? Then pray for such. Be specific.

When you start getting specific, as you present your requests to God, you'll discover that your one-minute prayers grow into five-minute and ten-minute prayers. Occasionally, you may go outside for a prayer-walk and find yourself talking to God for a half-hour or more—something you couldn't imagine yourself doing in the past. And those extended conversations (here's the bonus) will contribute toward your highest prayer goal of developing your relationship with God.

Prioritize the relationship. Present the requests.

Presume the Results

Let's go over John 15:7 one last time, paying close attention to the final phrase of this verse: "If you remain in me and my words remain in you, ask whatever you wish, and it will be given you." Jesus guarantees results when we ask him for something in prayer.

I can almost hear your objection. "Wait a minute," you're thinking. "Are you trying to tell me that if I ask Jesus for a silver Mercedes, or an executive position at work, or a date to the prom, or for the Cubs to finally win a pennant—he's going to give it to me?"

The best way to answer that question is by reviewing what we've learned so far. If your highest priority in prayer is a closer relationship with Jesus, do you really think you're going to be asking him for the kind of stuff that I just mentioned? I don't think so. The more you want *him*, the less those other things are going to matter to you. You'll find yourself praying about things that matter to Jesus.

"Okay," you say. "I'm with you when it comes to asking for a silver Mercedes, an executive position, a prom date, or a Cubs' pennant. But what if I'm asking God to heal my dad from cancer? There's no incompatibility between a request like that and a relationship with Christ, is there?"

No, there's not. But keep this in mind: If the most important thing to you is that you're being drawn closer to Christ—and that's the *primary* intent of your prayer—God may not always give you the *secondary* results that you're looking for. In the hypothetical case of your dad's cancer, his healing would be categorized as a *secondary* result.

Sometimes God won't give us the results we ask for: a healing from cancer, or a restored marriage, or a more understanding boss, or the complete removal of a certain temptation, or acceptance into the college of our choice, or a good friend to hang out with, or whatever. And the reason God won't give us the results we ask for, on many occasions, is because that wouldn't be the best way for us to be drawn closer to him. And that's the *primary* result that both God and we desire. Right? Every other result is of *secondary* importance.

So, does this lead us to stop praying about everything other than a more intimate relationship with Christ? (After all, everything else is of *secondary* importance.) No! Just the opposite. Because we understand that Jesus loves us so much that he's going to use everything we pray about as a means of drawing us closer to him, we pray with enthusiasm and confidence.

We are always going to get the *primary* result that we're after. We presume it. And often the Lord is going to throw in the *secondary* result as well, as a bonus. But whether he does or he doesn't, we still win.

If you're still having a hard time wrapping your head around this concept, let me put it another way that may be more familiar to you. A variety of Bible teachers have said that when God doesn't give us what we ask for in prayer, it's not because he hasn't responded.

He has. If God doesn't give you a "yes" right away, he is responding in one of three ways: no, slow, or grow. All three answers are for our good (and they rhyme, making them easy to remember). No, slow, or grow—simple, yet extremely helpful.

God says "no" to us when our request itself is wrong. As the Giver of every good gift (James 1:17), he's got something better in store for us.

God says "slow" when our timing is wrong. There may be nothing wrong with the request, but God wants us to wait for his answer. He wants us to persevere, to trust him, and to learn patience.

I remember a time when my kids were all preschoolers. Sue and I were praying for a "bugger" (a stroller that's pulled by a bike). We loved to go cycling together along a beautiful trail that runs beside our local river. But we couldn't do that unless there was a way to bring the kids along. So we prayed for a "bugger." And we searched the newspaper for a used, discounted model—since we didn't have the money for a new one. Nothing. I told the Lord, repeatedly, how reasonable I thought our request was. Still nothing. About a month after we began praying for a "bugger," however, we came home one day to find a brand new one parked in our garage. A gift from a good friend.

If the request is wrong, God will say, "no." If the timing is wrong, God will say, "slow." (And after some waiting, he may drop a brand new "bugger" in our garage.) If we ourselves are wrong, God will say, "grow." God's "grow" means that our character is in need of some maturing. God desires to shape who we are—and he can best accomplish that by not giving us what we've asked for.

No, slow, or grow. But our prayers are never without results. We can presume that this will always be true. So, ask!

Onto the Praying Field

1. One of the conditions that Jesus expects us to meet before he will answer our prayers is that we "remain" in him and allow his words (Scripture) to "remain" in us (John 15:7).

Why would this condition be so important to Jesus? How would meeting this condition impact the way in which you pray?

What is your current plan for ingesting God's Word on a daily basis? If you don't have a plan, put something in place right now.

2. Describe a time when difficult circumstances compelled you to connect with God in prayer.

Is there, at present, a problem in your life that God may be using to keep you dependent upon him? Take a moment to tell God that you are more interested in drawing close to him as you pray than in getting this prayer answered.

3. What two or three things have you been neglecting to pray about because they seem too small to bother God with? Pray about them now.

4. Can you think of a time when:

God said "no" to your prayer request—and you later realized that you had been asking for the wrong thing?

God said "slow" to your prayer request—and you later realized, after God provided for you, that your original timing had been wrong?

God said "grow" to your prayer request—and you later realized that, by withholding an immediate answer, God had matured your character?

9

Thank

Practice "Thank-You" Therapy

Have you ever had to go through physical therapy of any sort? Several years ago I broke a finger after falling off a ladder. I'd been sealcoating the brick fascia on my house, stretching with my brush to reach a place I'd missed, when my aluminum ladder twisted beneath me and I plummeted to the ground. (Did you notice how I blamed it on the ladder, not on my lack of coordination?)

As I brushed myself off, thankful that I hadn't broken my neck, I looked down at my left hand—my ring finger was bent to the side at a right angle and beginning to swell. I raced into the house, soaped up my finger at the kitchen sink, and tugged on my wedding band until I got it off. By then the room around me was beginning to spin and I dropped to the floor. A wave of nausea washed over me.

Hours later, I sat in a waiting room at our local hospital as a technician developed the film from my X-rays. When he finally showed up with the results, he passed them around for other medical personnel to see. I overheard a whispered, "Wow!" and a "Looks like an old man's break!" (translation: my finger had shattered as if the bone were brittle). These were not words of encouragement.

An orthopedic surgeon operated on the finger, putting it back together with the help of two metal screws. A week later, he took another X-ray to see how it was mending. Standing with his back to me as he stared at the X-ray, I heard him breathe a quiet expletive. I assumed that wasn't good news—and I was right. The screws had pulled out. Operation number two pulled the fragments of my finger back together, again, with the help of a metal plate and five screws. My finger was now capable of setting off an airport screening device.

After my finger healed, all that hardware had to be taken out in operation number three. This permitted me to start therapy. Ah, the joys of physical therapy! I had been warned ahead of time, by those who had recovered from hand injuries, that P.T. would be painful and grueling. But they had also insisted that I give it my 100 percent best effort. "You only do this one time," they had warned, "and if you don't do it right, you'll never get the full use of your finger back." Some of these folks even showed me their own twisted digits—the result of slacking off during therapy—to make their point.

So I worked hard throughout my weeks of physical therapy. And, although I can't completely straighten out that finger today, I can easily close my hand into a tight fist. That means, as several of my friends have pointed out, that I can still grip a golf club. Which is ironic, because I hate to golf. (Why ruin a good walk?)

Why this anecdote about my experience with physical therapy? Because the *T* of our regular CHAT with God is an engagement with therapy. Not physical therapy. Spiritual therapy. And when we don't vigorously and consistently offer thanks when we pray, we end up twisted on the inside.

We have already addressed the topic of giving thanks in prayer in previous chapters. We noted that it is one of the patterns (ch. 3) that can launch us into praying when we don't know where to begin. We mentioned several categories of blessings that we can scroll through as we offer thanks to God: physical and material blessings, spiritual blessings, relational blessings, and—yes—even trial blessings.

T-praying popped up a second time when we considered the promptings (ch. 4) that remind us to pray. When we're anxious in spirit, we ought to talk to God about it (Phil. 4:6–7). But pray always "with thanksgiving," Paul stresses. We took a close, but relatively brief, look at what that means.

Now, I'd like to study Philippians 4:6–7 in greater depth. This is, as I've already affirmed, one of my favorite texts in all of Scripture. It's well worth committing to memory and regularly meditating on. And since we have somewhat covered T-praying in general, I would like to focus our present discussion on the passage's specific context in which it tells us to thank God: trials.

Life's difficulties can twist and deform our spirits. "Thank-you therapy" (TYT) is how we prevent that from happening. It's how we maintain a sense of peace in troubling circumstances. I first heard someone use this expression years ago and have used it myself for so long that it feels like my own. (Credit actually goes to Don Baker who wrote a book with that title.)[1]

The apostle Paul promises us that if we will practice TYT, then "the peace of God—which transcends all understanding—will guard your hearts and your minds in Christ Jesus" (Phil. 4:7). A strong word, that verb *guard*. A military expression used in Paul's day, *guard* alluded to the protection provided by a garrison of Roman troops.

Philippi was a Roman city—and proud of it. Everything from its architecture to its administration had been modeled after that of the empire's capital city. And Philippi was a Roman military outpost, as well. Local citizens could sleep peacefully at night, knowing that no hostile outside force would dare mess with a city full of soldiers.

"The peace of God," Paul assures us, offers us a similar sort of protection. It will "guard your hearts and your minds" from all attacks. But, like many of Scripture's promises, this one comes with a condition. And the condition must be met by us if we want to experience God's impenetrable peace. Let's break down that condition into three things we must do.

Be Fearful of Nothing

What a place to start! Big help to be told, "Do not be anxious about anything" (Phil. 4:6). Isn't this akin to that old challenge: "Don't think about a pink elephant for the next minute"? What's the only thing that one is now able to think about? A pink elephant! (Okay, you can stop thinking about it. Just forget about those floppy pink ears, and long pink tusks, and trumpeting pink trunk. Do not continue reading until that pink elephant is completely out of your mind.)

You cheated. But I'll let you continue reading anyway. Paul's advice in this opening line seems to be psychologically impossible to apply. Nobody appreciates being told not to worry about his or her worries.

I can remember, as a child, those times when I needed to make a bathroom stop on a long car ride. We'd be headed from Chicago to a Florida vacation in the family station wagon, and my bladder would be ready to burst before we cleared Illinois. But my dad, intent on reaching Georgia by nightfall, would retort: "Just don't think about it!" Oh, that made me feel better immediately. Now I could hold it for another twelve hours. Right? Wrong!

Is "Do not be anxious about anything" a reasonable directive? In spite of everything I've just said, yes! How do I know that? Because God's Word would never ask us to do the impossible. God's Word would never command us: *Don't breathe!* We've got to breathe. Evidently, we don't "got" to be anxious.

I've been told that the command, "Do not fear" (twin to, "Do not be anxious"), is the most repeated command in Scripture. (Since I don't want to do the counting myself, I'll take this on faith.) Certainly God would not ask us, again and again, to do something that is impossible to do. We *can*—obviously, with God's help—put an end to fear and anxiety when they threaten us.

So, let's begin by not making excuses for our worrying. We don't have some special right to our fears. What are the most common reasons that people give to justify their anxiety? I'll tell you the two that I hear frequently (and sometimes personally use). The first is, "My circumstances call for a fearful response" (maybe not expressed in exactly those words).

We are willing to concede that some of our fears are ill founded and inappropriate. It is foolish, we'll admit, to fret just because our teenager is out fifteen minutes past his curfew, or because the electric bill was too high this month, or because our political candidate lost the election. Circumstances like these do not foreshadow the end of the world. We caution ourselves not to make mountains out of molehills.

But when we find ourselves facing something of a much more serious nature, a situation that any objective panel of judges would consider potentially tragic, acute anxiety seems to be entirely called for. In fact, we tell ourselves, only someone out of touch with reality would not be worried at a time like this.

Even tucked away in this secluded location where I have retreated to write, my peaceful repose has been interrupted three times in less than a week, by cell phone messages depicting others' dire circumstances. A friend's mother-in-law has been severely depressed and may be suicidal. A middle-aged single mom has been repeatedly threatened by her rebellious teenage son. A young couple's baby has had a spiked fever for almost a week, resulting in a ruptured eardrum. Do these people have a right to fear? Is anxiety a justifiable response to their predicaments? Would the apostle Paul have the gall to tell these friends of mine not to worry?

Joshua would answer these questions, "no," "no," and "yes." The Old Testament book that bears his name opens with our hero in a very tough spot. Moses has just died and the leadership baton has been passed to Joshua. How would you like to follow in the footsteps of Moses—who had gone toe-to-toe with Pharaoh, led his people out of 430 years of slavery, and parted the Red Sea? A guy who would go down in the history books as one of the greatest leaders of all time? Do you think you'd have a knot or two in your stomach?

How would you like to lead the ancient Israelites? They were several million in number, complained about everything, refused to follow orders, and had threatened to kill Moses on more than one occasion. Your turn at the helm. Fearful?

How would you like to face a mission as daunting as conquering the Promised Land? Wasn't it rumored that there were giants occupying this territory? Nothing but blood, sweat, and tears to look forward to. You worried yet? Are prebattle jitters allowed?

Listen to what the Lord repeatedly says to Joshua on this occasion—in just one chapter: "Be strong and courageous, because you will lead these people; Be strong and very courageous; Have I not commanded you? Be strong and courageous. Do not be terrified; do not be discouraged, for the LORD your God will be with you wherever you go; Only be strong and courageous!" (Josh. 1: 6–7, 9, 18).

We get the message, Lord. Doesn't sound to me like Joshua is given any wiggle room to worry. No license, even considering his extremely difficult circumstances, to wring his hands.

God calls us to fearless, anxiety-free living. Even when we find a condom in our teenager's jeans pocket. Even when the sump pump goes out during a thunderstorm. Even when we're out of work and nobody's responding to our resumé. Even when the chemo doesn't seem to be shrinking the tumor. Even when our biggest customer moves to a competitor.

God's Word does not say, "Do not be anxious—unless the circumstances warrant it." We are to be fearful of nothing. Which also overrides a second excuse that's often used to justify worrying: "It's just my personality to worry." Have you ever heard or used that one? Some people try to blame their anxieties on their temperament. They describe themselves as sensitive, or melancholic, or overly analytical.

I just finished reading a nonfiction book about rescue swimmers. They have just the opposite personality of what I've been describing. The Coast Guard may drop them out of a helicopter into sixty-foot waves, in shark-infested waters, to retrieve the survivors of an oil tanker explosion. And they go about their work like it's a day at the beach. They're unflappable.

But what about those whose God-given temperament registers at the other end of the spectrum? What about a Timothy? We learn from Paul's New Testament letters to this young man that he was raised by a mom and a grandmother. No mention of a manly influence in his life. And he must have been somewhat self-conscious about the age thing, since Paul had to encourage him not to let anyone look down on him because he was young (1 Tim. 4:12). And to top it off, Timothy was probably on the shy side, leading Paul to remind him that God had not given him a spirit of timidity but of power (2 Tim. 1:7).

Now, take a guy with this psychological makeup, and put him in the leadership position of a strategic church that's having problems with heretical teachers. Then tell him to straighten the whole thing out, facing down the bad guys like the actor Gary Cooper in the movie *High Noon.* That was Timothy's assignment! To give you an idea of how unsettling this mission must have been to Timbo, consider the fact that Paul had to counsel him to drink a little wine for his upset stomach (1 Tim. 5:23).

No coddling there! No permission granted to nurse any anxieties. Paul just points his young friend in the direction of the battle and gives him a push from behind. "Be fearful of nothing." Having a sensitive temperament doesn't legitimize worrying. God says, "Stop it!" And how does he expect us to do that?

Be Prayerful about Everything

How do you stop a bad habit? I'm sure you've heard the answer to this one before. The way to stop a bad habit is by replacing it with a good habit.

Back in chapter 3, I offered this very advice when I was describing the pattern of "body parts" praying. Actually, it was Paul who offered this advice: "Do not offer the parts of your body to sin, as instruments of wickedness, but rather offer yourselves to God, as those who have been brought from death to life; and offer the parts of your body to him as instruments of righteousness" (Rom. 6:13).

Do you follow Paul's argument here? If we want to stop sinning with our eyes, mouths, hands, and other body parts, then we've got to give our eyes, mouths, hands, and other body parts something

God pleasing to do with themselves. We *stop* certain behaviors by replacing them with other behaviors that we *start*.

How do we stop worrying? By replacing it with praying! It's impossible to miss this point in Philippians 4:6. Paul uses four different words—in one verse—to describe the cure-all for anxiety: *prayer, petition, thanksgiving,* and *requests.*

And how big does an anxiety need to be before it qualifies for prayer? If it's big enough to worry about, it's big enough to pray about. We don't put off phoning God like we put off phoning the doctor until our temperature is 104 degrees, or the bleeding won't stop, or the rash covers our entire body. The minute we sense the slightest twinge of anxiety, we get God on the prayer line.

At the risk of sounding like an emotional hypochondriac, let me reel off a few anxieties that I've prayed about in the past forty-eight hours—not because they were huge, but because they just *were.* I prayed about an upcoming phone conversation with a potential staff hire for a position we've had a hard time filling. I prayed about the pace of my son's relationship with his girlfriend. I prayed that I would get this manuscript to the publisher by the deadline. I prayed about the continuing pain in my left knee. I prayed about my seeming lack of discipline to lose a few extra pounds. I prayed for the wisdom to balance my too-busy schedule. If anything nagged me in the slightest way, it got prayed for.

Praying seems to do a couple of things to my fears. First, it identifies them. It brings them to the surface. It outs them.

My guess is that I don't appear to be a worrier to those who know me. I come across as a fairly confident person. I've already described myself like a duck that's gliding serenely across the pond, while under the waterline it's paddling feverishly. I tend do my fretting beneath the surface. I'm so good at concealing it that I can sometimes hide it from myself.

But I've learned to spot the telltale signs of my anxious spirit. The giveaways are irritability with other people, impatience with my circumstances, and the escaping of foul words from my mouth— when nobody's listening, of course. (Didn't Jesus say that the mouth speaks out of the overflow of the heart [see Matt. 12:34]?) When I spot these things in my life, I can very often trace them back to roots of anxiety. And the tracing back typically happens as I pray.

Let's say that I have just damned my coffee for spilling on my lap as I'm driving. Not my usual choice of words—but ones which, I'm embarrassed to admit, have occasionally passed through my lips. My standard response to such an outburst is almost always the immediate prayer: "Where in the world did *that* come from, Lord?" That's a sincere request on my part. And I expect God to answer in my spirit. His answer is most often the identification of some anxiety that has been subconsciously gnawing away at me. Now I can pray about *that*.

The second thing that praying does to my fears is take my focus off them (after they've been identified) and place it back on God. Prayer is a God-ward activity. At the risk of insulting your intelligence, let me point out that it is impossible to pray without bringing God to mind. And once God is in the picture, he puts our troubles in perspective.

Have you ever taken a camera shot that makes it look as if one person is holding another in the palm of her hand? My kids got a kick out of this. I'd position Rachel in the foreground, with her arm held out to the side and her hand palm up. Then I'd have Andrew stand about fifty feet behind his sister, directly over her open palm when viewed through the camera lens. It's all about perspective.

When we're worrying, our problems move to the forefront of our thinking—dwarfing all other considerations. But when we're praying, God is front and center. Our troubles are diminished and seen to be in the palm of his hand. This is why Paul encourages us to pray about everything that makes us anxious.

"Fine," you say. "But sometimes praying doesn't reduce the size of my anxieties. Sometimes it enlarges them. Sometimes I'm more worried *after* I've prayed than I was *before* I prayed." Have you ever experienced that? Maybe your teenage daughter promised to be home by eleven, and it's after midnight. Where is she? Why doesn't she answer her cell phone? Time to pray.

In your prayer, you remind God (in case he's forgotten) that your daughter is easily distracted when she's driving. And that it's

Saturday night—when there are more drunks on the road than at any other time of the week. And that a light drizzle is making the driving conditions dangerous. And that traffic fatalities are a leading cause of death among teenagers. When you say "amen," it doesn't seem as if the peace of God is now guarding your heart and your mind.

Why not? Because you have left the most important ingredient out of your prayer. You have not prayed *with thanksgiving*.

Be Thankful for Anything

I can remember one Halloween when we were going to have another family over for dinner. The dads were out with the kids trick-or-treating in the early evening, while Sue was making a big batch of chili for everybody to come home to. She looked at her recipe, and then added the amount of salt that was called for. But then the doorbell rang and she stopped cooking long enough to drop some candy in the bags of a ghost, a cheerleader, and a hobo.

Returning to the stove, Sue picked up where she'd left off with the recipe. It called for salt, so she added salt. Another doorbell interruption. She returned to the recipe and it called for salt. Doorbell . . . salt . . . doorbell . . . salt.

As we dove into the chili later that night, we found ourselves gulping down glass after glass of water. Our guests didn't want to appear rude by not eating the stuff, but it was making us all gag. Finally, Sue spoke up, acknowledging that she'd obviously done something wrong. That's when it dawned on her that she'd repeated the recipe's salt step a few too many times. The meal was thereafter referred to as "the chili from hell."

It's important to follow the recipe when praying. Our tendency is not to add too much of a certain ingredient to the mix. Our penchant is to leave something out completely. And it's a vital ingredient: thanksgiving. When we fail to present our requests to God, *with thanksgiving* (as Phil. 4:6 teaches us to do), our anxieties are more likely to increase than decrease. We'll find ourselves reaching for more water, as we choke on our concerns.

We must begin to practice "thank-you therapy." It doesn't come naturally to us. But when we make ourselves pray along these lines, the results are truly amazing. The peace of God really does begin to garrison our hearts and our minds.

I'd like to add two qualifiers to this habit of thanking God in our trials. The first is that we must learn to be *creative.* It is rarely easy to come up with things to thank God for when we are in a fearful situation. This will take some imagination on our part. God is not asking us to thank him *for* our troubles—it would take little creativity to merely spell them out. God wants us to thank him *in* our troubles, which requires that we envision all the good that could possibly be associated with them.

Let me give you an example of what I'm suggesting. A very personal example. As the senior leader of a fairly large church, I have a constant concern for the financial resources to sustain our ministry. We must raise millions of dollars every year in order to maintain three campuses, pay the salaries of our wonderful staff, support our international partners around the world, create outreach venues for sharing the good news of Christ, and meet the physical needs of the poor and destitute. If we have two or three weeks (or occasionally months) in a row with light offerings, I confess to getting worried. It doesn't take us long to find ourselves in a big hole.

If I pray about this matter without adding the appropriate thanksgiving, my agitation just increases. But how does a pastor thank God for his church being thousands of dollars behind in giving? Creatively! Here are some of the ways in which I've expressed my gratitude to God on these occasions. I've thanked him that our church has never—in the twenty-two years since we first opened our doors—ended a year in the red. I've thanked him for all the faithful people who are giving generously each week. (I just got an e-mail from a regular attender who's downsizing his house so that he can give more to the Lord's work. Yes!) I've thanked him for the great group of trustees who manage our financial resources with such care, skill, and integrity. I've thanked him for his Word, which provides me with wise stewardship principles that I use to challenge our congregation.

Do you see how *creative* thanksgiving goes? It may take quite a stretch of your imagination to come up with some good reasons to thank God in the face of whatever is threatening you. But start stretching. Don't settle for one or two reasons—come up with half a dozen. They may not be immediately apparent.

This brings me to the second qualifier for the practice of "thank-you therapy"—be *deliberate.* Make yourself apply TYT every time you are presenting a troubling request to God. Eventually it will become habitual. You'll automatically add thanksgiving to your anxiety-prompted prayers. But initially, it will feel awkward to do this. You may even feel like you're trivializing your concern by following it up with a handful of thank-you's. Do it anyway. Because God says to (Phil. 4:6). And because it works.

Thank God for the strength he's making available to you in your trial, for the related promises of his Word (such as his guarantee to make all things work together for the good of those who love him [Rom. 8:28]), for the lessons he's teaching you, for the people who are coming alongside you, for the wisdom to navigate through your conflict, for the doors he's opening to share the good news of Christ, for the opportunity to show Satan—as Job did—that you love God even when life's hitting the fan.

What bit of trouble do you need to pray about, right now, *with thanksgiving?* Be *creative* and *deliberate* as you identify reasons to praise God, even though: your position at work is being phased out, or your twenty-five-year-old daughter has just moved in with her boyfriend, or your migraines won't go away, or your mom's been diagnosed with Alzheimer's, or your house won't sell even though it's been on the market for over a year, or your favorite sin continues to trip you up.

Yes, thank God for the blessings that he's given you. That's the predominant way in which you'll practice the *T* of CHAT. But weave that *T* through the other aspects of your prayer, as well— especially through those requests that are provoked by anxiety and fear. "Thank-you therapy" will prevent you from developing a twisted or deformed spirit. Your heart and your mind will be well guarded by the peace of God.

Onto the Praying Field

1. Are you a worrier by temperament? What are the tell-tale signs that you are worrying about something? How do you tend to justify your right to worry?

   What sorts of things make you anxious? Is there any concern that you currently appear to be serenely gliding through—like a duck on water—but which has you churning furiously beneath the surface?

2. Write out Philippians 4:6–7 on a 3 x 5 card and carry it around until you have it memorized.

3. How does praying "with thanksgiving" about your anxieties keep your praying from becoming hand-wringing?

   What's the difference between thanking God "in" difficult circumstances and thanking God "for" difficult circumstances?

4. Identify three concerns that prompt you to worry (whether visibly or beneath the surface). Now come up with at least half a dozen things to thank God for "in" each of these situations.

5. Repeat the last exercise by praying with someone else for his/her concern(s) this week. Caution: Don't preach in your prayer. (*Dear Lord, help Jason to be thankful that he's even got a job during this time of relational conflict with his boss.* Jason won't appreciate that prayer!)

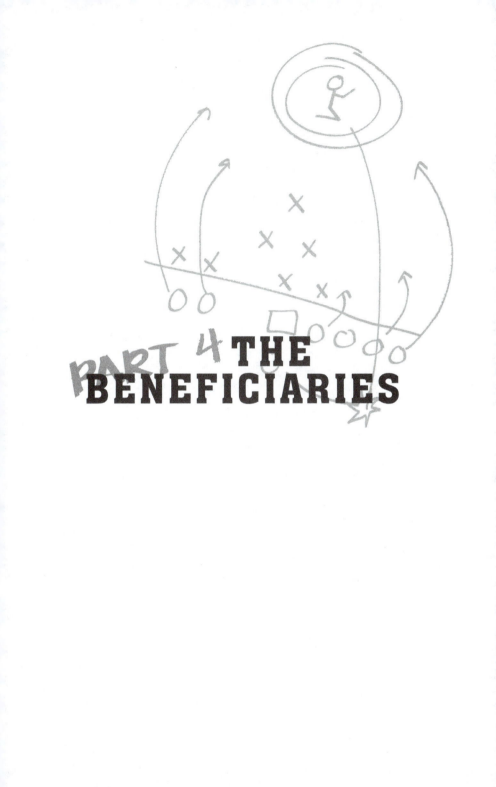

PART 4 THE BENEFICIARIES

10

Unbelievers

Open a Door, Your Mouth, and a Heart

One of the things I miss since my kids have grown up is the excuse to watch children's shows on TV. My favorite was *Sesame Street*. Talk about a creative learning experience! I loved the ways that humor and stories and wacky songs were used to teach basic concepts. Like the time that the lesson revolved around the letter *B*. Four Muppets in a rock band—looking a lot like John, Paul, George, and Ringo—crooned the song (with British accents, of course): "Letta B."[1] (If you're unfamiliar with the Beatles' hit "Let It Be," you are not as amused with this parody as I was.)

Another lesson that my kids and I learned from *Sesame Street* (and which we will never forget because of the way that it was drummed into our heads) had to do with the importance of *asking.* The emphasis here was on speaking up. Don't wait for mom and dad to guess what's on your mind. Ask. Ask them for help, or for comfort, or for whatever you need. The rap song that drove home this advice kept repeating the line: "All you have to do is ask, A-S-K, just ask!"

Back in chapter 8 we learned that this is also an important building block in prayer. It's the *A* of our daily CHAT with God. And, truth be known, this aspect of praying (Ask) probably comes to us more naturally than the other three (Confess, Honor, Thank). Our actual practice of prayer might be represented by the acronym: CHAAAAAT. We are usually not timid about asking God for money to pay the bills, or for wisdom to make a big decision, or for healing from a malignant tumor, or for resolution to a marital conflict, or for patience with our kids.

Because so much of our asking tends to revolve around our own personal needs, I'd like to focus, in the next few chapters, on praying for others. The Bible refers to this as *intercession,* and instructs us to engage in such "for everyone" (1 Tim. 2:1). While you may not be familiar with the noun *intercession,* you have probably heard its verb form *intercede* used occasionally. The dictionary defines it as: "to act as a mediator; to ask on somebody's behalf; to intervene." That's what we do when we pray for others. We bring their needs before Almighty God.

Let's begin with a group of people who are near and dear to God's heart. The apostle Paul will be our role model as we learn how to pray for these individuals. The beneficiaries of the praying that we now turn our attention to are those who are spiritually lost: *unbelievers.* Note the example that Paul sets for us in this verse: "Brothers, my heart's desire and prayer to God for the Israelites is that they may be saved" (Rom. 10:1).

What was at the top of Paul's prayer requests list? The salvation of unbelievers. Do we need to be praying a prayer like Paul's? That can be determined easily enough by answering a few diagnostic questions. Do you have friends and family members who don't know Christ personally? When was the last time you introduced someone to the Lord? Are you regularly building relationships with those in your neighborhood, workplace, or school who have not yet experienced God's saving grace? How bold are you in talking about Jesus with others? Has it been a week since he's come up in conversation with an unbeliever? A month? A year? Almost never?

If you're not satisfied with your answers to these questions, it should be obvious that something needs to change in your life. Jesus said that those who follow him would become "fishers of men" (Matt. 4:19). If you haven't been catching any people lately, please realize that this is a matter for prayer.

I love the story about the guy who was fishing illegally—with the help of dynamite! He'd light a stick of TNT, throw it in the water, and scoop up the stunned fish that were blown to the surface. When the local game warden heard of this activity, he went undercover and asked the "fisherman" if he could join him in his boat. Out on the water, the suspect took out a stick of dynamite and lit it. The game warden immediately pulled out his badge and shouted, "You're under arrest!" But the calm reply, as the fuse burned down, was, "Do you want to talk or do you want to fish?"

Most Christ followers would rather talk about fishing for people than actually do it. And it's not difficult to understand why. Our people fishing often meets with little success. Paul explains that so few spiritually lost people respond to the gospel because Satan has blinded their eyes—they cannot see the truth about Christ (2 Cor. 4:4). Only divine intervention can change this condition. That's why we've got to pray.

Someone passed on to me an outline for this sort of intercession called the "three-open prayer" (It comes from Ron Hutchcraft's book, *Called to Greatness*).[2] We pray for open *doors*—opportunities to engage in spiritual discussions. We pray for open *mouths*—boldness to speak up about Christ when the time comes. And we pray for open *hearts*—responsiveness to the good news we share.

Open Doors

As often as I've taught the three-open prayer to others, it still has a way of slipping to a back burner in my own life. I forget to pray it. I fail to A-S-K, just ask. I became aware of this oversight (for about the millionth time) just recently. Early one morning I had been dropped off at the San Jose airport in Costa Rica when returning from a missions trip. As I waited to board my flight I was anticipating the pleasure of being able to recline in my plane seat and catch a few more Zs. In the meantime, I opened my Bible and pulled out the reading schedule I'd been following.

That day's Scripture reading was Romans 10. As I reflected on the very first verse, I was immediately reminded of the three-open prayer. *Paul prayed for the salvation of others*, I wrote in my journal. *So should I.* That's when it hit me. *Oh, no. It would be just like God to seat me next to a spiritual seeker on my flight. But I want to sleep. My body craves sleep. If I ask God for an open door, he's liable to give me one—and that means good-bye to my nap.*

I somehow resisted the urge to close my Bible and journal without applying the day's text to my life. Instead, I told God (with a minimal amount of enthusiasm) that, if he would open a door for me to talk about Christ on the plane, I would willingly do so—even if it prevented me from dozing.

When I boarded the plane I discovered that I was seated on an aisle, right next to a pretty big guy. He had already pulled up the armrest between our seats so that he could spread into my space. Great! But he was fairly affable, and it didn't take me long to find out that he was an American golf pro who worked at a resort in Costa Rica. He was on his way to a business seminar up in the States.

As we talked, I could tell that he was very self-motivated. He explained to me that he had divided his life into four quadrants, and that he was trying to make progress in each of these areas. He wanted to grow professionally, relationally (family-wise), intellectually, and spiritually. That last category, of course, was of great interest to me. So I asked him the question: "What does it mean for you to grow spiritually?" He said that this included being kind to others, as well as developing his personal character.

Then he turned to me (I'm not making this up) and inquired: "What does growing spiritually look like for you?" I couldn't help but flash back to that prayer in the airport, asking God for an open door. He couldn't give me a door any more open than this one! For the next hour and a half my new friend and I talked about spiritual matters. I told him that my spirituality was founded on a personal relationship with Jesus. I explained the gospel, from start to finish, diagram included. He pushed back on a number of points—which made for a lively discussion.

No, he didn't become a committed Christ follower by the end of the flight. But we did exchange e-mail addresses and we've been writing back and forth. I've sent him a couple of Christian books. He's currently reading one of them out loud with his wife! Is that cool or what?

Paul solicited prayer from some Christian friends for the very thing that I've been describing. "And pray for us, too, that God may open a door for our message, so that we may proclaim the mystery of Christ, for which I am in chains" (Col. 4:3). Paul encouraged prayer for open doors. For opportunities to talk about Christ.

As I've made a practice of praying this prayer, I've noticed that there are two kinds of open doors that God provides. The first are spontaneous. And I've learned the hard way that I'd better be ready for these, if I'm praying the three-open prayer, because they come without warning. Sometimes they catch me by such surprise that I totally muff the opportunities that they present.

This is what happened to me when I took my car to the local mechanic. Glen has been repairing my vehicles for years, so we usually chitchat when I drop by. His favorite topic is fishing (about which I know nothing). Ice fishing, deep-sea fishing, fly fishing—Glen really lights up when I ask him if he's done any fishing lately. I regularly try to move the conversation around to something of a spiritual nature, but Glen seems to guess where I'm headed and quickly turns us to a more comfortable subject. Like fishing. On several occasions I've invited him to a special event at our church (e.g., a Christmas Eve service or a men's breakfast with sports hero speaker) but he hasn't been interested.

I was praying for an open door the last time I visited Glen with a sick car. But it came so unexpectedly that I didn't know what to do with it. It came at Glen's initiative. Before I tell you what he said, I've got to give you a little background information. Over the past year our church has been running one-minute commercials on local cable TV stations. Sue and I had to travel down to a studio in Tulsa to film these babies—and I wasn't too excited about the whole deal. I'm not a big fan of TV evangelism. But our outreach team at church talked me into doing the commercials because they believed that the ads might give us visibility in the community, as well as open up conversations with local friends about our church.

It worked! I was dropping my car off at Glen's shop and he said to me—out of the blue—"I saw your church's commercial on TV. Good job!" Here was Glen bringing up the topic of my church. You know what my rejoinder was? I said (and I cringe with embarrassment to repeat it): "Don't worry! I have no plans to become a TV evangelist." That was it! End of conversation. I beat myself up over that one for days afterward. I thought of all the things I could've said: "So, what did you think of our church?" Or: "Would a commercial like that tempt you to try us out?" Who knows where the conversation might have gone if I'd been ready for the open door.

The opportunities come spontaneously when we're asking God for them. This is not to say that a little baiting on our part wouldn't help. When Jesus conversed with a woman who had come to draw water from a well, he let slip that he had some living water she might be interested in. That's what I mean by baiting. And if we're praying for open doors there is a much greater likelihood that the bait will be taken. For example, at parent-teacher conferences I always told each of my kids' teachers that I so appreciated their work that I prayed for them. Sometimes they'd nervously change the subject. Sometimes they'd show an interest in what I'd just said.

Ask God for open doors. Don't be surprised when they come. Spontaneously—or with just a little push.

The second kind of open door we should be praying for is planned. We're deliberately working to create opportunities to share Christ by building relationships with others. But even though this is our plan, the development of these relationships and the opportunities that they present must still be a matter of prayer. Otherwise, we'll end up with friendship-evangelism that's all friendship and no evangelism.

Because I want the church that I lead to be reaching spiritually lost people, I am keenly aware that I myself must be a poster child for this mission. Where are the spiritually lost people that I, personally, am reaching? While some members of my church probably think that I have an advantage over them in this regard (after all, I'm a pastor), the truth is that full-time ministry handicaps me as an evangelist. All day long I'm hanging out with fellow Christ followers (my staff), planning church services and designing church programs. I'm envious of the guy who gets to spend nine to five surrounded by unbelievers in a "normal" work setting.

So, open doors that materialize from my daily environment are few and far between. That's why I'm constantly praying for new ideas about where I might develop personal relationships with spiritual seekers. When my son was in high school and played on the varsity soccer team, my bleacher-bum friendships with other parents provided many open doors for spiritual conversations. But now that those days are over, I'm looking for other ways to connect with neighbors and friends.

I can't say this strongly enough: *I regularly ask God to lead me into planned contacts with others that will give me opportunities to talk with them about Christ.* Should I join the Rotary Club? Volunteer to coach Little League (is that weird if I don't have a child on the team)? Throw a block party? Start a book club? (The last time I did, my across-the-street neighbor came to Christ!) Sign up for a ballroom dancing class? (A friend suggested this, but I haven't had the nerve to check it out yet.)

Open a door, Lord.

Open Mouth

When I think of bold evangelists, my friend Bill Hybels comes to mind. Bill is widely known for having been used by God to restore a passion to the Church (capital C) for reaching those who are spiritually lost. But Bill is equally committed to this task at a personal level. I remember having lunch with him, on one occasion, at a restaurant near Willow Creek Community Church. Bill was telling me how much he loved the challenge of bringing others to Christ. In fact, the bigger the challenge the more he loved it, he said.

"I like a guy who has no interest in church. I like a guy who's a self-made man and thinks he's got the world by the tail. I like a guy who pushes back on everything I say." By this time, Bill was making me a bit nervous. Not just because his voice was getting louder and louder. But also because he was beginning every sentence with the words, "I like a guy . . . I like a guy . . . I like a guy. . . ." I was worried that people might start looking at him—and, then, at me!

Bill would probably tell you that I've exaggerated this story for a laugh. But I'll tell you what I haven't exaggerated. He is one bold evangelist. Kind of makes me imagine what the apostle Paul must have been like. With this picture in mind, I am somewhat shocked by what Paul asked his friends to pray for as he shared Christ with others. "Pray also for me, that whenever I open my mouth, words may be given me so that I will fearlessly make known the mystery of the gospel, for which I am an ambassador in chains. Pray that I may declare it fearlessly, as I should" (Eph. 6:19–20).

Did I really read that? Did Paul really ask for the right words and for fearlessness as he told others of Christ? And did he really repeat his request for fearlessness a second time? Yup! Paul wanted prayer for an open mouth—for an ability to be articulate and bold.

Open doors won't do us any good unless we open our mouths to take full advantage of them. When opportunities arise to talk about Christ, that's exactly what we've got to do—talk! Often, the best way to fuel such a conversation is with good questions. Remember the open door I encountered on the airplane? Here was a guy telling me that one of the four ways in which he wanted to grow was *spiritually*! Would I match that open door with an open mouth? By God's grace I was able to return the volley with the question: "So, what does it mean for you, to grow spiritually?" We were off and running.

But I'd be the first to admit that conversations about spiritual matters don't always take off this easily for me. I mean, that guy's comment about wanting to grow spiritually was a softball-sized pitch that anybody could've hit. What do we do when the open door is not so . . . well . . . uh . . . open?

For starters, we should pray. (And I don't just say that because prayer is the theme of this book and I'm trying, at this point, to keep it from morphing into a book on evangelism.) Quietly thank God that a door of conversation has opened and ask him to now open your mouth in a way that moves the dialogue toward Christ. Pray like you understand that if God doesn't intervene, things aren't going anywhere.

Now it's time to step out in faith. If you believe that God has heard your prayer for an open mouth and that he will make you articulate and bold, *say something!* Volunteer some information about yourself that has a spiritual dimension to it. Mention something about your church, or an answer to prayer, or an insight you got out of your Bible reading that day. What could be more natural? I remember when it dawned on me that, as an avid reader, I was always telling people about a Grisham novel I'd just finished or a Rick Reilly editorial in *Sports Illustrated* that had made me laugh. Why not, just as casually, drop a comment about something I have recently read in the Bible?

Something else that has worked for me in opening up a spiritual conversation has been to say, "I'll be praying about that for you," when someone shares a personal hardship with me. (As I noted earlier, I will often volunteer to pray right then and there for a person who's confided in me. But if it seems obvious that such an offer would not fit the person or the setting at that time, I'll take this less intrusive approach of promising offhandedly, "I'll be praying about that for you.") Occasionally, I'll encounter someone who is gooned out by any mention of prayer. When one of my neighbors told me about a financial problem, and I said that I'd be praying for her, she quickly replied: "Oh, it's not *that* bad." A swing and a miss! But more frequently a reference to prayer will be warmly received and may move a conversation in a spiritual direction.

Good questions, as I've already pointed out, are also an effective way of transitioning from an open door to an open mouth. I bring this up again because I want to suggest an excellent book on this topic. As a staff member of Campus Crusade for Christ, Randy Newman has been generating spiritual conversations with university students for several decades. He's discovered that the best way to do this, in today's postmodern culture, is with provocative questions. He's written *Questioning Evangelism* to help the rest of us learn this approach. I can't recommend Randy's book highly enough.[3]

But we mustn't stop praying. Praying as we drop references to spiritual matters into our conversations. Praying as we casually offer to pray for others. Praying as we ask good questions. *Open my mouth, Lord. Open my mouth. Open my mouth.* Are you able to multitask? (My wife is chagrined that I can't fold laundry while I'm watching TV. Multitasking is not a strength of mine.) We must do two things at once in evangelistic encounters. We must keep talking to God, even as we're talking to others. *Open my mouth, Lord,* we pray.

What's next? What do you say once you initiate a spiritual conversation? You have two stories to tell: *Your* story and *His* story. *Your* story recounts the journey of your relationship with Christ. There's usually a "before" summary of life before Christ, a "point-of-decision" account (i.e., what prompted you to turn from sin to the Savior), and an "after" description of the transformation (i.e., in terms of character, relationships, priorities, and so on) that has occurred.

If you began to follow Christ at an early age, there may not be dramatic before and point-of-decision chapters to your story. But that's okay. Everyone has an after chapter. What does Christ mean to you today? What difference is he currently making in your life? It is worth rehearsing this part of your story out loud so that you will be ready to tell it well when the door opens. "Always be prepared to give an answer to everyone who asks you to give the reason for the hope that you have" (1 Pet. 3:15). Are you prepared to tell your story? When the opportunity comes to launch into it, don't forget to pray a silent, *Open my mouth, Lord.*

Your story should dovetail into *His* story (although *His* story may be reserved for a future conversation if it seems better to wait with it). *His* story is the gospel. The gospel has often been summarized in several basic points, which drive home: our sin and its repercussions; Christ's death on the cross to atone for that sin;

salvation received by faith, as a gift from God. (I strongly disagree with those who denigrate printed gospel-summary presentations, such as the *Four Spiritual Laws* booklet.⁴ These tools are not, as their accusers claim, mechanical or trite—unless one uses them in a mechanical or trite fashion.)

I personally like to use the bridge diagram when talking about the gospel with others. This gives me the opportunity to draw a picture on a napkin, or on a blank page out of my Day-Timer, or on whatever else is available. (My golf pro friend on the airplane actually offered me the back side of a business contract he was negotiating for my drawing!) This gives people a visual aid, as well as something they can take with them at the end of the conversation.

The bridge diagram consists of: two cliffs (us on one, God on the other); a great canyon (the sin that separates us from a holy God); arrows that reach from our cliff to God's—but which fall short (representing all our attempts to merit salvation); and a cross that bridges the two cliffs (Jesus' sacrificial death). I have the person with whom I'm talking draw a little stick figure somewhere on the diagram (to indicate where he or she is now, spiritually speaking—to the far left of the bridge, or ready to step across it, or already to the right of it).

Just like with *your* story, *His* story requires some practice in order to be able to tell it well. Whenever I use the bridge diagram, I throw in Bible verses and colorful illustrations as I'm drawing each point. And just like *your* story, *His* story requires the accompaniment of much prayer. Back to multitasking. What a challenge for me to draw, and talk, and pray—*Open my mouth, Lord*—at the same time. (Now I'm juggling three activities!)

After I have had an opportunity to present the gospel to someone, I usually follow it up, a few days later, with a book. (I explain that books are my "love language," which typically results in them being received with appreciation.) If someone is struggling with intellectual questions, I'll usually give them a copy of something that Lee Strobel has written—*Case for Faith* is my favorite.⁵ Lee is a former Yale Law School grad, financial affairs editor at the *Chicago Tribune*, and agnostic. Good credentials, in the minds of the skeptics that I talk with. But he came to faith in Christ after wrestling with hard questions—questions he addresses in his books.

Rick Warren's *The Purpose Driven Life* is another one of my favorite giveaways.[6] (The book has some weaknesses, but it's not heretical, as some conservative commentators have tried to make it out to be.) Its position at the top of the best-seller lists has made it easy to pass along to unbelievers. And it definitely explains the gospel within its pages. Recently, I have also been buying Chuck Colson's *The Good Life* in bulk, as gifts for spiritually seeking friends.[7] Chuck is a fantastic storyteller. The gospel gets woven into his tales in a captivating way.

If my spiritual conversation has occurred with a person whom I met in passing and may never see again, I always ask for a business card or personal address. This allows me to send a book or two, along with an "I enjoyed meeting you" note. Sometimes I never hear from them again. (Not even a thank-you for the $19.95 or whatever I spent on the book.) But occasionally I get return letters that let me know my books have left their mark.

And what do I do as I'm putting the books in the mail. I pray! I pray that God will use Lee Strobel's, or Rick Warren's, or Chuck Colson's open mouth.

Open Heart

Back to Romans 10. After Paul tells us how passionately he prays for the salvation of others (v. 1), he explains why. The folks in the circles he traveled in were crazy religious. (This summary of the next few verses is in the NIV—Nicodem Interpretive Version.) They believed that they could achieve a right standing with God based upon their compliance with God's laws. "Not a chance!" Paul retorted. "You may be good people, but you're not *that* good."

Then Paul explained that Christ is the "end" of the law, and that right standing with God now comes by believing (v. 4). In what sense did Christ put an end to the law for us? In the sense of the law being used as a means of salvation. It's true that the law can measure our righteousness. But the result is not good news. According to the law's yardstick, none of us measures up to God's standards. And the law is powerless to do anything to change that.

When I was a boy, my dad would measure my height by standing me up against a two-by-four stud in the basement. The wood was marked with feet and inches, and he would put a pencil line by the spot to which I'd grown. But I recall that in junior high it seemed as if I couldn't grow fast enough. I was the very last kid cut from the basketball team, after the coach said he needed someone who was at least five feet tall. (No, in those pre-growth-spurt days, I couldn't even clear four feet, eleven inches.) I would measure myself almost every week against that basement stud—but I always fell short (pun intended). And the stud itself could do nothing to help me grow.

God's law is like that. Every time we stand our lives up against it, it says: "Nope! Too short." "All have sinned," Paul points out a few chapters earlier in Romans, "and fall short of the glory of God" (Rom. 3:23). We don't measure up. And the law can't change that fact. But Christ put an end to the law being used as a means of establishing one's righteousness before God. Christ himself became that means by dying on the cross to pay for our moral failings, and by rising again to offer us his righteousness as a gift. A gift that's received by faith.

Boy, does this honk off religious people. And nice people. You would think they'd be happy over what Christ has done. But they're not. They're insulted. Their pride chafes at the report that they are not good enough to meet God's required standard on their own. They're certain that if they just stand straight against the stud of God's law, square their shoulders, and stretch their necks—they'll reach the acceptable mark. But it ain't gonna happen.

Now do you understand why it's so important for us to pray as we share the good news of Christ with others? To many of them, it doesn't sound like good news. They'll immediately reject it. They'll close their hearts to whatever we have to say. Only God can make them receptive. Only God can open their hearts.

I was on vacation, several months ago, down in Florida. Sue and I were staying in a friend's condominium on the gulf shore beach. One day as I was swimming in the condo's pool, I struck up a conversation with a couple who were sitting nearby in lounge chairs. I'd seen the guy doing some fishing in the surf that morning, so I asked him if he'd had any luck. (For a guy who doesn't do any fishing, I sure end up talking about it a lot—usually as I'm people fishing.)

We were really hitting it off. I had an open door. So I began to pray for an open mouth. In a matter of minutes I discovered that this couple lived about thirty minutes away from me back home—in the very community where our church had just started an extension campus. This gave me the opportunity to tell them about this new ministry in their neighborhood, about its growth from 150 to more than 700 people in the first year, about the lives that were being changed. And as I talked, and they politely listened, I kept praying for open hearts.

But they shut down the conversation at that point. They let me know that they were religious, thank you, and not interested in anything beyond their brand of "churchianity." An open door, followed up with an open mouth, is no guarantee of an open heart. We've got to realize what we're up against and pray, pray, pray for God's intervention.

Sometimes God will open a person's heart even as we're talking to him or her. Other times it's as if God answers this prayer for an open heart retroactively by leading us to a person whom he has already prepared to be receptive. We move from open door to open mouth, and, as we begin to pray for an open heart, God says: "Done! I opened it before you even got here." Ever had that happen to you?

When I walked across the street to invite my neighbor to a six-week book club, I had carefully prepared what I wanted to say. I'd deliberately chosen a book that was not, overtly, Christian. It was a John Maxwell book on leadership that I thought might appeal to my neighbor, since he had recently taken on some management responsibilities at work. The guy expressed an immediate interest, but then he abruptly asked: "Is this a spiritually based book?" I was so afraid of scaring him off that I quickly mumbled something about it alluding to spiritual principles but that it was mostly about leadership and had been on the *New York Times'* best-seller list. "Oh," he replied. "I was hoping it was spiritually based since my wife and I have just started a journey down that road."

What a rebuke! The Spirit spanked me good with those words. I'd been so proud of my efforts to create this book club open door. But God was a couple of steps ahead of me in my neighbor's life. God had already created an open heart. Before I'd even prayed for one. So when you get to this third step in the three-open prayer, asking God for an open heart, don't be surprised if he's beat you to the punch. You may be talking to a prequalified candidate.

In *A Passionate Life*, Mike Breen and Walt Kallestad call this kind of a responsive individual a "person of peace."[8] This designation comes from the account of Jesus sending out seventy-two followers to announce his coming kingdom. As they entered various towns, they were to look for a "man of peace"—someone who would welcome their message and show them hospitality. If they didn't find a man of peace they were to move on until they did (see Luke 10).

Breen and Kallestad see this as a principle to be applied to our evangelistic efforts today. We pray, every day, for God to lead us to a person of peace. And then we look until we find one. Open door, open mouth, but *closed* heart? Keep looking. Open door, open mouth, *open* heart? Ah, you have just found your person of peace, whom God has prepared in advance for just such an encounter.

A-S-K, just ask. Learn to pray the three-open prayer. Pray it with regularity. Ask God for open doors. Ask him for an open mouth. Ask him for an open heart. You may want to pray this prayer with particular people in mind. I periodically make up a new VIP list of spiritually lost people who I am befriending in the hopes of sharing Christ with them. I keep my list to just five names on a three-by-five-inch card, so that they'll receive focused prayer. And I update that card every once in a while to reflect those with whom I currently have the greatest potential for contact.

Onto the Praying Field

1. How long has it been (honestly) since you have talked about the gospel—God's plan of salvation—with someone who does not have a relationship with Christ? In what ways would prayer lead to those sorts of conversations?

2. Do you have daily contact with spiritually lost people that could result in open doors? If not (e.g. because you work for a Christian organization or spend a lot of time on your own), where could you find some "ponds" to do "people-fishing"?

3. Make a list of five people who need Christ that you will begin to pray for. Next to their names, write down a topic of conversation or a transitioning line that might help you move a conversation with them in the direction of spiritual matters.

4. Look back over your conversations with unbelievers this past week. See if you can spot two or three open doors that you missed. What could you have said that might have allowed you to walk through that door?

5. As a witness for Christ, do you tend to be overly bold or overly silent? If overly silent, why? Begin praying, during conversations, for an "open mouth."

   This week look for an opportunity to tell a non-Christ follower that you will be praying about a concern that he/she has raised. What response did you get?

6. Pick up a copy of Randy Newman's *Questioning Evangelism* or Bill Hybels's *Just Walk Across the Room* and determine to read it (after you've finished *Prayer Coach*, or course).

7. Practice telling your own conversion story (before–the decision–after) until you can present it in three minutes. Find a Christian friend who will listen to it and give you feedback.

   Pray for an opportunity (and the boldness) to share your story with someone who needs Christ. What happened?

8. Find out if your church has an evangelism training seminar and sign up for it (even if it's just a refresher of stuff you already know).

11

Children

Don't Let Them Leave Home without It

I am an unabashed eavesdropper. Most pastors are. It's how we collect human-interest illustrations for our sermons. I find myself frequently listening in on others' conversations in restaurants, on airplanes, at ballgames. The men's locker room at the health club where I work out provides me with great material. One of the favorite topics of conversation in this venue is kids. Dads love to talk about their children.

What these fathers have to say about their sons and daughters falls into four categories. First, and no surprise, is sports achievements. Men regularly regale each other with stories from the previous week's big athletic events—the ones in which their boys caught the winning touchdown passes and their girls scored a 9.8 on their gymnastics routines. They brag about which colleges are offering scholarships. They leave the impression—these middle-aged, overweight, somewhat out-of-shape dads—that it was their athletic genes that got passed on to their offspring.

Sports achievements. It's always about sports. I can't recall a single time when I've heard a dad brag that his son played a cello solo in the school's orchestra concert. Even if the boy had distinguished himself accordingly, his father would probably keep it to himself in the men's locker room. The other guys are not going to be impressed with the fact that he may be raising the next Yo-Yo Ma. (The only yo-yo they're familiar with is a child's toy on the end of a string!)

Dads, secondly, talk about their kids' grades. Not necessarily the grades themselves—but what the grades represent in terms of their chances of getting into the college of choice (which is often the old man's alma mater).

And why is it important to get into the college of choice? Because, thirdly, fathers want their children to eventually land good jobs. "Good," I've learned from my eavesdropping, means jobs that will pay well. Money is the bottom line, the measure of success. I even heard one dad boasting (honest to goodness) that his son had moved to Las Vegas and was raking in big bucks as a professional poker player at a casino! Now, that's something to put in the family's Christmas newsletter.

The fourth category of dad-talk revolves around sons finding nice girls, and daughters finding nice boys to settle down with. "Nice" includes (judging from the conversations): attractive, gainfully employed, racially compatible, and able to produce an abundance of grandchildren.

I'm not making this stuff up. These are the dreams that fathers— at least the ones in my locker room—have for their children. And I often walk away thinking to myself, *That's it? These are the most important things that these guys hope for? Kids who produce trophies, grades, money, and babies?* It's not that I lack any interest in these things. It's just that I want so much more for my children. I believe that God made them for a purpose, that he has a divine plan for their lives. I long to see them make a Christ-honoring impact on their world.

And that's why it's so critical for me, as their dad, to pray for them. What I desire for my children won't just happen. In fact, as I'll point out later in this chapter, there are evil forces at work in this world that are determined to keep my two daughters and one son from experiencing what I've just described. There's a spiritual war going on for the control of their lives, so I'm going to battle on their behalf in prayer.

This is what Jesus has done—and is doing—for me. John 17 records a lengthy prayer that Jesus prayed for his immediate disciples, as well as for those who would become his followers over time. Although we have labeled a brief excerpt from Jesus' Sermon on the Mount as "The Lord's Prayer" (Matt. 6:9–13), many have argued that this extended intercession of John 17 is more deserving of that title.

Whatever we call John 17, it is the sort of prayer that an intensely loving parent would want to pray for his or her children. And so I am going to use it as a model for moms and dads to learn from. We'll note five aspects of Jesus' intercession; he prays a priority prayer, a prototype prayer, a personal faith prayer, a protection prayer, and a people prayer.

Priority Prayer

John's Gospel devotes a great deal of space (ch. 12–19) to describing the week of Jesus' "passion" (i.e., death on the cross). Some have even called the fourth gospel "a passion story with an introduction." This is a bit of an overstatement, but, ironically, there are voices in the evangelical community today claiming that we have put too much emphasis on Jesus' death and not enough on his life. They argue that we need to balance our view of Jesus as Savior with a view of Jesus as Role Model. But if we have been disproportionately focused on the cross and its payment of sin's penalty, it is because Scripture directs our attention to such.

Jesus' prayer in John 17 took place smack dab in the middle of this narrative of the closing events of his life. Shortly after saying "amen," he was arrested in the garden of Gethsemane and led away to be crucified. Remarkably, with his crucifixion just hours away, Jesus took time to pray. For others! I can understand him prayerfully asking the Father to take the upcoming cup of a tortuous death away from him, as recorded by the other gospel writers (Matt. 26:39; Mark 14:36; Luke 22:42). But to be so concerned for his followers at this time that he prayed for them at length (the entire chapter of John 17) just amazes me.

Jesus' example teaches us that interceding for others must become a priority for us, no matter what else is on our plate. Can moms and dads excuse a lack of prayer for their kids because they have too many other important things to attend to? There's showing up at the job, paying the bills, keeping up with household chores and repairs, taxiing kids around, and grabbing a little bit of R&R in front of the TV. When is a parent supposed to find time to pray—other than quickies—for the children?

If you've ever read Stephen Covey's best-selling *Seven Habits of Highly Effective People*, you are familiar with his four-quadrant diagram for identifying important/urgent, important/non-urgent, non-important/urgent, and non-important/non-urgent activities.[1] (It's really less confusing than it sounds.)

At one end of the spectrum are those activities that are important/urgent. If it's April 14, for example, and you haven't paid your taxes yet, this would qualify as something that is important/urgent. We have a tendency to get these sorts of things done. At the other extreme are those activities that are non-important/non-urgent—like reading today's newspaper. No big deal if we don't get around to it. Right?

But between these two extremes, says Covey, is the most critical category of activities: those that are important/non-urgent. Because they are non-urgent (i.e., we're under no pressure to complete them), we have a propensity for putting them off. And off . . . and off. If we put them off long enough, these important/non-urgent tasks may just become urgent. If we don't brush our teeth today, for example, we probably won't get cavities tomorrow. But if we don't brush our teeth tomorrow, and the next day, and the day after that—well, we're going to pay for our neglect at the dentist.

Praying for our kids is an important/non-urgent task, although there may be times when a crisis makes it very urgent. It's easy to let praying slide because no apparent disaster results from skipping a day or two of intercession. But if we rarely get around to prayer for our children, we are denying them the blessings and protection that God provides only when he is asked for such. (Remember James 4:2: "You do not have, because you do not ask God.")

Randy Travis, one of my favorite country singers, describes some of the benefits of a parent's intercession in his song "When Mama Prayed."[2] Thank God for praying mamas. But our kids need praying papas, too. Praying for our children *has* to become a priority.

More important than helping them with their homework. More important than cheering them on from the sidelines of a soccer game. More important than shopping with them for a new pair of jeans. Praying for our children has to become a priority. And priority is spelled t-i-m-e. If something is truly important to us, we make time for it. (It may be a good idea, at this point, to go back to ch. 1 and reread the section on the prayer buster of "no plan." Then decide, today, when and where you're going to start praying for your kids.)

Prototype Prayer

Edith Schaeffer learned how to pray from watching Dr. Hoste. Edith and her late husband, Francis, are relatively famous in Christian circles as the founders of L'Abri Fellowship. L'Abri was begun in the mid-1950s as a retreat center in the Swiss Alps. It became known as a place where young spiritual seekers who were asking intellectually difficult questions could find answers. Francis Schaeffer was an astute theologian, philosopher, and commentator on contemporary culture. Hundreds of skeptics have discovered a personal relationship with Jesus at L'Abri.

Edith was L'Abri's supreme hostess. The listening ear who drew out inquirers. The art lover whose decorating touches gave the place the feel of home. The one whose prayers solicited miracle after miracle from God—from money to pay the bills to the salvation of those who had been spiritually lost. And Edith claims that she learned to pray by watching Dr. Hoste.

Edith grew up in China, where her parents were missionaries with the China Inland Mission (directed by Dr. Hoste). For four hours every morning, he would pace the compound grounds and pray, by name, for his entire team, their families, and the people they ministered to. When she was four year old, Edith looked up at his six-foot frame and asked if she could join him on his walk. Dr. Hoste agreed—on the condition that she not talk, so that he could pray. What amazed her, as she listened to him converse with God, was his mention of her own name in prayer. This convinced her that she must matter to God—and it led to her becoming a lifelong intercessor.[3]

Jesus' prayer in John 17 is introduced with the words: "After Jesus said this, he looked toward heaven and prayed." After Jesus said *what*? The closing verses of John 16 tell us that Jesus had just warned his disciples that they would have trouble in this world. Then he turned from talking to them and immediately began talking to the Father. This means that, when Jesus began to pray, these guys were looking on. He modeled for them how praying is done.

You might recall that the only time—ever—Jesus' disciples asked him to teach them something was the occasion when they expressed an interest in learning to pray (Luke 11:1). What had stimulated this curiosity on their part? They had just observed Jesus praying. They wanted to be able to do what they had just seen Jesus doing.

When Jesus prayed, his intercession served as a prototype, a model, for his disciples to follow. This is a second lesson that parents can pick up from John 17. We not only need to pray *for* our children, we need to pray *with* them. This is how they will learn to pray. What have they gained, thus far, from watching and listening to us talk to God?

Some parents never ski outside the wake of repetitive prayers that are offered strictly before meals and at bedtime. "For what we are about to receive may the Lord make us truly thankful. Amen." How many times have we numbly rattled off something like that, seconds before everyone grabbed for the biggest steak? What does that teach our children about prayer?

When I was growing up, my family always followed up the breakfast meal with a brief reading from the Bible and an accompanying devotional book. Then we would go around the table, each of us taking a turn at praying. Although these were supposed to be extemporaneous prayers, they sounded pretty canned over time. All three of my siblings and I had set lists of a few items each that we would routinely reel off in the same words, at record speed, with monotoned voices, day after day after day.

When my own children got to be old enough to pray around the family table, I noticed that their prayers had this same tendency to become rote. I remember the day when I finally put a ban on the word *good*. They were beating this adjective to death when they prayed. "Lord, help me to have a good day, and do good [should've been *well*] in school, and make good friends, and thank you for this good meal. . . ." Good grief! When I couldn't take it anymore, I outlawed the word. "Nobody is allowed to say *good* when you pray. You'll have to come up with something else." This resulted in stammered praying for a time. One would think I'd taken away the whole dictionary. But at least it broke them out of their rut.

Here's something else I did, of a much more positive nature, to teach my kids how to be more thoughtful and sincere when they prayed. Rather than leaving it up to them to pray about whatever came to their minds (which ended up being the same old, same old), I'd assign them topics. And I'd suggest several aspects of each assigned topic to cover when they prayed.

I might say, "Rachel, why don't you pray about our upcoming family vacation." I would then add: "Ask God to protect us as we travel, and to help us get along with each other, and to refresh us with this trip, and to open up conversations about Jesus with the people we meet." I was supplying the creativity in prayer that Rachel lacked at that age of her life. If I'd left it entirely up to her, she would have prayed: "Lord, help us to have a good vacation. Amen."

As my kids got older, I did less *telling* when it came to the details of their prayers and more *asking*. "Rachel, why don't you pray about our upcoming family vacation. What sorts of things do you think you ought to include in your prayer?" Please note that, at this point,

I still assigned the major topic itself. And I continued to do that, even after my kids became teenagers, so that we wouldn't neglect to pray about important stuff that they might not think to bring up: a family member going through divorce, a big outreach event at church, a crisis at work, a stressor at school, or an international ministry partner in Bangladesh. But after assigning such a topic to someone, I'd then ask that person to suggest some specifics that he or she might want to include in praying for it.

I was training my kids, little by little, to use their imaginations as they approached prayer. Eventually, instead of just assigning the topics that I had brought up, I asked for volunteers. "Who wants to pray for Grandpa's open heart surgery? Who wants to pray for Emily's SAT test?" And so on. I'd even throw it open for additional topics (although still personally mentioning the "biggies" that I didn't want us to miss). "What else can we pray for?"

Once the major topics have been divvied up, and the particulars of each have been discussed, it's time to pray. When it's mom's or dad's turn, it's important for them to keep in mind that they are not only praying *to* God, they are also praying *in front of* their children. They're demonstrating how it's to be done. Their prayers should be brief and specific and passionate.

It's our job, as parents, to teach our kids how to pray. They learn by watching and listening to us pray, as well as by participating in times of prayer that we direct. If we're just letting prayer "happen" in our homes, there's a good chance that it isn't—or that it's become mechanical and lifeless.

Personal Faith Prayer

It's time to consider the content of Jesus' prayer in John 17. In the opening eight verses of this chapter (you may want to hit "pause" here and take a moment to read them), Jesus describes how he has revealed his Father to the world. This has resulted in some professing belief in him. To this responsive group, Jesus says, he has given eternal life. And then he defines this term: "Now this is eternal life: that they may know you, the only true God, and Jesus Christ, whom you have sent" (v. 3).

What is foremost in Jesus' mind as he prays for others? *Eternal life.* He wants people to know God and God's saving grace. What ought to be the prime concern of moms and dads as we pray for our children? That our children might come to faith in Christ.

Is this at the top of our prayer lists? If our prayers for our children were monitored and we were given a monthly listing of the topics we have covered while interceding for them, what would be on that report? Most parents pray with regularity that their kids would: make friends at school, stay away from drugs and alcohol, get good grades, obey better at home, be kept from harm, and avoid sexual activity. Great. Some important items on that list. (Parents of pre-schoolers may want to add potty training and sharing toys.)

But how often do we pray for our children to know God? How often do we pray that they would fully surrender their lives to Christ, so as to experience the eternal life that only he can give? Do we just assume that this will happen because they're enrolled in a Christian school, or because they're active in the church's youth ministry? Our children's salvation is too important to be taken for granted. We should pray about this matter as if their eternal destiny were at stake—because it is!

Have you ever heard of Dewitt Talmage? I only came across his life story because I'm an insatiable reader of biographies—and I happened to pick up his. Talmage was the Rick Warren of the early 1900s. Talmage pastored a church in Brooklyn whose auditorium seated over five thousand—and it was packed every Sunday. His sermons were printed each week in newspapers across the country, reaching a hundred million readers. He was the personal friend of presidents and prime ministers—and even a Russian tzar.

Scores of people, in the early twentieth-century, got their start in a relationship with God through the preaching of Dewitt Talmage. So, how did he himself come to personal faith in Christ? Talmage was the twelfth child born to his parents. Every Saturday afternoon, his mother disappeared for a few hours. Everyone assumed that she was taking a breather and grabbing some much needed personal time. But after she died, the family discovered through her journals where their mom had been spending her Saturday afternoons all those years. She'd been meeting with five other moms to pray for their children. Specifically, for their salvation.

Not surprisingly, every one of Talmage's siblings eventually chose to follow Christ. I love that story. The only thing I'd want to change about it is that I wish a group of dads had been meeting to pray for their kids. We expect this sort of activity from moms. But wouldn't it be inspiring (maybe "shocking") to hear about some dads who were regularly getting together to pray that their sons and daughters would come to know God in a life-transforming way?

And let's not settle for them merely making a decision to trust Christ. The *personal faith* prayer expresses a longing for much more than this. Christ wants *disciples*, not *decisions*. So, moms and dads must pray for their children to have an ongoing hunger for God's Word, for genuine worship, for fellowship with other believers, for a bold witness, for a life of service. They must pray for their kids to be sold out to the Lord.

I'll never forget the night that I tucked my oldest daughter, Emily, into bed and noted that she was troubled about something. She was about five years old at the time. "What's wrong?" I asked her. Her answer caught me totally by surprise. "I don't want to be," she shared with me, "a casual Christian." I fought the urge to break into a grin at this dramatic confession of hers.

I knew that she had picked up the expression "casual Christian" from a song that we often played in our home in the late 80s. The lyrics express an aversion to living a "lukewarm life" and a strong desire to "light up the night" for Christ. I was so overjoyed to hear my young daughter voice this passion to become a fired-up follower of Jesus. It was, and continues to be, an answer to my prayer for her.[4]

Protection Prayer

In the next section of Jesus' prayer (John 17:9–19), he seems most concerned for the protection of his followers. "They are still in the world, . . . Holy Father, protect them by the power of your name. . . . While I was with them, I protected them and kept them safe by that name you gave me. . . . My prayer is not that you take them out of the world but that you protect them from the evil one" (v. 11, 12, 15).

Here is a fourth lesson to be applied to the practice of parent prayer. We are right to be concerned for the protection of our children, and to daily ask the Lord to provide such. The bigger they get, the greater our natural tendency to pray for their safety. Especially after they've gotten their driver's license!

Emily, my "I don't want to be a casual Christian" daughter, drives with a lead foot. As a teenager, she was somewhat careful not to speed around town because our vintage station wagon (with racks for bicycles and a canoe on top) was easily recognizable. But occasionally she just had to "put the pedal to the metal." Well, one icy winter day she did that while taking a corner and ended up in a ditch. When we got the call, she quickly informed us that she wasn't hurt and that the car didn't look too badly damaged.

We raced to the scene and saw "mother ship" nose down in a very steep gully. It took two tow trucks, pulling from different angles, to get the car out. By that time, there were a number of emergency vehicles on the scene. We'd done a pretty good job of tying up traffic. Not a few of those motorists were attending our church at the time, so they wanted to hear all about "the accident" the next Sunday.

I think that little escapade made Emily a more conscientious driver (for a week or so). I know that it made me a more conscientious prayer. I was reminded of the importance of interceding for my daughter's protection every time she walked out the door. But is that the sort of protection that Jesus prayed for his followers in John 17—even if it is the kind that parents constantly pray for their kids?

Another look at Jesus' prayer reveals that he had bigger perils than fender benders in mind when he asked the Father to protect believers. He mentions the dangers posed by both the world ("the world has hated them, for they are not of the world any more than I am of the world" [v. 14]) and Satan ("protect them from the evil one" [v. 15]). Here we have two of three "Evil Axis" powers (the world, Satan, and—not referred to here—the flesh) that are constantly threatening Christ followers.

Who will protect our kids from these treacherous enemies? Only God can. When he's asked to do so. Who's asking on behalf of our children? Aside from parents (and maybe an occasional grandma or youth pastor), I don't know of anyone who's praying spiritual protection around our sons and daughters. Moms and dads, this is our job. We'd better not neglect it.

We all know that Satan is a formidable foe. But so is the world. It attacks our kids through peer pressure, advertising, music, movies, and clothing styles. It is relentless. And beyond that there is the enemy within—the flesh. That inbred sinful nature that incites rebellion, selfishness, dishonesty, lust, and a whole lot more.

How do we pray for our kids along these lines? What should prayers of protection include? Let me give you some suggestions to get you started. First off, I've prayed that my children would hate sin; that they'd find it distasteful. Proverbs 8:13 says that "to fear the LORD is to hate evil." I have known people to get physically sick because of an internal revulsion for the sin that they are concealing. When David covered up his sin with Bathsheba, he later confessed: "My bones wasted away through my groaning all day long. . . . my strength was sapped as in the heat of summer" (Ps. 32:3–4). I've asked God to make my kids miserable when they sin.

Second, I've prayed that my kids' sin would quickly come to light. That they'd be found out. An advantage of having more than one child is that they frequently rat on each other. Sometimes this was done deliberately, to get a sibling in trouble. Other times the information just leaked out. But I would frequently warn my children: "You will not be able to keep your sin a secret. Mom and Dad are going to find out. God will see to that."

And God did. I remember a time when I took my car into the repair shop. My mechanic, who knew my vehicle quite well, laughingly told me how it had passed him on a main street in town that week—doing about twenty miles an hour over the speed limit! Ah, my daughter with the lead foot was busted. I had a little talk with her about her driving later that day.

Third, I've prayed, and still pray, that my two daughters and one son would have quick-to-repent hearts. Listen to what King David had to say on this score: "Then I acknowledged my sin to you and did not cover up my iniquity. I said, 'I will confess my transgressions to the LORD'—and you forgave the guilt of my sin. Therefore let everyone who is godly pray to you while you may be found" (Ps. 32:5–6).

Does the last line of this text infer that there may come a time in our lives when God can*not* be found? I believe that the answer to that question is "yes." Not because God is hiding from us, but because our hearts have become so hard that we are no longer seeking him. I've seen this callousness in kids—and I pray earnestly that it will never take root in mine. I ask God to make them deeply sorry for every harsh word that escapes their lips, for every lustful detour on the Internet, for every shading of the truth, for every selfish act. I know that they will sin. So I pray that sin will break, not harden, their hearts—and that they will cry out to God: "Create in me a pure heart, O God" (Ps. 51:10).

Fourth, I've prayed for my children what Jesus taught me to pray for myself regarding temptation: "Lead us not into temptation, but deliver us from the evil one" (Matt. 6:13). This prayer doesn't exempt my kids from all temptation. It works more like a bulletproof vest (according to what I know about these protective devices from reading detective novels). A person who is shot while wearing such a vest is still left bruised by the slug's impact. But his or her life is saved.

My antitemptation prayers for Emily, Rachel, and Andrew, in a similar way, seem to lessen the impact of the shots they take. God protects them from being tempted in times of vulnerability, or he puts Christian friends in their path to warn them, or he thwarts their foolish efforts to pursue a wrong path. I'm not sure how it works. I just know that God takes the deadly edge off the temptations my kids face when I pray for them. And so I'll keep on praying for their protection.

People Prayer

The final segment of Jesus' John 17 prayer is a plea that his followers would experience relational oneness: He prays "that all of them may be one, Father, just as you are in me and I am in you. . . . I have given them the glory that you gave me, that they may be one as we are one. . . . May they be brought to complete unity to let the world know that you sent me and have loved them even as you have loved me" (vv. 20–23). Interpersonal harmony is the closing theme of Jesus' prayer.

Harmony in relationships is the fifth lesson that parents can learn from the Savior's example. As we pray for our children we should be interceding for their relationships. This is such a big part of their lives. They will be significantly shaped by their interactions with others. And their attitudes and skills in this regard will greatly influence their success in life.

I've found it helpful to bring to mind the various categories of relationships that my kids are engaged in as I pray for them. I begin with their relationship with me. Yeah, that's probably a bit self-serving. But my children will "enjoy long life on the earth" if they obey and honor their parents—that's the prerequisite for such happiness (according to Eph. 6:2–3).

Then I pray for their relationships with authority figures. They're never going to learn to submit to God if they refuse to submit to teachers, coaches, police officers, bosses, librarians, and anyone else who tells them what to do.

Sue and I have tried hard, over the years, to avoid taking our children's side in any conflict with an authority figure. Oh, there have been times when we've wanted to give one of their teachers or bosses a piece of our mind. But we've done our best not to show this irritation to our kids. We want them to respect those in authority—even when the authorities are wrong, or unfair, or overly demanding. Although God is none of these things, there will be times in our kids' lives when he appears to be so, and must be obeyed regardless. So, I pray that they will learn to obey him by practicing a compliant responsiveness to human authorities.

Then I pray, of course, for my children's friends. I ask God to give them Christ-following buddies who will fan into flame their own love for the Lord. Positive peer pressure is such a blessing at this stage of their lives. After Paul warned young Timothy to "flee the evil desires of youth," he underscored the importance of hanging out with the right friends, by adding, "and pursue righteousness, faith, love and peace, along with those who call on the Lord out of a pure heart" (2 Tim. 2:22).

Recently, Sue and I ran into a Christian couple whose daughter, Amy, had been a best friend of our daughter, Rachel, during high school. As we caught up on family news with this mom and dad, Sue noted to them: "Amy and Rachel got each other through public high school, didn't they?" That observation brought back memories of how hard and lonely it had been for these two attractive girls to follow Christ in the midst of a very secular and antagonistic environment. We were so glad that they'd had each other. An answer to prayer.

Of course, we also wanted our kids to have friends who needed Jesus. That was certainly an advantage—a risky one—of being in the public school. We prayed that Emily, Rachel, and Andrew would be influencers, and not influencees. We prayed that they would live in a way that would make the gospel attractive. We prayed that they would be bold in talking about Christ, and in inviting friends to church.

Parents. Authority figures. Friends. Another category of relationships that became a topic of our prayers, believe it or not, was future spouses. It's never too early to begin asking God for the right life partners for our kids. And speaking as a dad who has recently married off two daughters, I can't begin to tell you how incredibly gratifying it is to see them tie the knot with guys who love and serve God.

They didn't just fall into these relationships. They were prayed into them. That meant praying, during their dating years, that they would value the right traits in guys, that they would stand for sexual purity, that they would not get wrapped up in one relationship to the exclusion of other friendships, and that their top priority in a serious relationship would be a shared commitment to Christ.

Sue and I would be the first to admit that we did not pray for our kids with as much consistency as we should have. But, by God's grace, we logged a lot of hours of intercession. The best praying, I'm sure that Sue would agree, took place when we did it together.

I've mentioned several times that our favorite praying venue is the path along the river near our home. If we start at the Mac-Donald's in downtown Batavia and head north along the east bank of the river, we can cross over to the west side at Fabyan Park for the return trip. One hour, three miles, and countless requests for our kids. We've covered that route hundreds of times (still do) and our children have benefited in ways that they will never know. If we didn't pray for them like this, who would?

Onto the Praying Field

If you're not a parent, put the following into practice with nieces and nephews or with the kids you teach at your church.

1. What sorts of things do you typically pray for your kids? How frequently do you engage in structured prayer for them (i.e., not just when needs arise)? Regularly? Occasionally? Rarely? If not regularly, what gets in the way of such?

2. When do you pray *with* your children? Describe the format of these times. Is this format effective in teaching them how to pray? What should you do differently?

    What bad patterns in your children's praying would you like to change?

    What three or four things would you like to involve your kids in praying for?

3. Are you certain that your children have put their trust in Christ for salvation and are following him? If not, how could you remind yourself to pray regularly for this? When will you make time to have a conversation about salvation with them?

4. Reread the portion of this chapter that cites our kids' need for protection, and list the specific dangers that are mentioned. Pray about these for each of your children.

5. Reread the portion of this chapter about people, and pray for your kids' relationships with those in each category.

6. How could you team up with your spouse to pray more regularly for your children?

Leaders

Protect the Quarterback

everal years ago I experienced one of my life's most uncomfortable moments. I was attending a men's conference at a large stadium in Indianapolis. There were more than fifty thousand guys there, including a sizable group from my own church. This weekend rally culminated in a session that was aimed at honoring pastors. So they asked all the church leaders in the arena to come to the main floor.

I didn't move. Truth is, I looked around for a hole to crawl into. But hundreds of pastors were making their way down the aisles, and my own friends dragged me from my seat and pushed me out into the traffic. I didn't have any choice but to go.

There are at least a couple of reasons why I find this sort of recognition personally embarrassing. First, because I'm an introvert by temperament. Whenever I point this out to members of my church, their initial reaction is disbelief. How could an introvert speak in front of thousands of people every weekend? Simple. I direct the attention to God's Word. I hide behind the Bible. My sermons are not about me, so I am not self-conscious when standing in front of a crowd at our church services.

But this stadium rally was an entirely different matter. Not only were all eyes on us pastors as we made our way to the main floor, the conference emcee was leading the crowd in a standing ovation by swinging a towel over his head (like at a sporting event?) and screaming at the top of his lungs. I was mortified.

The second reason that this praise fest made me uncomfortable was because I prefer affirmation that's communicated to me in personal and specific terms. Being cheered by fifty thousand guys who had never met me was meaningless. For all they knew, I might have been a lousy pastor, totally undeserving of their hoopla. For that matter, I might have robbed a bank on my way to the conference—and here they were screaming their lungs out for me.

By way of contrast, I recently got a card from a man in our church. It was only two lines long (probably an epistle for him). The first line read: "Your messages give me hope." I knew his situation, and why he needed hope. I was so profoundly moved by his expression of appreciation that I thumb tacked that card to the bulletin board over my desk. I don't mind being the recipient of genuine praise. But I don't want to be group-hugged by people I don't know.

Ironically, as I nervously shifted from one foot to the other on the main floor of that stadium, wishing I were some place else, I looked around at the other pastors and was surprised to see that some of them had tears in their eyes. Some of them were even openly weeping. That's when it struck me that not every church leader is wired like me (disinterested in large group affirmations). Nor do they all receive the constant flow of positive feedback that my church generously gives me. Some of these pastors had probably not heard an encouraging word in months. They would take whatever affirmation they could get, even if it came from total strangers.

And, in fairness to the ministry that sponsored this event, let me hasten to add that they challenged the thousands of spectators who were cheering for their pastors to continue this practice once they returned home. Not by leading their congregations in standing ovations, but by starting up prayer ministries that would specifically support their senior leaders. A man from my own church did that very thing within a matter of weeks. He signed up guys to pray for me on a regular basis. He even divvied up this group into smaller clusters that would pray, on a rotating basis, during the 40 minutes of every service when I am preaching.

At first, my aversion to being the center of attention almost prompted me to request that this prayer be redirected from me to our church as a whole. Not only do we have scores of programs that deserve prayer, we also have hundreds of staff and volunteer leaders who would benefit from being prayed for. But while I was considering the prospect of redirecting this intercession, God impressed upon me that I should welcome it instead.

No, I don't want to be the sole beneficiary of prayer at Christ Community Church. I encourage our congregation to pray for all our programs and leaders. On the other hand, I am not about to turn down others' offer to pray specifically for me. This does not fuel my sense of self-importance. Just the opposite, it constantly reminds me, in the words of the old spiritual: "It's me, it's me, it's me, O Lord, standin' in the need of prayer. Not my brother, not my sister, but it's me, O Lord, standin' in the need of prayer."

There are unique demands that a senior pastor faces in leading a church. In this chapter, I would like to convince you that these leaders are "standin' in the need" of focused prayer. If your church already has a group that intercedes regularly for the pastor, join it! If such a group doesn't exist, start one! At the very least, put your pastor somewhere near the top of your own personal prayer list.

Here, then, are eight good reasons to pray for the "point guy." Let me quickly add that most of these same reasons apply to praying for strategic Christian leaders outside of your church. I pray, on a regular basis, for people like Franklin Graham, James Dobson, Bill Hybels, Rick Warren, John Maxwell, and others, because they have an enormous spiritual impact upon hundreds of thousands of people.

God's Word Commands It

Every year, just before the National Day of Prayer, we are reminded of Paul's exhortation: "I urge, then, first of all, that requests, prayers, intercession and thanksgiving be made for everyone—for kings and all those in authority, that we may live peaceful and quiet lives in all godliness and holiness" (1 Tim. 2:1–2). When Paul challenges Christ followers to pray, he singles out one group in particular that should not be missed: Leaders!

Paul specifically draws attention, within this group, to civil authorities—starting with the king (or president, or prime minister, or not-so-benevolent dictator). This passage is trotted out on every National Day of Prayer. It makes a good case that we have a responsibility to pray for our senators, governors, mayors, police chiefs, and all other elected officials.

But Paul's "all those in authority" must also include spiritual leaders. Including the senior pastors of our churches. Certainly the rationale that Paul gives for praying for civil leaders would apply to church leaders. Paul intimates that leaders are the people who set the tone for our environment. While civil leaders impact cities, states, and countries, spiritual leaders influence churches and Christian organizations. And, as go leaders, so go the people they lead.

The Bible frequently recognizes this critical role that church leaders play, encouraging us to honor them. Paul instructs the Thessalonians "to respect those who work hard among you, who are over you in the Lord and who admonish you. Hold them in the highest regard in love because of their work" (1 Thess. 5:12–13). Our spiritual leaders, our pastors, are to be held in the highest regard.

Honoring leaders does not come naturally to Westerners. In a democratic culture, where everyone has a voice and a vote, we are fond of pointing out that nobody is more important than anybody else. We are egalitarian to a fault. This realization especially struck me when I was visiting with our ministry partner in Bangladesh recently. Everywhere we went, this ministry director was treated like royalty—as were we, his guests. We were greeted with garlands of flowers, and banners, and marching bands, and standing ovations. At one point I turned to my wife and said, "This is a great place to be a leader!"

Eastern culture calls for the honoring of leaders. We could learn something from them. I'm not suggesting that the church's worship band should play "Hail to the Chief" every time the pastor walks onto the platform to preach. But in recognition of the huge responsibility this leader has to set the tone for the church, one significant way to hold him in highest esteem would be to put him at the top of your prayer list.

Pray for your pastor to be honored, affirmed, encouraged, and respected.

A Quarterback Takes Unusual Hits

A recent article in *Sports Illustrated* described what makes a certain quarterback so phenomenal. This guy is known for his willingness to stand in the pocket (i.e., within an area where he is protected by his teammates) until one of his receivers breaks into the open. He waits, and waits, and waits—until just the right moment to release the ball.

However, on the occasions that he's forced to wait too long, the defenders eventually get to him. And this particular guy has taken some devastating hits. Oh, it's not like a quarterback is the only guy on the team who ever gets pounded. Linemen, and running backs, and wide receivers all get their bell rung from time to time. But hits on the quarterback are so jarring, that there's even a special name for them. They're called "sacks." The defense keeps track of their "sacks" with pride. The quarterback is their primary target.

The same thing happens in a church. Everybody takes hits. The minute that Christ followers roll up their sleeves and start serving in some ministry, or sharing the gospel with their friends, or leading a small group, or contributing their financial resources, they run into spiritual opposition. The enemy tries to put a stop to them.

But I believe that this is particularly true of pastors. I believe that the enemy singles out spiritual leaders for special treatment. He goes after quarterbacks. Peter wrote that, "your enemy the devil prowls around like a roaring lion [or a menacing linebacker] looking for someone to devour" (1 Pet. 5:8). Peter knew this from firsthand experience. He had been devastatingly sacked the night he'd denied Jesus, and he still winced every time he recalled that hit.

Interestingly, Jesus had a dozen disciples whom he'd been mentoring. These men (minus Judas, of course) were destined to become the church's founding leaders. But Peter was the obvious quarterback of the group. And Satan knew that. Which is why he singled Peter out as a primary target of attack.

Was Peter destroyed by this hit? No. What saved him? Prayer. Remember the story? Jesus had told Peter at the Last Supper that, "Satan has asked to sift you as wheat." What an ominous warning! Fortunately, Jesus quickly added: "But I have prayed for you, Simon, that your faith may not fail" (Luke 22:31–32). Jesus prayed for Peter!

Pray for your pastor to be protected from the focused attacks of Satan.

People Are Shaken When a Leader Falls

Several years ago, I received a special mailing from a Christian organization that frequently sends out helpful materials to pastors. It was a taped interview with the founder of this ministry, whose radio program is heard around the world. He was warning pastors to avoid sexual temptations—specifically, to steer clear of pornography on the Internet.

The moderator of this interview was the founder's right-hand man. A few days after the tapes were put in the mail to pastors, this guy made national headlines by confessing to an extramarital affair! The secular media had a field day with that one. Here's a Christian organization that is known for its promotion of family values, and one of its most noted leaders had been cheating on his wife. I wondered how many people were disillusioned by that news. How many Christ followers didn't want to hear another word from that ministry? How many unbelievers were confirmed in their suspicion that "all Christians are hypocrites"?

From time to time, when I'm facing the pressure of some relentless temptation, I make myself play out, in my imagination, the likely repercussions of a moral fall. What would happen if I slept with another woman, or I stole money from the church treasury, or I visited pornographic Web sites—and I was found out?

The reputation of Christ Community Church would be seriously damaged. We would definitely make the headlines of Chicago's suburban newspaper. Hundreds of people who have found Christ at our church would be left reeling. My unbelieving neighbors and friends that I've shared Christ with would have another reason to reject him. Fellow staff members and volunteer leaders would have a mess to clean up—in the midst of their pain. The many men whom I've discipled would be left wondering if anything I'd taught them could be trusted. And my family—I don't even want to go there in my imagination.

It's a terrible thing whenever any Christ follower takes a moral spill. But when a Christian leader falls, the repercussions are extraordinarily tragic. The fallout is enormous! Just look at the history of Israel's kings. When they were godly men (a rarity), the people were godly. But when they behaved wickedly, the whole nation wandered from God.

Pray for your pastor to stay far from sin and to walk in obedience to God's Word.

People "Buck Up" against Authority

I recall an occasion when word reached me through the church grapevine that a certain woman in our congregation couldn't stand me. *What's not to like*? I thought. The odd thing about this case was that I didn't even know the lady—and she didn't know me. So what could I have possibly done to offend her?

I ran this question by a counselor on our staff, someone who had periodically met with this disgruntled woman. "What's the deal?" I asked him. "What have I done wrong?" His answer surprised me: "Nothing." And then he went on to explain without violating confidences by giving away personal details. "It's not you," he said, "that really bugs this woman. It's your position of authority. In fact, everyone who's had a rocky relationship with parents or is struggling with authority is going to have bad feelings for you." That was a happy thought. I thanked him for sharing it with me.

This is one of the joys (sarcasm intended) of leadership. A lot of folks don't want to be led. It goes with the territory. Some years ago I read a book about the fatal errors that managers make. One of their biggest mistakes, according to this expert, is trying to be good pals with those they oversee. That never works because there's a built-in adversarial element to every leader-follower relationship. The leader is the boss, the one who gets the final say. That has a tendency to rub people the wrong way.

Oddly enough, this book pointed out, people only buck *up*. They don't buck *sideways*. What he meant by that is that their peers hardly ever experience their disdain. Co-workers may even say: "Oh, he's a great guy to work with." The buckaroos don't make life miserable for others horizontally. They only cause problems for the poor sucker who's got to manage them.

This same sort of tension exists in the church. The toughest part of a pastor's job is leading and managing people. There are many days when I wish I could just hide out in my office, prepare messages from the Bible, preach them on the weekends, and then retreat to my study. No leadership demands.

Or maybe I ought to resign my position as a senior pastor and become a seminary professor who presents classroom lectures, but doesn't have to manage a staff. Or I could become a traveling consultant, using my two decades of experience to coach other pastors with advice that I myself no longer have to put into practice. Fly in and fly out. Sounds nice. (My apologies to seminary professors and traveling consultants whose job descriptions I have oversimplified to make my point.)

I don't want to leave you with the wrong impression. I serve a great congregation and partner with a wonderful staff. But leading often wears me out. The people problems. I don't enjoy dealing with someone who is upset because he got left out of a decision, or because she feels her salary package is inadequate. I don't like explaining to a critic why our music is "so loud," or why our capital campaign is raising money for a youth facility, or why we won't marry them if they're not both believers. I get tired of trying to motivate people to do what they are supposed to do.

Hebrews 13:17 instructs Christ followers to obey their spiritual leaders and submit to their authority so that "their work will be a joy, not a burden." Leading would be a total blast if there were no relational conflicts to sort out. But because there will always be some who "buck up," pastors could use some extra prayer.

Pray for your pastor to be given wisdom, patience, perseverance, and grace in facing people problems. And pray that those he leads will be loyal, understanding, and supportive.

A Poor Family Relationship Disqualifies a Leader

The apostle Paul asks the question: "If anyone does not know how to manage his own family, how can he take care of God's church?" (1 Tim. 3:5). Evidently, a healthy relationship with one's spouse and children is a necessary qualification for those who want to be spiritual leaders. Thankfully, I'm not required to be a perfect husband and dad in order to lead others. But it does appear as if my home life must be pretty much on track if I want to be a pastor.

You need to know that this puts a unique pressure on me—and on all others who serve in a similar role. There are times, for example, when I'm not getting along with Sue (the cat's now out of the bag, eh?). And, because of that, I find myself wishing that I were a doctor, or an insurance salesman, or a schoolteacher. Any other profession. Why? Because one doesn't have to resolve all conflicts with his wife in order to be successful at these other jobs.

But I've got to be reconciled with Sue before I can get any work done. The nature of what I do for a living demands it. This really bugs me sometimes. If I were a carpenter, I could still build a house even though I was mad at Sue. But as a pastor, I can't preach a sermon, or make a big ministry decision, or give wise feedback to a staff member when I'm honked off at my wife. God won't be in it.

The same is true of my relationship with my kids. If I'm at odds with them, or if I'm not doing a good job as a parent, I shouldn't be trying to spiritually lead others. This doesn't mean that I am responsible for producing children who always exhibit godly behavior. No, they will sometimes choose to take another path—in spite of my best parenting efforts. They "wear their own faces" with respect to these bad choices. But it is my duty to do everything possible to lead my kids to Christ, to ground them in God's Word, to set boundaries for their behavior, and to provide discipline that's both loving and firm.

I picked up a new book to read last night. It's one that my daughter Rachel and her husband, Jameson, gave me for Father's Day. They know my love language. Books! As I opened the cover, I noticed a note that Rachel had penned on the front page. I must have missed it before. It read: "Thank you for being a role model to us—always willing to put others first, willing to confess when you've fallen down, and willing to learn and grow."

I'm not sure that I've fully lived up to Rachel's billing. And I don't cite her overly generous commendation to brag on myself. The point I want to make is this: If I hadn't been a role model for Rachel, if she couldn't hold me in high esteem in this regard, then I wouldn't be qualified to lead my church. God's sets the bar high. No way could I clear it without the prayers of others.

Pray for your pastor's marriage and parenting.

The Preacher Is a Conduit for God's Word

Ever play that old party game, "Telephone"? Everyone sits in a circle and someone whispers a message into the ear of the person on his left. She then passes it on to the guy who's sitting next to her.

On and on it goes, until the message has made its way completely around the circle. The last person to receive it then states it out loud. It's amazing—and usually quite funny—how twisted a single sentence can become as it's transmitted from one person to another. "The cows are running out of grass and the farmer doesn't know what to feed them" becomes "The cars are running too fast—the karma is too slow to lead them."

Pastors (and strategic Christian leaders) spend a good deal of their time listening to God, so that they'll have a message to share with those they lead. If they don't hear God accurately, or they garble his message when passing it on, a lot of people get misdirected.

That's why James warns aspiring spiritual communicators: "Not many of you should presume to be teachers, my brothers, because you know that we who teach will be judged more strictly" (James 3:1).

That should give us leader-teachers pause. God does not take our public speaking lightly—and neither should we. Our preparation should be saturated in prayer. Not only our own, but the prayers of everyone whom we can possibly recruit to the task. The story of Dr. Wilbur Chapman has inspired me along these lines.

Chapman was a fairly young man when he became, at the end of the nineteenth century, the senior pastor of a large church in Philadelphia. After one of his first sermons, an elderly gentleman—who was also a wealthy patron of the church—let him know that his preaching was a bit weak, and that he was quite young to be pastoring such a significant ministry. But the old guy promised to pray for Chapman. The new pastor wrote him off as a crank.

Before long there were ten people joining this senior citizen in prayer before each Sunday service. The group continued to grow. In fact, it multiplied, becoming twenty, then forty, then eighty, then a hundred and sixty, and so on. In addition to this general band of prayer supporters, Chapman had almost twenty elders who would meet with him in a back room before the service, lay their hands on him, and pray. Not only did this give him joy and confidence as he went out to speak, it also produced tangible results. During one three-year period at the church, over a thousand people—most of them men—made public decisions to trust and follow Christ.

With so much at stake when a pastor preaches, it is critical to pray that he gives a clear and powerful message from God. Speaking for myself, I know that there are a number of things that can keep me from being the conduit that I need to be. Let me list them here so that you will know how to better pray for your own pastor (and for well-known communicators, such as Franklin Graham and company).

Sin can prevent me from hearing God speak as I prepare a message. What's worse, sin can prevent me from realizing that sin is preventing me from hearing God speak. Follow? If there is unconfessed sin in my life, I can go through my regular routine of putting a sermon together, totally oblivious to the fact that my thoughts are not being directed by God. Sin is like earwax that must be removed in order for God's voice to come through loud and clear.

Busyness is another detriment to sermon preparation. There are so many other demands crowding a pastor's agenda that study time can get squeezed out. We need to go back frequently to Acts 6 and remind ourselves that the primary role of a spiritual leader is to study God's Word and to pray (see vv. 2–4). No amount of staff managing, vision casting, program evaluating, or resource raising can take the place of these two priorities. If we are too busy to spend significant time in God's Word, then we are too busy.

Theological laziness is another temptation that pastors sometimes succumb to. We are so concerned about being culturally relevant, or seeker sensitive, or postmodern hip in the crafting of our messages, that we don't pay enough attention to being theologically accurate. Are our applications coming out of a correct interpretation of Scripture? Or are we forcing them onto the text? We must heed the apostle Paul's warning to Pastor Timothy: "Do your best to present yourself to God as one approved, a workman who does not need to be ashamed and who correctly handles the word of truth" (2 Tim. 2:15).

Still another inhibitor to my being able to preach God's Word in a life-transforming way is my failure to allow it to first transform my own life. I must practice what I preach if I want others to practice what I preach. Authenticity empowers communication. If I am going to teach on evangelism, for example, it is critical for me to be able to use illustrations from my own life (recent ones) of sharing Christ with others. I myself must be a poster child for whatever truth I'm hoping to get across. Try keeping this up on a weekly basis!

Finally, if I am not filled with the Holy Spirit, my preaching will be anemic. What a contrast with the early disciples' preaching: "After they prayed, the place where they were meeting was shaken. And they were all filled with the Holy Spirit and spoke the word of God boldly" (Acts 4:31).

And so we have come full circle, reminded again that prayer is the key to a leader's success—in this case, to his or her effectiveness as a conduit for God's Word.

Pray for your pastor's teaching ministry—an ability to hear God's voice, time in the study, theological accuracy, the personal application of truth, and the filling of God's Spirit.

Spiritual Readiness Requires Consistent Discipline

My brother-in-law, John, is a trumpet player. A serious trumpet player. He has a Ph.D. in trumpet, teaches trumpet at a university, and plays trumpet for a variety of symphony orchestras.

I was at my parents' house one Christmas holiday when John and his family were in town for a visit. After greeting everyone else, I asked, "Where's John?" I was told that he was in the basement. Practicing. When he joined the rest of us later for dinner, I expressed my surprise that he was practicing his trumpet on Christmas day.

"How long do you practice?"
"Four hours a day."
"Every day?"
"365 days a year."
"Holidays included?"
"Even Christmas."

Wow! That's the discipline required to play the trumpet at his level. Being a spiritual leader requires an equal commitment to personal discipline. Paul challenged Pastor Timothy to be prepared to do his job, "in season and out of season" (2 Tim. 4:2).

Oh, to be a major league baseball player who has the winter off (allowing him to occasionally skip workouts and eat jelly donuts)! Pastors are never off. I have a sense that I am always on call. I run into people who attend my church at the store, at local restaurants, on the bike path, when I'm picking up a DVD at Blockbuster. Often a simple "hello" evolves into a lengthier conversation in which people ask me for counsel or prayer.

I can't say on these spontaneous occasions, "You know, I'm not walking with God at just this moment. If you'll call me tomorrow at the church office, I'll have had my morning quiet time by then and be fully connected with God." No! That doesn't cut it. I have to be ready to pastor *in season and out of season.*

Even as I write these lines, I'm hiding away at an undisclosed location five hours away from home. (I'd tell you where, but then I'd have to kill you.) But I still practiced my usual routine, early this morning, of reading God's Word, and spending some time in prayer, and singing a few worship songs.

Not just because I love God (which is my prime motivation). But because I've got to stay in shape spiritually. And I've got to be ready for whatever comes my way today. And that could include an emergency call from my church; running into one of my volunteer leaders who owns a summer home up here ("up here" is the only hint you'll get); a spontaneous conversation about Christ with the guy I've been baiting at my favorite lunch spot; writing the next chapter of this book; or a temptation to do something stupid while I'm incognito.

Pray for your pastor to consistently practice important spiritual disciplines.

Without a Vision the Church Flounders

All good leaders are vision casters. I love what Marcus Buckingham says in *The One Thing You Need to Know.* Buckingham is a brilliant Cambridge graduate who has spent years researching and writing about great leaders. He says that all great leaders need to know "how to rally people to a better future."[1] That sounds to me like a definition of vision casting.

And it also sounds a lot like what the apostle Paul was doing throughout his New Testament epistles. As Paul challenged individuals to take on Christ's character, and churches to take on Christ's mission, he was rallying people to a better future. He was vision casting. This is the job of every pastor. (I'd cite the familiar phrase, "without a vision the people perish" at this point. But the King James rendering of Proverbs 28:18 is misleading—the verse isn't about vision, so I won't use it. See the New International Version for a more accurate translation.)

The senior pastor should be the biggest cheerleader for the church's mission. He should live it, talk about it, sleep on it, enthuse over it.

In Sam Walton's biography, I was amused to learn that the Wal-Mart founder's family got irritated on vacation when their dad insisted on stopping at every department store along the way. He would run inside, armed with a spiral notebook and pen, and jot down anything he observed that could be applied to making his Wal-Marts better.[2]

I smiled at this anecdote because I could identify with it. I'm constantly thinking about the church. How could we do a better job of worshiping God, of teaching Scripture, of engaging our people in ministry, of reaching the spiritually lost, of caring for the destitute? When I travel, I'm eager to check out other churches, or to tour historic sites where Christ's kingdom has been advanced.

Some time ago, when I was passing through London on a twenty-four-hour visit, the friends I was with got out their city maps and Tube schedules to decide what sights to take in. One person wanted to stop at Parliament. Another wanted to see Windsor Castle. When it came to my turn for input, I said, "John Wesley's house." They looked at me as if I had two heads.

Not exactly the sort of place that the double-decker tour buses stop at. But, hey, Wesley was one of the greatest evangelists of all time. He used to preach outside the entrances to the coal mines as men arrived at 5:00 a.m. for work. In the American colonies in the mid-1700s, his circuit riders were planting churches across the frontier. His brother, Chuck (okay, Charles), wrote some of the most moving hymns in history. I wanted to see the dude's house. You got a problem with that?

Pastors love the church. They are passionate about the church's mission. They want others to catch their excitement and jump on board.

Pray that your pastor would be zealous for the church and compelling in promoting its mission.

Now that you know how to pray for your pastor—get started!

Onto the Praying Field

1. Choose three Christian leaders to pray for each day of this coming week. One of them should be your pastor. The other two may be point people of national or foreign ministries that you support. Here is what to pray for, as specifically as possible:

Day 1: That they would be honored, affirmed, encouraged, and respected.

Day 2: That they would be protected from the focused attacks of Satan, stay far from sin, and walk in obedience to God's Word.

Day 3: That God would give them wisdom, patience, perseverance, and grace in facing people problems, and that those they lead would be loyal, understanding, and supportive.

Day 4: That their marriages and parenting would be God-pleasing and wise.

Day 5: That, in preparation for teaching God's Word, they would hear God's voice, protect their time for study, be kept from theological error, personally apply the truth, and be filled with God's Spirit.

Day 6: That they would consistently practice important spiritual disciplines.

Day 7: That they would be zealous for the church and compelling in promoting its mission.

2. Copy these seven days' worth of prayer topics onto a 3 x 5 card, and keep that list in a place where you will be reminded to pray regularly for leaders.

3. Drop a note to one of the three leaders that you prayed for to let him/her know of your intercession. It will be a tremendous encouragement!

13

Accountability Partners

Be Your Brother's (or Sister's) Keeper

I'm about to take a huge gamble here. I'm about to get real vulnerable with you and tell you about something terribly stupid and sinful that I did six or seven years ago (not that I haven't done anything stupid and sinful since then). My point in relating this incident is to underscore the importance of this chapter's topic: accountability partners.

But I realize that my transparency could backfire. You could conclude, after reading the following, that I'm not qualified to dispense godly counsel, or to write a book on prayer, or even to be a pastor. I'm willing to risk that, hoping that my openness will be of some help to you.

The terribly stupid and sinful thing that I did was to rent a video that I had no business watching. (Some of you are shocked, while others are shaking your heads and saying, "That's it?") My wife was out of town for a few days, and I was wandering the local Blockbuster's aisles (never a wise thing to do) when I came across the section of foreign films. What caught my attention was that most of these movies were not rated. The reason that I was struck by this fact was that the elders and staff of my church had made a commitment not to watch R-rated movies. But nobody had said anything about movies with *no* rating.

My flesh (NIV: sinful nature) immediately seized upon this loophole and I picked up a video that looked like it might have some steamy scenes in it. I took it home. I wasn't disappointed. (Let me hasten to add, so your imagination doesn't run away with you, this was *not* an X-rated movie. But there was enough nudity in it to have earned it an R rating, had it been rated.) The momentary pleasure quickly gave way to a deep sense of guilt. Now what?

Fortunately, I instantly knew "now what." I had recently begun meeting with an accountability partner. One thing we talked about openly with each other was sexual temptation. He was bound to ask me when we got together next: "Have you deliberately put before your eyes any unwholesome images?" (This question comes directly from Ps. 101:2–3: "I will walk in my house with blameless heart. I will set before my eyes no vile thing.") I decided to beat him to the punch. Instead of waiting to be asked, I called him on the phone and confessed what I'd done.

I don't remember all the details of our conversation, but I know that as it concluded, after he had assured me of God's forgiveness, he gently stated that I would have to tell both my wife and our elders about the video. I had broken my word to them. Those confessions were painful and humiliating. And cleansing.

What if I had kept my transgression to myself? What if I had reasoned that all I needed to do was confess my sin, confidentially, to God—and he would forgive me (true, but not the whole truth about confession)? I believe that when we keep our dealings with sin a private matter, we are more likely to stray into the same paths of unrighteousness again and again. Compounding our guilt and sense of failure. Better to put it on the table, in the presence of a trusted and godly friend.

Is there biblical support for this practice? (Some militant Protestants and ex-Catholics are already objecting: "I don't need a priest. I can go directly to Jesus!") Yes. James 5:16 puts it this way: "Therefore confess your sins to each other and pray for each other so that you may be healed. The prayer of a righteous man is power-ful and effective."

No, we don't need a professional priest. But we do need some-one who will listen wisely to our confession. And pray for us. This is what a good accountability partner can do. I am going to make a case, in this chapter, for the importance of having a structured account-ability relationship with another Christ follower. This relationship is about more than just prayer. But prayer is a critical component of it. Your accountability partner will become a major beneficiary of your intercession, just as you will benefit from his or hers.

The goal of this relationship is to help each other stay on God's path—and return to that path when a detour has been taken. We must stop neglecting this responsibility with the Cain-like objection: "Am I my brother's [or sister's] keeper?" (Gen. 4:9). Yes, as a matter of fact, I am. And so are you.

Paul instructs us, "Brothers, if someone is caught in a sin, you who are spiritual [not perfect, just walking with God at the time] should restore him gently. But watch yourself, or you also may be tempted. Carry each other's burdens" (Gal. 6:1–2). How do we re-store a friend who has wandered into sin? Through open and honest dialogue. Getting in his or her face, if necessary. And prayer.

We can find numerous examples of accountability partners, of sorts, in Scripture. In an earlier chapter, we considered Nathan's confrontation of David. This prophet risked his own life in ap-proaching the king about Bathsheba. The repercussions of David's sin were spelled out in no uncertain terms. Repentance was called for. Forgiveness was proffered. A plan of restoration was laid out. And David's humble response returned him to God's path.

Or consider the time that Paul played accountability partner to the apostle Peter. Peter had been visiting the church in Galatia, which was made up of a lot of new Gentile believers. Peter had no qualms about hanging out with these guys—until some of his Jew-ish buddies showed up. Suddenly, Peter became extremely Jewish, distancing himself from his Gentile brothers and sisters.

When Paul arrived on the scene and observed all this, he was livid. (You can read about it in Galatians 2.) Peter's behavior was doing a disservice to the gospel, which welcomes everyone into God's family on the basis of simple faith in Christ. Paul had no reservations about taking Peter to task on this score, like a good accountability partner would.

Do you have a Nathan in your life? Or a Paul? Someone who will speak the truth to you when you may least want to hear it? Someone who longs to see you return to God's path when you've wandered from it? Do you have an accountability partner who is not only willing to confront you, when necessary, but who is also committed to praying for you?

People frequently ask me when I mention this subject: "How do I get started in this kind of a relationship?" Read on. I'm going to put the cookies on the bottom shelf. This is really practical stuff.

The Parameters of an Accountability Partnership

I want to be careful not to oversell my product here. There are limits to what an accountability partnership can do for us. We need to approach such a relationship with realistic expectations.

Take my cell phone. What it does best is allow me to make and receive calls. (Oh, and I like the voicemail and phonebook features, too.) But the makers of my cell phone want me to use it for so much more. My 211-page owner's guide (I'm not kidding) teaches me how to use it for playing games, taking pictures (still shots and video), listening to music, connecting with the Internet, keeping my daily schedule, hosting conference calls, sending text messages, setting cutesy ring tones, and making dinner. Okay, it can't make dinner. But it wouldn't surprise me if the next generation of cell phones could!

I don't need a cell phone that can do all that stuff. In fact, I find all those auxiliary features to be somewhat distracting. (I realize that I am showing my age with this analogy.) Just give me a cell phone that handles incoming and outgoing calls.

Accountability partnerships do a few things well. We need to put some boundaries on what we expect from these relationships so that they can accomplish what they are designed for. Here are a few parameters to consider.

1. The Topics

Have you ever watched the TV show *Monk*? It's about a San Francisco police detective who's got OCD (obsessive-compulsive disorder). Because the series airs on cable TV, and we don't have cable TV, we had never seen it. Until we discovered that previous seasons are available on DVD at our local library. Now, we're addicted.

Monk is brilliant at a crime scene. But he's unbearably annoying everywhere else. He's a perfectionist, a neatnick, and a phobiaholic. There's hardly a thing he doesn't fear. Fortunately, for Monk, he's got a therapist who patiently listens to him ramble on and on about his concerns. Whatever comes to his mind. Stream-of-consciousness stuff.

This is not what one does with an accountability partner. Accountability is different from therapy. Accountability assumes that the participants are relatively healthy . . . uh . . . sinners. They don't need long-term counseling; they need occasional correcting. Accountability partners don't focus on disorders; they focus on disciplines.

There are several topics—four, to be exact—that my accountability partner (I'll just call him my AP from here on out and save some ink) and I discuss every time we get together:

Walk with God: Are you connecting daily with God through Bible study and prayer? Where are you reading in Scripture? What applications are you making?

Battle with sin: What's your biggest source of temptation these days? If it's lust, how are you doing with Internet pornography, fantasies about women you know, masturbation, magazine racks at the airport, etc.? (Other favorite sins are checked up on in a similarly detailed fashion. No skimming over the surface.)

Investment with family: Are you getting along with your wife? Have you resolved the conflict that you shared last time? Have you spent quality time with your kids this past week? What issues do you need to address with them?

Balance with work and other priorities: Are you overworking? How do you plan to cut back? How are your workplace relationships? What are you doing for exercise and recreation? Are you eating healthy and keeping your weight in check?

We always cover these four topics. And we rarely wander onto other subjects. These topics are like the gauges on the dashboard of our car. If they are registering positive information, there's a good chance that things are in overall, decent working order.

2. The Truth

Accountability partnerships work only (I can't believe I have to say this) if both partners are willing to be ruthlessly honest with each other. Everybody nods in agreement to this ground rule. But not everybody practices it.

In the slightly more than twenty years that I have shepherded Christ Community Church, I have had to let two staff members go because of serious moral issues. Really serious. Ironically, in both cases they had APs. They had APs that they were barefaced lying to every time they got together. I still can't believe it. Neither can their APs.

There are a number of Christian books out there that talk about the importance of having an AP, more for men than women. Most of these books include a sample list of questions, as I provided above, to routinely ask your AP. And most of them close their list with a final set of inquiries that goes something like this: "Have all your previous answers been truthful? Have you lied to me about anything? Are you withholding important information from me?"

I hate to admit to being so crass, but I will occasionally use a vulgar term to ask guys (I only do this with men) if they have been lying to me as we've talked about a sin issue in their lives. Have you been ____-____ing me? The inclination to cover up is so strong that it seems to take a shocking expression like that (from the lips of a pastor, no less) to draw out an honest response. And I have frequently had men hang their heads in shame after my no-holds-barred, earthy inquiry and admit that, yeah, they'd been deceiving me.

Demand the truth from your AP. And demand it from yourself.

3. The *To* (Instead of *For*)

I mentioned in the last chapter having read a book about the fatal errors that managers often make. Here's another one, as I remember it: Misguided managers try to be responsible *for* people, instead of *to* people. Let me explain the difference, using the Nathan/David confrontation as an illustration. Nathan (a good manager) didn't take it on himself to fix David by offering all sorts of remedies for dealing with the king's lust and adulterous inclinations. He just blew the whistle on David, expecting the king to take the necessary steps to correct the situation himself.

Do you see the difference between those two approaches? Nathan didn't see himself as being responsible *for* David's behavior (the way that some parents blame themselves when their teenagers do something bad). Therapists would probably call that a form of codependency. It's a no-no. But Nathan did see himself as being responsible *to* David in the sense of being obligated to confront him.

Your job is not to fix your AP's misbehavior. (Although, there may be a bit of prescribing called for, as we'll see in a moment.) Your job is to invite honest confession, call for necessary changes, check up to see if progress is being made, and pray like crazy. That's being responsible *to*, not *for*, your AP.

4. The Two (And Only Two)

You've heard the expression, no doubt: "Two's company, three's a crowd." (Probably first uttered, under his breath, by a guy whose girlfriend's mother insisted on chaperoning their date.) Here's my version of that line, as applied to the subject at hand: "Two's an accountability partnership, three's a small group."

Accountability partnerships work best as one-on-one relationships. There just isn't enough time for everybody to share, in depth, when the group grows to three or more. And the communication doesn't take place eyeball to eyeball, as it does when there are only two people involved.

What's more, if you share something in my small group (community group, life group, discipleship group, whatever you call it), I won't necessarily feel a personal responsibility to follow up with you. After all, there are others in the group who heard you say what you said. Surely one of them will check back with you. Probably someone who's closer to you than I am. Or so I reason. But I don't reason that way with my AP. When he divulges things to me, I write them down. I later use that list to pray for him and to check up on him.

A couple of years ago my AP and I tried to add another guy to our twosome. We had good intentions. This Christian brother had been a local pastor, but had stepped down from his job due to a moral fall. I had been part of a team that had supervised his reconciliation with his wife and church, and his eventual restoration to ministry. A great story of God's redeeming grace. But like anyone who has been living a double life for a time, this guy still needed to learn how to be honest and vulnerable with others.

My AP and I believed that we could provide him with the ideal context in which to practice that kind of openness. That's what our relationship had been about for over a half dozen years. We invited him to join us. And it worked—for him. This guy thrived in his newfound accountability. He brought things out into the open that needed to be dealt with. He listened empathetically to my AP and me when we shared. He was a sweetheart.

But it did something—I'm not sure exactly what—to the dynamics of the relationship that I'd previously had with my AP. We weren't quite as open with each other as we'd been before. Or maybe it was that we both wanted this other brother to succeed and so were focusing our attention on him. I don't know.

It just felt like when Sue and I have had company stay too long at our house—and we needed them to leave so that we could catch up with each other. So I asked our new guy to leave. To find his own AP. I was very tactful about it, of course. And, you know what? He got hooked up with a great AP, and Mark (my AP) and I returned to normal.

The Particulars of an Accountability Partnership

Now that you understand some basic boundaries that must be respected in order for an accountability partnership to flourish, you are ready to get started. Here are a few simple steps to keep in mind as you begin. (Forgive the alliterated outline. I'm trying to break the habit with the help of a recovery group.)

1. Pick

Choose a partner. This person does not have to be a good friend or someone with whom you'd want to do family vacations. A common mistake that I see men make when selecting an AP is to hook up with someone who is a best bud—or potentially so. The trouble with the best bud approach, however, is that the friendship often gets in the way of the accountability. Instead of spending time together asking one another tough questions, two good ole boys end up shooting the breeze about mutual interests. (I imagine that it works the same way with women.)

My AP and I haven't made much effort to get together socially. We rarely meet outside of our bi-weekly accountability appointment. We don't have a lot in common with each other. I'm a number of years older than he is. We have different hobbies. Mark earns a living as an architect; I have a hard time drawing a straight line. Our wives don't hang out together. He lives a good distance—two towns away—from me. Mark has four kids, the oldest of which is in high school. I have three kids, the youngest of which is in college.

But I love Mark! He's been a great AP for me. Our meetings are a priority to him—he works his schedule around them. He's a wise sounding board. Sometimes he consoles me, sometimes he kicks my butt. And I know that I'm at the top of his prayer list.

Let me suggest a few qualities to look for in an AP. First and foremost, this person must be able to keep confidences. You don't want to share your struggles with your AP—and then discover that everybody knows about them. That happened to me once. Not with Mark, with Gary. In the third grade.

Gary asked me, as we rode bikes home from school one day, if I had a girlfriend. I didn't want to tell him, but he badgered me until I did. I confessed that I was in love with Jill. The next morning all my school friends greeted me with the chant: "Jimmy and Jill, sittin' in a tree, k-i-s-s-i-n-g." You know the rest of the rhyme. I could've killed Gary. It was a long time before I shared the intimate details of my life with anyone. APs have to be tight-lipped.

Second, look for someone who is at the relatively same stage of Christian experience as you are. If one of you is significantly further down the road in a relationship with Christ than the other, this is likely to become a discipling or mentoring relationship instead of an accountability partnership.

Third, find an AP who's available. You don't want to have to keep canceling and resetting appointments because of conflicts with schedules.

Fourth, choose nervy over nice. Is this person willing to ask questions that may make you uncomfortable? Will he or she be bold enough to give you frank feedback? Does he or she have the tenacity to check up on you in areas where you have confessed a need for change?

A frequent complaint I hear from men about their AP is: "He's not tough enough with me." I keep reminding guys of how the writer of Proverbs describes the dynamics of a robust accountability relationship: "As iron sharpens iron, so one man sharpens another" (Prov. 27:17). Can you visualize this? What happens when iron is used to sharpen iron? Sparks fly! Things heat up. This is what you need from an AP if you want to be well honed.

Where do you find a person who meets the qualifications that I've been describing? I'd recommend that you start by considering someone in your small group. (If you're not currently in a group, this is another good reason to join one.) You already know this individual to some extent. And you're both pursuing spiritual growth. Any candidates in your group?

I'll warn you ahead of time that asking someone to be your AP is a little like asking him or her to date you. You are risking rejection. You may be tagged as being "way too serious" in seeking this sort of a relationship. Remember dating? (Maybe you're still there.) I asked Sue out the fall semester of our freshman year at college, and it only took me a few weeks to determine that I wanted more than a friendship. Unfortunately, she wasn't looking for someone to go deep with, in an exclusive relationship. She just wanted lots of buddies. Ouch! (Thank goodness she eventually changed her mind on this score.)

You may have to do a bit of fishing before you find a person who bites on this idea of an accountability partnership. Don't give up. And don't scare the fish away by trying to set the hook too soon. (I can't believe I'm using a fishing analogy. I never fish. Never.) Grab a cup of coffee a few times together. Just to talk. (I'm back on familiar ground with coffee. I do coffee.) Don't propose an accountability relationship until you've got a sense that this individual would be a good partner.

2. Plan

I've spent a lot of time talking to you about the importance of picking the right AP because that's the most critical step in the process. We can move more quickly through steps two through six.

Coming up with a plan for when and where you will meet with your AP is your next order of business. Those who think that they can just wing it, those whose time and location for getting together are a moving target, those who constantly promise that they'll "call each other next week and try to get something on the calendar," never succeed in establishing an accountability relationship. Without a plan, you will fail.

So, for starters, I'd recommend that you connect with your AP at least twice a month. A weekly meeting is usually an unrealistic expectation for busy people. On the other hand, if you go for more than two weeks without getting together, you will have too much to catch up on. Your sweeping summaries of what's been going on in your lives will gloss over specific situations that need to be addressed. Let me illustrate.

Recently, I stepped into my garage and pushed the button for the electric door opener. Nothing happened. Not a good way to begin the day. I pulled out a ladder and climbed up to take a look at the motor. It took me about ten seconds to realize that I had no idea what I was looking for. Fortunately, however, I did see something that proved to be helpful. I saw an 800 number for the manufacturer. When I called for technical assistance, the first question I was asked was general: "What's wrong with your garage door opener?" And my response was just as general: "It doesn't work!"

The technician couldn't help me based upon such a broad synopsis of my problem. He needed details. So he walked me through a step-by-step diagnosis of the malfunctioning equipment. We eventually got my garage door opener up and running.

If my AP and I let too much time go by before we meet, our recaps of our lives tend to be much too general to do each other any good. Let's say, for example, that Sue and I have had a big argument. But the next time I see my AP is three weeks—twenty-one days—later. When he asks me, "How are things going with Sue?" I reply, "Okay." The argument has long been forgotten. Or even if I do remember it and say, "Sue and I had a blow-up a few weeks back," I can't recall any of its details (the reason I was angry, the hurtful things I said, the grudge I carried for a while). I don't get to the root of the problem with my AP.

However, if I'm meeting with Mark just a couple of days after that argument, I'm able to fully recount it and benefit from his counsel and prayer. That's why it's important for us to get together at least twice a month. We have a standing appointment every other Monday, at 1:00 p.m. If one of us is going to be out of town at that time, we either reschedule for another day that same week or we arrange to touch base with each other by phone.

Let me suggest that, if a set meeting time doesn't work for you—because you travel or you're constantly switching shifts—you and your AP should at least pull out your calendars and decide on the date of your *very next* rendezvous. Short-term planning is better than nothing.

Where should you meet? Choose a place that affords you some privacy. Mark and I get together at my house, where I'm studying on Mondays. He's able to leave his office for an hour and a half to join me. We used to do our accountability over lunch at a nearby restaurant. But we changed locations for several reasons: eating takes up too much time and is a distraction, talking about personal struggles (like that argument with Sue) is uncomfortable when the lady sipping her French onion soup at the table two feet away may be eavesdropping, and praying earnestly for each other just doesn't happen in a public restaurant.

Here's one final tip if you've got yourself a great AP but the two of you just can't seem to coordinate a time and place for meeting. Assuming that you both go to the same church, arrange to get there an hour before the weekly service for your accountability appointment. Or if you're in the same small group (as previously recommended), grab a cup of coffee together afterwards. (Just watch out for that eavesdropping lady—she's now sipping her latte at the table two feet away.)

3. Pace

All right, I promised to be briefer with these succeeding steps. It's time to pick up the pace. And speaking of pace, be careful not to get bogged down in the conversation with your AP. It's easy to do. Watch out for slow starts. Begin your meetings on time, open with prayer, then one of you jump right in with a succinct review of your life along the lines of the agreed upon topics.

I'm not saying that you should never ease into your time together with small talk. But I'll warn you that if you give small talk an inch, it will take a mile. You'll banter about last night's baseball game, or the clothing sale at a local store, or the vacation you just returned from. And—surprise—when you glance down at your watch you notice that twenty minutes have passed. Nothing criminal about that. But if you've only got an hour to an hour and a half with your AP, every other week, you'd better make every minute of it count.

So, as abrupt as it may feel, open briefly in prayer and then one of you start scrolling through how you've been doing with regard to the accountability topics. Don't skip any of them. But don't spend so much time on any one of them that the others are skimmed over.

What happens if a major issue surfaces? Do you stick to the pace? If your AP's teenage daughter is threatening suicide, do you try to keep the conversation moving so that you can get to other concerns? No. That's when you throw the clock out the window. In fact, there may be occasions when your AP is facing something that's so huge that you forego spending *any* time on yourself in that particular meeting.

My only caution is that you should not allow this to become a regular pattern for your times together. Both of you need consistent accountability, which you'll miss out on if your meetings are frequently dominated by a single issue. Keep referring to that list of topics as an outline for your conversations.

4. Probe

Imagine that you are a major league baseball player who has a hard time hitting a curveball. Would you step up to the plate, turn to the catcher, and say: "There's something I think you guys should know—I can't hit a curveball"? Of course not! You wouldn't breathe a word of it. Maybe the opposing pitcher would eventually discover your weakness, but you certainly wouldn't volunteer the information.

Here's the strange thing about accountability partnerships. You have a responsibility to provide your AP with the very questions that will expose your sinful tendencies. Have you been watching too much TV? You tell your AP: "Ask me, next time, how much TV I've watched." Are you neglecting your kids? You tell your AP: "Ask me, next time, if I've spent quality time with my kids." Is there an attractive woman flirting with you at work? You tell your AP: "Ask me, next time, if I've kept my distance from so-and-so." It's that simple.

Don't play by the "don't ask/don't tell" rules of the military. You are not allowed to keep your struggles or shortcomings to yourself until your AP figures out the right questions to draw them out of you. You provide those "Ask me, next time" questions.

Mark and I are always doing this with each other. I'll say to him: "I'm going to be traveling this week. Ask me, next time, if I've stayed away from airport magazine racks and hotel in-house movies." Or: "I've been staying up too late reading. Ask me, next time, if I'm getting to bed at a decent hour." Or: "I'm really honked off at So-and-so. Ask me, next time, if I've resolved things with him."

This is full disclosure. And if Mark's questions are too broad to pin me down, I pin myself down. Let me give you an example of this. When Mark asked me, not too long ago, the Psalm 101:2 question—"Have you put any unwholesome images before your eyes?"—I could tell him, truthfully, "no." But that wasn't the whole truth. So, I told him the rest of the story.

I told him that I'd borrowed a DVD from a friend that week, who'd handed it over to me with the words: "I can't remember if there's a scene or two in this movie that you'll want to fast-forward through." I deliberately chose not to ask my friend for a further explanation—because I didn't want to hear about junk in the movie that might trouble my conscience enough to keep me from watching it.

Fortunately, there was no junk in the movie. But if there *had* been, I could've justified myself afterwards by saying, "I didn't know *that* was going to be in there." How lame. How deceitful. I ratted on myself to Mark. Even though his original question hadn't nailed me, I nailed myself. Voluntarily.

Don't settle for superficiality with your AP. Ask each other probing questions. Give each other full-disclosure answers. Don't forget that the Lord wants "truth in the inner parts" from us (Ps. 51:6).

5. Prescribe

My first job out of college was as a youth pastor in a quaint New England town. I was recently married at the time. One day I was troubled by something that I'd done. (No more details. I've done enough confessing in this chapter.) I wanted to get it off my chest, to talk about it with somebody. But I didn't want to share it with Sue or with anybody in the church because I was brand new to these relationships.

That's when I was struck by a novel idea. One of my friends in town was a young Catholic priest. We occasionally worked out at the gym together. I could tell him about my wrongdoing. He listened to confessions for a living, right? He'd know exactly what to say to me. So that's what I did. I went and spilled the beans to Father John. And you know what he told me? Not much. He said that my sin was understandable given my circumstances. And he told me to put it out of my mind. That was it.

I was so underwhelmed by that experience. I'd wanted my priestly friend to confirm the sinfulness of my behavior, to lead me in prayer seeking God's forgiveness, and to give me some counsel as to how to avoid a similar transgression in the future. Instead, he gave me a "boys will be boys" and a slap on the back. No help at all.

It's very easy for an AP to become nothing more than a sympathetic ear. Men frequently tell me that, when they confess their sins to their AP, all they get in response is commiseration. The AP says something like: "I hear you, bro. I struggle with the same thing myself." No help at all. No help with the sense of guilt and failure. No help bringing about a desired change.

What do these guys really want from an AP? They want an AP who will confirm their suspicion about the ugliness of their sin and its offense to a holy God. They want an AP who will lead them to God's throne of grace for a thorough cleansing. They want an AP who will give them some suggestions about how to avoid this trap in the future.

I had a friend (not my AP) who repeatedly confessed to me that he struggled with lust at the health club where he worked out. He had a membership at a very upscale gym where young, good-looking women in skimpy outfits exercised. You know what I told him? I told him to go lift weights some place else. "Lust is serious business," I reminded him. "It will fill you with spiritual darkness (Matt. 6:23) and destroy your faithfulness to your wife (Matt. 5:28). Jesus expects you to gouge out your eye if it leads you into lust—in other words, vacate your current health club." That's not a verbatim quote of what I said to this guy—but it's pretty close.

Mark and I have given each other permission to prescribe whatever next steps we feel should be taken when one of us has confessed to some sin. I opened this chapter by relating a time when I watched an indecent video. Mark's prescription on that occasion required that I divulge what I'd done to both Sue and our church's elders. Gulp! That was bitter medicine to swallow. But it was better, in the long run, than if Mark had just listened, assured me of God's forgiveness, and let the matter drop. His prescription stimulated genuine change.

Over the years, we have counseled each other to do some hard things. To apologize. To put together a budget. To serve our wives with a willing spirit. To lose weight. To download responsibility at work. To install a filter on the PC. We're not content with commiseration. We're shooting for transformation.

6. Pray

This last step goes without saying in a book on prayer. But I'll say it anyway. Because it's not unusual for an accountability partnership to become all share and no prayer.

If you frequently close your meetings with, "Well, we've run out of time to pray, but at least we now know what to pray for each other," you need to put a lid on your chitchatting. Every meeting, set a deadline for transitioning from talking to praying.

And take notes when your AP is giving you an update. This is not simply to communicate that what he's sharing is important to you. It will also enable you to pray specifically for him at the close of your meeting and over the following week or two.

I am my brother's keeper.

Onto the Praying Field

1. Do you have an accountability partner (AP) with whom you meet on a regular basis for prayer? If not, what hurdles will

you have to overcome to begin such a relationship? If you have an AP, how would you rate your current quality of interaction?

2. List four areas of personal discipline for which you would like some accountability, and three questions you would like to be regularly asked about each.

3. What would tempt you to be less than truthful with an AP? How could you ensure complete openness and honesty in this relationship?

4. Who would be your best prospects for an AP? Begin to pray about this selection. Review the characteristics that you should be looking for in an AP according to this chapter. Set a deadline for broaching the subject with a candidate.

5. What day(s) and time(s) would work out best for you to meet on a regular basis with an AP?

6. Once you have chosen an AP, have him/her read this chapter and discuss it with you.

7. For what issue do you most need immediate accountability? What specific question would you like your AP to begin asking you to check up on this matter?

14

Satan

Dress for Success

One of my favorite musicals (it's a fairly short list) is *Fiddler on the Roof*. It's the story of Tevya, a Jewish peasant who lives in a small Russian village at the beginning of the twentieth century. Tevya loves to talk to God about the problems in his life—everything from his sick milk cow to the five daughters he must marry off.

And Tevya has a rabbi who is also known for his praying. This religious teacher can rattle off a blessing for any situation in life. On one occasion he's asked: "Rabbi, is there a blessing for the tzar?" He has to think about that one for a moment. How do you pray for a dictator who is cruelly persecuting the religious group that you belong to?

But the rabbi was able to come up with a blessing. "May God bless and keep the tzar—far away from us."[1]

The tzar was the beneficiary of that rabbi's prayer in the same way that Satan can be made the beneficiary of some of our praying. I'm obviously using the word *beneficiary* in a tongue-in-cheek fashion here. This term is usually used to describe an individual who profits (benefits) in a good way from somebody else's action. But quite literally the word simply means, "one who receives." So, I'm going to suggest that it is possible for Satan to be on the receiving end of our prayers. They will definitely impact him. And, in that sense, he will be one of their beneficiaries.

Please don't argue with me theologically or linguistically on this point. You don't have to agree that "beneficiary" is the best label to pin on Satan with respect to our prayers. Just let me stretch this word to make it serve my purpose. The purpose of demonstrating the importance of prayer in our daily battle with the evil one.

This battle is described in Ephesians 6, a passage that I've already mentioned a couple of times. The believer's six-piece armor is pictured here. Have you begun to regularly pray on this protective suit yet? (This is one of the patterns that I recommended back in ch. 3.) If you haven't felt compelled to do this, it may be that you need a fuller explanation of the danger that you're in. A danger that makes the wearing of one's armor an absolute *must*. Let me summarize Paul's counsel in Ephesians 6:10–20 in the form of three warnings.

Don't Be Naïve!

There are several things, in the opening verses of this passage, that Paul cautions us not to be naïve about. The first is *our diabolical enemy*. It's always dangerous to underestimate an adversary. And this adversary is not one to be taken lightly.

But before we unmask this foe, let me remind you that Christ followers face opposition from two other sources as well. We don't want to pin all the blame for the spiritual conflict in our lives on a diabolical enemy. In fact, if we want to get a good look at the most persistent troublemaker we deal with, all we have to do is gaze into a mirror. As Pogo once said in the Sunday comics, "We have met the enemy and he is us."[2] The biblical term for the vexatious *enemy* that Pogo was referring to is "the flesh" (NIV: "the sinful nature"). We are, in our flesh, our own worst spiritual enemies.

Sinning has been our natural inclination for years. It's become an ingrained habit. We do it without thinking. Our inherent propensity is to disobey God. If God's Word says, "Do this" or "Don't do that," our flesh responds: "Nah! I'll just do what I want to do." Most of the spiritual battles in a Christ follower's life will be provoked by his or her own sinful nature.

Now, the good news is that once we surrender our lives to Christ, his Spirit comes to reside in us and to empower us to overcome the tyranny of our flesh. We can rebuff those internal impulses to sin. In the words of an old hymn, Jesus "breaks the power of cancelled sin, he sets the prisoner free."[3] Our sins were cancelled in a judicial sense—forgiven, wiped away—the moment we trusted Christ to save us. But now he wants to break their ongoing power to control us on a daily basis. He wants to break the power of our flesh.

Our second spiritual enemy is the world. The Bible uses this expression to refer to the influences in our social environment that prompt us to leave God's path of righteousness. The world can confront us in the form of peer pressure, or movies, or bosses' expectations, or advertising, or school textbooks. The world promotes values, priorities, and moral standards that are contrary to God's.

Sometimes our flesh and the world join forces—like in tag-team wrestling—to oppose us. For example, my sinful nature loves to covet. I always wants more. Especially more stuff. The world comes along and fans that coveting into flame by providing me with a mailbox full of catalogs, friends who are always buying cool things that I now want, a local mall for my recreational shopping, and ballgames on TV that constantly break for enticing commercials.

Our flesh and the world are formidable allies. Our flesh loves to rage, so the world provides us with violent movies and aggravating motorists. Our flesh loves to lust, so the world provides us with Internet porn sites and immodestly dressed co-workers. Our flesh loves to pig out, so the world provides us with all-you-can-eat buffets and expense accounts that beg to be used.

And if this perilous collaboration between spiritual enemies one and two were not enough, Ephesians 6 tells us that spiritual enemy three is even more dangerous—and lurks around every corner. Paul identifies him as "the devil" (v. 11), admonishing us to put on our armor so that we can take our stand against his schemes. The devil is God's archenemy. If we can believe in an unseen God, it should not be difficult to believe in an invisible devil. Believing in the devil does not make one a superstitious wacko.

C. S. Lewis was a die-hard atheist, teaching at both Cambridge and Oxford in the early twentieth century. When he became convinced of the truth of the Christian faith, he began to express his newfound convictions in writing. The Chronicles of Narnia, a series of children's stories about a Christlike lion named Aslan, endeared Lewis to readers. But his *Screwtape Letters*, another work of fiction, was far edgier.

Lewis created an imaginary correspondence between a senior-level demon, Screwtape, and his bumbling nephew, Wormwood. He mixed great fun with biblical insight. But he made it absolutely clear that evil adversaries do actually exist. Demons are for real! And one of their strategies is to convince us that they aren't. As Screwtape tells Wormwood: "The fact that 'devils' are predominantly comic figures in the modern imagination will help you. If any faint suspicion of our existence begins to arise in his [i.e., the victim's] mind, suggest to him a picture of something in red tights, and persuade him that since he can't believe in that (it's an old textbook method of confusing them), he therefore cannot believe in us."[4]

Do you believe in the devil and his cohorts? The Bible never pictures him with horns, pitchfork, and red outfit. We're told, rather, that he was once one of God's angels. That makes him a created being, and in no way (thankfully) equal in power to God. Motivated by pride, the devil challenged God for his job, lost the contest, and was banished from heaven. (For an Old Testament recap of these events, check out Isa. 14:12–15 and Ezek. 28:11–19, where a description of the rise and fall of the kings of Babylon and Tyre point to the bigger story of Satan.)

We must not be naïve to the schemes of this diabolical enemy, the apostle Paul warns us. And then he sounds an even more ominous note by pointing out that our wicked foe has an army of accomplices: "Our struggle is not against flesh and blood, but against the rulers, against the authorities, against the powers of this dark world and against the spiritual forces of evil in the heavenly realms" (Eph. 6:12). Some commentators go into great detail about the distinctions between these four categories of demons. But the Bible, in fact, does not give us enough information to distinguish these groups from each other.

Paul's point, in using four designations for demons, seems to be simply to underscore his warning that we face a fearsome enemy. Only a fool would take the devil and company lightly. They are a tremendous force for evil. People who go through their day without a thought for an unseen adversary are perilously naïve.

What is our diabolical enemy up to in our lives? What does he hope to accomplish? Well, if you are a Christ follower, he has already lost the biggest battle—the one to hold your soul captive to sin and death and hell. But that does not mean that he has conceded the overall war. From this point on, his goal is to drive a wedge between you and your Savior. He wants to do as much damage to this relationship as possible and to sabotage your effectiveness in service to Christ.

There are a number of ways in which he can accomplish these purposes. He tempts you into sin (working hand in hand with your flesh and the world), so as to undo the work of God's Spirit who is persistently conforming you to Christ's image (Rom. 8:29). He keeps you from spending time in Scripture, which is your source of spiritual nourishment and knowledge of God (Ps. 1:2–3; 2 Tim. 3:15–17). He muzzles your witness, so that others will not hear the good news of Jesus from you. He diverts your time, energy, and resources into temporal pursuits instead of into Christ-focused ministry. Paul doesn't want us to be naïve about this relentless, diabolical enemy.

Here's a second thing that Paul doesn't want us to be unaware of: *our personal weakness.* He opens this passage about spiritual armor by exhorting us to "be strong in the Lord and in his mighty power" (Eph. 6:10). God's power, in contrast to our weakness, has been a repeated theme throughout this New Testament epistle.

Paul reminds us, again and again, that the Christian life is not difficult—it's impossible! There is no way that we can live it in our own strength. We have got to learn how to tap into God's power.

Consider these previous references to that power: "I pray also that the eyes of your heart may be enlightened in order that you may know . . . his incomparably great power for us who believe" (Eph. 1:18–19); "I pray that out of his glorious riches he may strengthen you with power through his Spirit in your inner being" (Eph. 3:16); "Now to him who is able to do immeasurably more than all we ask or imagine, according to his power that is at work within us" (Eph. 3:20). We get the message! But, just in case we've missed it, Paul wraps up this letter with: "Finally, be strong in the Lord and in his mighty power" (Eph. 6:10).

Friends, we mustn't think for a single minute that we can handle a diabolical enemy in our own strength. We will lose every battle if we do not learn how to appropriate the power of God.

Our naïveté in this regard reminds me of a funny story that my friend Eric has told me about his college baseball days. Eric played ball for a small college. There were barely enough guys on the team to cover all the positions. One day their schedule had them matched up against a much bigger school that had invested a good deal of money and manpower in its baseball program. They showed up with three squads of twenty players each. All of them wore beautiful uniforms and cocky smiles. Their winning record was intimidating.

Amazingly, as the game entered the ninth inning, Eric's team was in the lead. One out. Two outs. The next batter hit a pop ball to the third base side. Eric, the third basemen, moved under it. But his catcher also chased down the ball. A fraction of a second after the ball plopped into Eric's mitt, the catcher ran into him like a truckload of bricks. To everyone's astonishment, Eric held on to the third out. Game over.

But the collision had been jolting. So jolting that Eric was later treated for a concussion at the local hospital. So jolting that, when Eric first struggled to his feet, he did something rather foolish. He taunted the opposing team. He was only a few yards from their dugout, and all sixty of them had begun screaming profanities at him when he'd come up with the ball. So Eric—in his stupor—decided to take them on. With all the sense knocked out of him, he headed for their bench. With blurred vision, on wobbly legs. "You wanna piece of me?" he called out.

Fortunately, Eric's teammates got to him before the opposing players did. They wrestled him to the ground and then dragged him away. "Those guys saved my life," Eric concluded his story with a big grin on his face. From the sound of it, they probably did.

Paul doesn't want any of us to be so daft as to think that we can take on the devil—along with rulers, authorities, powers of this dark world, and spiritual forces of evil in the heavenly realms—in our own strength. We can't afford to be naïve about our diabolical enemy, or about our own weakness. Or third, about *our coming crisis*.

When Ephesians 6:13 instructs us to put on the full armor of God, it is so we will be able to stand our ground "when the day of evil comes." What is this "day of evil" that Paul refers to here? Bible scholars tell us that Paul probably did not have in mind some worldwide, cataclysmic, eschatological event. The day of evil that's coming our way will be just an ordinary day when Satan will strike us with extraordinary force. He'll make his temptations extra tempting, his discouragements extra discouraging. He'll catch us when we are most vulnerable.

Satan is getting ready to attack us. Are we getting ready to repel him? Paul mentions his "schemes" (v. 11). He's sneaky. He knows when and where we are most susceptible. What would it take for him to bring you down? A little more alcohol than you're drinking now? A serious health problem? A conflict that goes unresolved in your marriage? A personal achievement that leads to pride?

Your day of evil will come. As a matter of fact, you'd best think in terms of days—plural. Because Satan won't limit his assaults to one twenty-four-hour period. He'll come after you again and again. Don't be naïve to your diabolical enemy, or your own weakness, or your coming crisis.

Don't Be Naked

Remember the children's fable about the emperor with no clothes? Once upon a time there was a very egotistical king who asked his personal tailor to create a new outfit for him. The king wanted to look good for an upcoming royal parade. The tailor was more than a little bit flustered by this request. He knew that he'd better come up with something impressive for the king to wear, or he himself might be wearing a noose around his neck. But day after day his mind drew a blank.

The morning of the big parade, he had nothing to show the king. Nothing. That's when the idea struck him: *Why not show the king nothing—and tell him that it was something?* So he informed the king that he had designed a magnificent suit of invisible clothes. He appealed to the king's vanity, stating that these were the only invisible clothes in the whole realm. And the king, who was a sucker for flattery, bought the story. He eagerly put on his new outfit and strutted down Castle Street at the head of the parade. He assumed that everyone was staring at his latest threads—but they were actually staring at a whole lot more! (He thought he was cool. But they wondered if he was cold.)

What does this fable have to do with Ephesians 6? Maybe you've already guessed. I'd like to make the observation that we often prance through our day spiritually naked while we imagine ourselves to be fully clothed. And that's because we don't take the time to put on the armor, which God intends for us to wear (see vv. 14–17 for a detailed description of that armor).

How do we don this outfit? I gave you instructions for doing so (see ch. 3) when I recommended the use of several patterns that are helpful in launching us into prayer. Borrowing words from the hymn, "Stand Up, Stand Up for Jesus," I encouraged you to: "Put on the gospel armor; each piece put on with prayer." At the beginning of every day, deliberately pray on each of the six pieces of armor that Paul mentions.

Let's briefly review those pieces (it would be a good idea to memorize them), and elaborate on what is meant by each. The belt of truth tops the list. Truth matters a great deal to God. It's one of his divine attributes. Scripture even calls him "the God of truth" (Isa. 65:16). And Jesus, God's Son, identifies himself as "the way and the truth and the life" (John 14:6).

God wants our lives to be marked by truthfulness. Conversely, he hates deceit of any kind. Commandment nine on God's list of top ten moral imperatives prohibits lying (Ex. 20:16). When the writer of Proverbs tells us that there are seven things that the Lord absolutely detests, two of them have to do with dishonesty: "a lying tongue" and "a false witness who pours out lies" (Prov. 6:16–19).

Lies come in all shapes and sizes. We can be guilty of dishonesty even if we haven't told a huge whopper. There's the little lie that gets us out of trouble. The exaggeration used to make a point. The flattery we dish out so that others will like us. Those are all lies. Have you ever shown up late for work, announcing: "The traffic was terrible!" Maybe the traffic *was* terrible—but the real reason for your tardiness was the fact that you overslept and didn't get started on time. Your half-truth was a lie.

We don't even have to open our mouths to practice dishonesty. The guy who waits for the rest of the family to go to bed so that he can sneak onto the Internet and view pornography is living a lie. So is the woman who discreetly slips her new clothing purchases into her closet without telling her husband about this latest splurge. So is the high school student who turns in test answers or an essay that isn't entirely his or her work.

When we pray on the belt of truth, we begin by confessing to God every word or act of deceit from the previous twenty-four hours. And then we ask him to make us ruthlessly honest—so that we will speak only what is completely true, and behave in private as the people we appear to be in public.

The breastplate of righteousness is the second piece of armor on Paul's list. Keep in mind that our standard of righteousness is the character of Christ. So praying on the breastplate of righteousness entails asking God to make me more like Jesus (and acknowledging where I'm most obviously falling short). A brief checklist of Christlike characteristics is that "fruit of the Spirit" inventory in Galatians

5:22–23: "love, joy, peace, patience, kindness, goodness, faithfulness, gentleness and self-control."

Let me warn you that God may not answer this prayer in the way that you expect him to. I used to think that getting a fresh infusion of Christ's righteousness in my life was like taking my car in for an oil change. They drain out all the black cruddy stuff and then refill the crankcase from a hose that's connected to an unlimited supply of Quaker State's best 10W–40. Then away I go!

In the same way, when my life is lacking in love, let's say, I just ask God for Christ's love, and then imagine him inserting his divine hose into my heart and turning on the flow. I expect to walk away from such a prayer with a fresh compassion for everyone I encounter—a desire to give each of them a hug. Instead, the very next person I run into is a demanding wife (this is just a hypothetical illustration), or a disgruntled employee, or a rude salesclerk, or an overly vigilant traffic cop. I feel like slugging, not hugging. What happened to that love-of-Christ infusion?

The fact is: God never seems to answer my prayer for Christ's righteousness by pouring it into me like the folks at Jiffy Lube pour fresh oil into my car. Instead, his response comes in the form of a challenge. If I pray for Christ's love, he sends me someone who's difficult to even like. If I pray for Christ's faithfulness, he puts me in an impossible situation that makes me want to quit. If I pray for Christ's patience, he gives me traffic jams, mile-long checkout lines, and the Chicago Cubs.

Don't get me wrong. It's still God who must supply me with whatever aspect of Christ's righteousness I've requested. I can't work it up on my own. But his provision doesn't seem to alleviate my need to struggle. Paul expressed this same balance in his epistle to the Philippians, saying "it is God who works in you to will and to act according to his good purpose"—immediately after challenging them to "work out your salvation [i.e., growth in righteousness] "with fear and trembling" (Phil. 2:12–13).

God works *in* as we work *out*. He supplies as we struggle. Don't forget that as you pray on the breastplate of righteousness.

The gospel shoes must be put on next. Paul requires that our feet be "fitted with the readiness that comes from the gospel of peace" (Eph. 6:15). The gospel of peace is the good news that peace with God—forgiveness and reconciliation—has been made possible through Christ's sacrifice upon the cross (see Rom. 5:1 and Col. 1:20). Once we have prayed on our gospel shoes, we are ready to take this message to others. We are prepared to run into, rather the away from, opportunities to talk about our Savior.

Lon Allison and Mark Anderson, in their book *Going Public with the Gospel,* cite surveys which show that only one Christ follower in twenty actually shares his or her faith with others. "How is this possible?" the authors ask incredulously. "These people are living a life in disobedience to the commands of Jesus. They demonstrate with their self-centered lifestyle that they are not loving their lost neighbors. . . . If anyone knows that his or her friends, coworkers and relatives are lost and on their way to hell but refuses to share with them the truth that could change their eternal destiny, he or she may not be a Christian."[5]

Those are strong words! If it's been a very, very long time (if ever) since you have explained to someone how to experience peace with God, do you know what is holding you back? Maybe you have attributed your reluctance to share the good news to a lack of opportunities, boldness, articulateness, or heartfelt desire. But what's behind these deficiencies? Prayerlessness. You haven't been praying on the armor of gospel shoes, and so your enemy has been defeating you in this matter.

It's quite possible that you are so defeated when it comes to introducing others to Christ that you no longer care (or realize) that you are defeated. Sharing the gospel is a nonissue to you. That's defeated. But, if it's any consolation to you, even the great apostle Paul—who spread the good news of Jesus Christ all across the first-century world—confessed his need for more courage and initiative to carry out his mission. Paul had to pray on his gospel shoes every day. And he asked his friends to intercede for him along these same lines.

How does one pray on the gospel shoes? This would be a good time to review the three-open prayer (see ch. 10). We must pray for open doors (opportunities to talk about spiritual matters), open mouths (boldness to interject Christ into these conversations), and open hearts (a responsiveness to what we say).

Now we are ready to pick up the shield of faith, our fourth piece of armor. The faith that Paul is referring to here is not saving faith. It's not the initial faith that we place in Christ when we ask him to forgive our sins and give us eternal life. The faith that Paul has in mind here is an ongoing confidence in God. Satan attempts to undermine this assurance by shooting flaming arrows at us (Eph. 6:16).

What are these flaming arrows that can set us ablaze if we're not protected by our shield of faith? Difficult circumstances. Seemingly unanswered prayers. Unfair criticism. Physical fatigue or illness. Loneliness. Generic discouragement. Relational conflicts. These kinds of things take aim at our faith-inspired optimism. They call into question God's concern for us. Does he really care? Is he paying attention to what's going on in our lives?

We must identify each flaming arrow in order to prayerfully extinguish it with our shield of faith. Once we have put our finger on what's troubling us, we can talk to God about it. We can ask for protection, or wisdom, or perseverance, or joy, or a thicker skin, or healing, or a friend, or whatever it is we need. Of course, what we need most is a confident faith in God.

Sometimes, as I'm praying for a shield of faith, I imagine God handing it to me but my arm being too weak to hold it up. What good is this shield if I don't have the strength to lift it? So I pray for that as well. I ask God to invigorate me so that I can raise my shield to stop Satan's arrows.

Two pieces of armor to go. Let's put on our headgear: the helmet of salvation. "Salvation" is such a broadly inclusive word. When we first prayed, "Dear Jesus, I surrender my life to you as Savior and Lord," God poured out more blessings upon our lives than we could ever comprehend. Our sins were forgiven. We were adopted into God's family. Our eternal destiny was secured in heaven. The Holy Spirit came to dwell in us. We were endowed with spiritual gifts—supernatural abilities. We gained access to God in prayer. The list goes on and on. All of these blessings fall under the heading, "salvation."

So, what does it mean to put on the helmet of salvation? Well, what does a helmet protect? A person's head, right? His or her mind, thoughts, attitudes. When I pray on the helmet of salvation, I am asking God to turn my attention away from what it has been stuck on and to refocus it on my spiritual blessings.

What have I been thinking about? Have I been mentally preoccupied with resentment toward someone who's offended me, or with a desire for a caramel frappuccino, or with a problem at work, or with my son's misbehavior, or with my vacation plans, or with my need to get the lawn mowed before it rains?

Not all of these musings are bad. Some are quite necessary. But they are not the thoughts that God wants to dominate my mind. Paul wrote to the Colossians: "Since, then, you have been raised with Christ, . . . Set your minds on things above, not on earthly things" (Col. 3:1–2). That's just another way of saying (as I understand it), "Put on the helmet of salvation."

And, practically speaking, the way that I do this is by deliberately reciting some of those blessings that are associated with my salvation. I pray (right out loud): "Lord, you've forgiven my sins—putting them as far from me as the east is from the west. I am now your son, and there is an eternal inheritance waiting for me in heaven. Your Spirit is living in me as my Counselor, Perfecter, Intercessor, Teacher. You have given me a mission, a purpose for living." By the time I'm done reviewing my salvation's benefits package, I have a whole new perspective on life. My helmet is in place, protecting what's going on in my head.

Paul does not leave us wondering what he means by the sixth and final piece of armor: the sword of the Spirit. He comes right out and tells us that this is *the word of God* (Eph. 6:17). When I initially saw the word *sword*, I immediately imagined the sort of broadsword that would be used by a knight in a King Arthur movie. I pictured it to be long and heavy. A bit difficult to wield, but it could knock your enemy into the next time zone if you were lucky enough to connect with it.

But, according to historians, the Roman soldier's sword was rather short. And he didn't swing it like Bobby Bonds swings a baseball bat. He controlled it dexterously in close, hand-to-hand combat. The key to this sword's effectiveness was the skill of the soldier who used it.

To arm oneself with the sword of the Spirit is to become skillful in the handling of God's Word. (See 2 Tim. 2:15.) Do you read Scripture daily? I was watching the DVDs of a Christian leadership conference recently—the biggest conference of its type in the country, and one that is broadcast around the world. To my dismay, the host of this conference recommended that his listeners might want to make Bible reading a regular habit. Why would I be dismayed by such great advice? Because he felt it was necessary to say this to a gathering of *leaders.* Shouldn't Bible reading be a given for these folks?

God's Word is the only offensive weapon in a Christ follower's armor. We can't expect to achieve spiritual victories if we aren't capable of using it well. That means reading it daily—following some sort of a systematic schedule. That means memorizing key portions of it. That means keeping a journal in which we write down personal applications for the insights we have gleaned. That means praying as we walk through each step above.

Six pieces of armor. Are we wearing them, or running around naked? Each piece gets put on with prayer.

Don't Be Napping

It doesn't take a Bible scholar to figure out Paul's major emphasis as he closes the passage. Take a pen and circle the words *pray, prayers,* and *praying* in Ephesians 18–20.

And PRAY in the Spirit on all occasions with all kinds of PRAYERS and requests. With this in mind, be alert and always

243

> keep on PRAYING for all the saints. PRAY also for me. . . . PRAY
> that I may declare it [the gospel] fearlessly, as I should.

Paul mentions prayer five times in three verses. And, if that's not enough to drive home his theme, look at how often he uses the word *all* or *always* in verse 18. Four times! Paul is not only encouraging us to pray, he's exhorting us to do a lot of it. This is the key to overcoming our enemy.

And Satan knows it. Remember, "Satan trembles, when he sees the weakest Christian on his knees"? The devil has no desire to be a beneficiary of our prayers. He will do everything possible to keep us from praying. His best strategy, to our shame, seems to be the inciting of drowsiness whenever he catches us in the mood for prayer. Here's another old adage: "Satan is never too busy to rock the cradle of a sleeping Christian." Our enemy induces napping when we should be praying.

Remember what Jesus was doing just hours before his crucifixion? He took his disciples to one of their favorite outdoor hangouts: the garden of Gethsemane. He explained to them that they were about to engage in a fierce spiritual conflict. He warned them to pray, or else. Then he moved off for some privacy and started praying himself.

What did the disciples do? Did they pray? No, they napped. Three times Jesus returned to these guys and found them asleep (see Matt. 26:36–46). Each time he warned them that if they didn't start praying they'd be woefully unprepared for what was ahead. He used that line on them that we still use today to rouse ourselves ("the spirit is willing, but the body is weak"), admitting that the best of our intentions are worthless if we don't back them up with actions. But they continued to nap.

Then the soldiers came to arrest Jesus. And the disciples weren't ready. Peter is a prime example of how someone behaves who is not prayed up when everything hits the fan. First, he wildly hacked off a guy's ear with his sword (*not* the sword of the Spirit). Then, he ran for his life. Finally, he disowned his best friend.

All of Peter's buddies also performed like losers. Which brings to mind a favorite saying of my kids: "You snooze, you lose." Now, in our house this means that the last piece of pizza will be gone if you don't grab it right away. But, with respect to the disciples, it meant that napping instead of praying resulted in them being totally defeated. *You snooze, you lose.*

This is serious business. A wiser Peter later wrote that our diabolical enemy "prowls around like a roaring lion looking for someone to devour" (1 Pet. 5:8). Prayerlessness is a dangerous condition. If we want to experience spiritual victories we must wake up and start praying. Today! Go back through this book a second and a third time. Study it with a small group. Pick out some things to put into practice.

I recently read an article about Jerry Jenkins, coauthor of the *Left Behind*[6] series. Jerry has written over 150 books, many of them biographies of famous people. Several years ago, he helped Billy Graham compile his memoirs. During that process, he asked the renowned evangelist, "What's the secret of your success?" Graham gave him two responses: daily Bible study and constant prayer.

Jerry pressed for a further description of this second ingredient. "I know that Scripture says to pray constantly," he countered, "but that's just figurative language. Nobody can actually *do* that." Dr. Graham quietly replied: "I'm doing it right now. I've been praying throughout this conversation."

What has made Billy Graham such a tremendous man of God? Prayer. Why has he been able to redirect the eternal destinies of so many people by introducing them to Christ? Prayer. How has he been able to maintain a life of such moral integrity when other leaders have fallen? Prayer.

Prayer. It's time to stop talking about it and to start doing it.

Onto the Praying Field

1. Do you tend to underestimate or overestimate your spiritual enemy? Explain.

2. In what ways is your flesh most likely to assert itself? What influences of the world (peer pressure, entertainment, boss' expectations, advertising, etc.) are you most susceptible to?

3. How does Satan most effectively undermine you? (Review the chapter for a description of his tactics.) If you were Satan, how would you attack you?

4. Describe your last "day of evil"—a time when all hell seemed to break loose in your life. How could you have been better prepared to face it?

5. Carefully review what this chapter has to say about the six pieces of spiritual armor in Ephesians 6. Now pray that armor on—one piece at a time.

6. As you conclude this book on prayer, how are you doing? Are you praying more often and more effectively?

   What have been your three or four best takeaways from this study?

   What insights do you still need to put into practice?

A to Z List of Biblical Names, Titles, and Attributes of God the Father, Son, and Holy Spirit

A

able (Dan. 3:17; Matt. 9:28; Rom.
    16:25; 2 Cor. 9:8; Eph. 3:20;
    2 Tim. 1:12; Heb. 7:25)
abounding in love and faithfulness
    (Ex. 34:6)
Adam, the last (1 Cor. 15:45)
advocate (Job 16:19; 1 John 2:1)
all (Col. 3:11)
Almighty, the (Job 5:17)
Alpha (Rev. 1:8; 21:6)
Amen, the (Rev. 3:14)
Ancient of Days (Dan. 7:22)
Anointed One (Ps. 2:2; Acts 4:27)
apostle and high priest (Heb. 3:1)
architect and builder (Heb. 11:10)
atoning sacrifice (1 John 2:2)
author and perfecter of our faith (Heb.
    12:2)
avenger (2 Sam. 22:48; Ps. 94:1)
awesome (Ex. 15:11; Neh. 1:5; Dan.
    9:4)

B

baby (Luke 2:16)
banner for the peoples (Isa. 11:10)
beauty (Ps. 27:4; Isa. 33:17)
Beginning, the (Rev. 21:6)
Branch of the Lord (Isa. 4:2)
Bread of Life (John 6:35)
breath of the Almighty (Job 32:8; 33:4)
bridegroom (Matt. 9:15)
bright, Morning Star (Rev. 22:16)
brightness (Ps. 18:12)
brother (Heb. 2:11)
brother of James, Joseph, Judas, and
    Simon (Mark 6:3)

C

carpenter (Mark 6:3)
Chosen One (Luke 23:35)
Christ, the (Matt. 16:16)
comforter (2 Cor. 1:4)
commander of the Lord's army (Josh.
    5:15)

compassionate (Ps. 103:8)
confidence (Ps. 71:5)
consolation of Israel (Luke 2:25)
Counselor, Wonderful (Isa. 9:6)
covenant for the people (Isa. 42:6)
Creator of the ends of the earth (Isa. 40:28)
crown, glorious (Isa. 28:5; 62:3)

D

defender (Ps. 68:5)
deliverer (2 Sam. 22:2; Ps. 18:2)
desired of all nations (Hag. 2:7)
despised by men (Isa. 53:3)
diadem, a royal (Isa. 28:5; 62:3)
dwelling place (Ps. 90:1)

E

eagle that leads his people (Deut. 32:11)
End, the (Rev. 21:6)
eternal life (John 11:25; 17:3)
Everlasting Father (Isa. 9:6)
everlasting to everlasting (Neh. 9:5)
exalted (Ex. 15:1; Job 36:22; Isa. 6:1)

F

Faithful and True (Rev. 19:11)
familiar with suffering (Isa. 53:3)
Father (Matt. 11:25)
father of the fatherless (Ps. 68:5)
Fear of Isaac (Gen. 31:42)
fire, a consuming (Deut. 4:24)
First, the (Isa. 44:6; Rev. 22:13)
firstborn among many brothers (Rom. 8:29)
fortress (Pss. 18:2; 91:2)
foundation (1 Cor. 3:11)
fountain of life (Pss. 36:9; 87:7)
friend (Job 16:20)
friend of tax collectors and sinners (Matt. 11:19)

G

gardener (John 15:1)
gate for the sheep (John 10:7)

gift, indescribable (2 Cor. 9:15)
giver (James 1:17)
Glory (Ps. 106:20; Jer. 2:11)
GOD
    Most High (Gen. 14:18)
    of Abraham, Isaac, and Jacob (Ex. 3:16)
    of all comfort (2 Cor. 1:3)
    of all the kingdoms of the earth (2 Kings 19:15)
    of gods (Deut. 10:17)
    of heaven and earth (Ezra 5:11)
    of our fathers (Deut. 26:7)
    of peace (Rom. 16:20; 1 Thess. 5:23)
    who does wonders (Ps. 77:14)
    who sees (Gen. 16:13)
gracious (Isa. 30:18; Neh. 9:17)
guarantee (2 Cor. 1:22; 5:5; Heb. 7:22)
guide (Ps. 48:14)

H

he who turns blackness into dawn (Amos 5:8)
head of the body, the church (Col. 1:18)
head over every power and authority (Col. 2:10)
heart-searcher (Rom. 8:27; Rev. 2:23)
heir of all things (Heb. 1:2)
help in trouble, an ever present (Ps. 46:1; Heb. 13:6)
help of the fatherless (Ps. 10:14)
hiding place (Ps. 32:7)
high priest, a merciful and faithful (Heb. 2:17)
him who is able to keep you from falling (Jude 24)
him who is able to present you before his glorious presence without fault and with great joy (Jude 24)
holiness, our (1 Cor. 1:30)
holy (Lev. 11:44; Josh. 24:19; 1 Sam. 2:2; Isa. 6:3; Rev. 4:8)
Holy One (Isa. 43:15; Luke 1:35; 1 John 2:20)

Holy Spirit (Ps. 51:11; John 14:26)
home (Pss. 84:3–4; 90:1)
hope (Ps. 71:5)
horn of my salvation (2 Sam. 22:3; Ps. 18:2)
husband, my (Isa. 54:5; Jer. 3:14; Hos. 2:16; 2 Cor. 11:2)

I

I Am (Ex. 3:14; John 8:58)
Immanuel, God with us (Matt. 1:23)
immortal (1 Tim. 1:17)
inheritance, their (Ezek. 44:28)
intercessor, my (Job 16:20; Isa. 53:12; Rom. 8:26)
invisible (1 Tim. 1:17)

J

Jealous (Ex. 34:14)
Jesus (Matt. 1:21)
Judge of the earth (Ps. 94:2; 2 Cor. 5:10; 2 Tim.4:8)
just (Deut. 32:4)
justifier (Rom. 3:26)

K

keeper (Ps. 121:7; cf. also John 10:29)
key-holder (Rev. 1:18)
kind, kindness (Isa. 54:8; Luke 6:35; Eph. 2:7)
King (Pss. 24:7; 44:4; 47:7; 74:12; 95:3; Jer. 10:10; Dan. 4:37)
kinsman-redeemer (Ruth 3:9)
knowing (Psalm 139)

L

Lamb of God (John 1:29)
lamp, my (2 Sam. 22:29)
Last, the (Isa. 44:6; Rev. 22:13)
Lawgiver (James 4:12)
leader (Isa. 55:4)
life eternal (1 John 5:20)
life, our (Col. 3:4)
light of the world (John 8:12; 1 John 1:5)
lily of the valleys (Song 2:1)

Lion of the tribe of Judah (Rev. 5:5)
living water (John 7:38)
longsuffering (Jer. 15:5)
Lord (Luke 2:11)
Lord, Most High (Ps. 7:17)
Lord of Lords (Rev. 19:16)
love (1 John 4:8)
lover (John 3:16)

M

magnificent (Isa. 28:29)
Majestic Glory (2 Pet. 1:17)
majestic in power, holiness (Ex. 15:6, 11)
Majesty on high (Heb. 1:3)
Maker of all things (Jer. 10:16)
Maker of heaven and earth (Ps. 146:6)
man (Acts 2:22)
Man of Sorrows (Isa. 53:3)
manna (John 6:49–50)
Master (Luke 5:5; 2 Tim. 2:21)
mediator (1 Tim. 2:5)
merciful (Heb. 2:17)
Messiah (John 1:41)
Mighty God (Isa. 9:6)
Morning Star (2 Pet. 1:19; Rev. 22:16)

N

name above all names (Phil. 2: 9–10)
Nazarene (Matt. 2:23)
need meeter (Phil. 4:19)

O

obedient son (Luke 2:51; Phil. 2:8; Heb. 5:8)
offering (Rom. 8:3)
offering and sacrifice to God (Eph. 5:20)
Omega (Rev. 1:8)
one and only Son (John 1:14; 3:16)
one greater than Solomon (Matt. 12:42)
owner (2 Cor. 1:22)

P

pardoner (Mic. 7:18)
Passover Lamb (1 Cor. 5:7)

249

pasture (Jer. 50:7)

patient (2 Pet. 3:9; Rom. 9:22)

peace, our (Eph. 2:14)

perfecter (Heb. 12:2)

physician (Luke 4:23)

portion, my (Ps. 119:57)

possession, their (Ezek. 44:28)

potter (Isa. 64:8; Rom. 9:21)

power of God (1 Cor. 1:24)

praise of Israel (Ps. 22:3)

priest forever (Heb. 5:6)

Prince and Savior (Acts 5:31)

Prince of Peace (Isa. 9:6)

promise, the Father of (Acts 1:4)

Prophet, the (John 7:40)

purifier (Mal. 3:3)

Q

quieter (Ps. 23:2; Zeph. 3:17)

R

Rabbi (John 3:2)

Rabboni (John 20:16)

radiance of God's glory (Heb. 1:3)

ransom for all (1 Tim. 2:6)

reaper (Rev. 14:15)

reason for our hope (1 Pet. 3:15)

Redeemer, my (Job 19:25; Ps. 19:14)

refiner (Mal. 3:3)

refuge and strength (Ps. 46:1)

refuge from the storm (Ps. 9:9; Isa. 25:4)

resting place (Jer. 50:6)

restorer (Ps. 51:12; Lam. 5:21; 1 Pet. 5:10)

resurrection and the life (John 11:25)

revealer of mysteries (Dan. 2:29)

reward, your very great (Gen. 15:1)

righteousness, our (Jer. 23:6; 1 Cor. 1:30)

Rock of my salvation (Ps. 89:26)

rock of offense (1 Pet. 2:8)

Root and the Offspring of David (Rev. 22:16)

rose of Sharon (Song 2:1)

ruler over the kings of the earth (Rev. 1:5)

S

sacrifice (Eph. 5:2)

salvation, my (Ex. 15:2; Ps. 27:1)

sanctuary (Isa. 8:14)

Savior (John 4:42; Acts 13:23; 1 Tim. 4:9)

scepter (Num. 24:17)

seal (Eph. 1:13)

seeker (Ps. 119:176; Luke 15:4; 19:10)

servant, holy (Isa. 53:11; Acts 4:27)

shade (Ps. 121:5)

shelter (Pss. 31:20; 61:4; 91:1)

Shepherd and Overseer of your souls (1 Pet. 2:25)

Shepherd of the sheep (John 10:11; Heb. 13:20)

shield for me (Ps. 3:3)

Son of God (John 1:49; 1 John 4:9)

Son of Man (Matt. 12:40; 24:27)

song, my (Ps. 118:14)

sovereign Lord (Hab. 3:19; Luke 2:29)

sower (Matt. 13:3)

Spirit of

grace (Heb. 10:29)

holiness (Rom. 1:4)

life (Rom. 8:2)

truth (John 14:17; 15:26)

wisdom and understanding (Isa. 11:2)

spring of living water (Jer. 2:13)

star (Num. 24:17)

stone, a living (1 Pet. 2:4)

stone that the builder rejected (1 Pet. 2:7)

strength (Pss. 18:1; 28:7; 46:1; 73:26)

stronghold, my (2 Sam. 22:3; Pss. 9:9; 27:1; 43:2)

sun (Luke 1:78; Ps. 84:11)

support, my (2 Sam. 22:19; Ps. 18:18)

sustainer (Ps. 55:22; Isa. 46:4)

sword, glorious (Deut. 33:29)

T

teacher (Mark 9:17; John 3:2)

thirst quencher (John 4:13–14)

tower from the enemy (Ps. 61:3)

trap and snare (Isa. 8:14)
treasure (2 Cor. 4:7; Col. 2:3)
truth, the (John 14:6)

U
unchanging (James 1:17)
unique son of God (John 3:16)

V
victor (Ps. 45:4; 1 Cor. 15:54)
vindicator (Ps. 24:5)
Vine, the (John 15:5)
voice of the Lord (Ps. 29:3)

W
warrior (Ex. 15:3)
waters, gently flowing (Isa. 8:6)
way, the (John 14:6)
wisdom from God (1 Cor. 1:30)

witness to the people (Job 16:19; Isa.
55:4; Rev. 3:14)
Wonderful (Isa. 9:6)
Word of God (Rev. 19:13)
Word of Life (1 John 1:1)
worthy (Heb. 3:3; Rev. 5:12)

X
xalted (Ex. 15:1; Job 36:22; Isa. 6:1)

Y
Yahweh. see I Am (Exodus 3)

Z
zealous (Ezek. 39:25)
Zion's King (Pss. 2:6; 9:11)

Notes

Chapter 1: Obstacles: Fail to Plan, Plan to Fail

1. George Duffield Jr., "Stand up, Stand up, for Jesus," 1858. Music by George J. Webb, 1837.

Chapter 2: More Obstacles: Can You Hear Me Now, Lord?

1. Rory Noland, "Holy Spirit Take Control" (S. Barrington, IL: Ever Devoted Music, 1984).

Chapter 3: Patterns: Get into a Rut

1. John Goldingay, *Walk On: Life, Loss, Trust, and Other Realities*, rev. ed. (Grand Rapids: Baker Academic, 2002), 97.

Chapter 4: Promptings: Pray When the Spirit Says Pray

1. Bill Thrasher, *A Journey to Victorious Praying: Finding Discipline and Delight in Your Prayer Life* (Chicago: Moody, 2003). Bill has overseen the Master's Program in Spiritual Formation and Discipleship at Moody since 1990.

2. William Cowper, "What various hindrances we meet." See entire poem at Fire and Ice: Puritan and Reformed Writings, http://www.puritansermons.com/poetry/cowper7.htm.

Chapter 5: Passion: Say It Like You Mean It

1. Bill Gothard, *The Power of Crying Out: When Prayer Becomes Mighty* (Sisters, OR: Multnomah, 2002).

2. Steve Blow, "Gunman Faces Off with Prayer's Power," *Dallas Morning News*, October 28, 2001.

3. C. H. Spurgeon, *Morning and Evening*.

4. Gothard, *Power of Crying Out*, 13.

5. Ibid., 60–61.

Chapter 6: Confess: Pull Sin up by the Roots

1. Mark McMinn, *Why Sin Matters: The Surprising Relationship Between Our Sin and God's Grace* (Wheaton, IL: Tyndale, 2004), 20.

2. C. S. Lewis, *The Screwtape Letters* (Old Tappan, NJ: Fleming H. Revell, 1976), 67.

3. Robert Lowrey, "Nothing but the Blood of Jesus," 1876.

4. Elvina M. Hall, "Jesus Paid It All," 1865. Music by John T. Grape.

Chapter 7: Honor: Enter His Courts with Praise

1. Stephen Arterburn and Fred Stoeker, *Every Man's Battle: Winning the War on Sexual Purity One Victory at a Time* (Colorado Springs: Waterbrook, 2000).

2. David McCullough, *John Adams* (New York: Simon & Schuster, 2001), 327.

3. C. S. Lewis, *Reflections on the Psalms* (New York: Harcourt Brace, 1958), 94–95.

Chapter 8: Ask: Value the Relationship over the Request

1. George MacDonald, "The Word of Jesus on Prayer," in *Unspoken Sermons Second Series* (London: Longmans, Green, 1885). Accessed at Christian Classics Etheral Library, http://www.ccel.org/ccel/macdonald/unspoken2.v.html.

2. Larry J. Crabb, *The Papa Prayer: The Prayer You've Never Prayed* (Nashville: Integrity, 2006).

Chapter 9: Thank: Practice "Thank-You" Therapy

1. Don Baker, *Thank-You Therapy* (Wheaton, IL: Victor Books, 1989).

Chapter 10: Unbelievers: Open a Door, Your Mouth, and a Heart

1. Sesame Street Beetles, "Letter B," lyrics by Christopher Chef, on *Songs from the Street: 35 Years of Music* (Sony Wonder, 2003).

2. Ron Hutchcraft, *Called to Greatness: Becoming a Lifeline for Those Who Need Hope* (Chicago: Moody, 2001).

3. Randy Newman, *Questioning Evangelism: Engaging People's Hearts the Way Jesus Did* (Grand Rapids: Kregel, 2004).

4. *Have You Heard of the Four Spiritual Laws?* (San Bernardino, CA: Campus Crusade for Christ, 1965).

5. Lee Strobel, *The Case for Faith: A Journalist Investigates the Toughest Objections to Christianity* (Grand Rapids: Zondervan, 2000).

6. Rick Warren, *The Purpose-Driven Life: What on Earth Am I Here For?* (Grand Rapids: Zondervan, 2002).

7. Chuck Colson and Harold Fickett, *The Good Life* (Wheaton, IL: Tyndale, 2005).

8. Mike Breen and Walt Kallestad, *A Passionate Life*, rev. ed. (Colorado Springs: Nexgen, 2005).

Chapter 11: Children: Don't Let Them Leave Home without It

1. Stephen Covey, *The 7 Habits of Highly Effective People: Powerful Lessons on Personal Change* (New York: Free Press, 2004).

2. Randy Travis, "When Mama Prayed" on *Rise and Shine* (World Entertainment, Inc., 2002).

3. Edith Schaeffer, *The Life of Prayer* (Wheaton, IL: Crossway, 1992), 161–62.

4. DeGarmo & Key, "Casual Christian" on *Commander Sozo and the Charge of the Light Brigade* (DKB Music, 1985).

Chapter 12: Leaders: Protect the Quarterback

1. Marcus Buckingham, *The One Thing You Need to Know: About Great Managing, Great Leading, and Sustained Individual Success* (New York: Free Press, 2005).

2. Sam Walton and John Huey, *Sam Walton, Made in America: My Story* (New York: Doubleday, 1992).

Chapter 14: Satan: Dress for Success

1. *Fiddler on the Roof,* motion picture directed by Norman Jewison (1971).

2. I Go Pogo, http://www.igopogo.com/we_have_met.htm. See also Walt Kelly's Pogo, http://www.pogopossum.com.

3. Charles Wesley, "O for a Thousand Tongues to Sing," 1739.

4. C. S. Lewis, *The Screwtape Letters* (Old Tappan, NJ: Fleming H. Revell, 1976), 45.

5. Lon Allison and Mark Anderson, *Going Public with the Gospel: Reviving Evangelistic Proclamation* (Downers Grove, IL: InterVarsity Press, 2003).

6. Tim LaHaye and Jerry Jenkins, *Left Behind* (Wheaton, IL: Tyndale, 1995).

Scripture Index